ODE TO JOY

Biblical Abbreviations

OLD TESTAMENT

Genesis	Gn	Nehemiah	Ne	Baruch	Ba
Exodus	Ex	Tobit	Tb	Ezekiel	Ezk
Leviticus	Lv	Judith	Jdt	Daniel	Dn
Numbers	Nb	Esther	Est	Hosea	Ho
Deuteronomy	Dt	1 Maccabees	1 M	Joel	Jl
Joshua	Jos	2 Maccabees	2 M	Amos	Am
Judges	Jg	Job	Jb	Obadiah	Ob
Ruth	Rt	Psalms	Ps	Jonah	Jon
1 Samuel	1 S	Proverbs	Pr	Micah	Mi
2 Samuel	2 S	Ecclesiastes	Ec	Nahum	Na
1 Kings	1 K	Song of Songs	Sg	Habakkuk	Hab
2 Kings	2 K	Wisdom	Ws	Zephaniah	Zp
1 Chronicles	1 Ch	Sirach	Si	Haggai	Hg
2 Chronicles	2 Ch	Isaiah	Is	Malachi	Ml
Ezra	Ezr	Jeremiah	Jr	Zechariah	Zc
		Lamentations	Lm		

NEW TESTAMENT

Matthew	Mt	Ephesians	Eph	Hebrews	Heb
Mark	Mk	Philippians	Ph	James	Jm
Luke	Lk	Colossians	Col	1 Peter	1 P
John	Jn	1 Thessalonians	1 Th	2 Peter	2 P
Acts	Ac	2 Thessalonians	2 Th	1 John	1 Jn
Romans	Rm	1 Timothy	1 Tm	2 John	2 Jn
1 Corinthians	1 Cor	2 Timothy	2 Tm	3 John	3 Jn
2 Corinthians	2 Cor	Titus	Tt	Jude	Jude
Galatians	Gal	Philemon	Phm	Revelation	Rv

ODE
TO
JOY

Homily
Reflections for
Sundays and
Holy Days:

Cycle C

HAROLD A. BUETOW, PHD JD

ALBA·HOUSE   NEW·YORK

SOCIETY OF ST. PAUL, 2187 VICTORY BLVD., STATEN ISLAND, NEW YORK 10314

ST PAULS

Library of Congress Cataloging-in-Publication Data

Buetow, Harold A.
    Homily reflections for Sundays and Holy Days / Harold A. Buetow.
        p.   cm.
    Includes bibliographical references.
    Contents: Cycle C — Ode to joy.
    ISBN 0-8189-0729-0
    1. Church year sermons. 2. Catholic Church — Sermons. 3. Sermons,
American.
    BX1756.B826H66   1997
    252'.6 — dc21   97-20679
                                          CIP

Produced and designed in the United States of America by the
Fathers and Brothers of the Society of St. Paul,
2187 Victory Boulevard, Staten Island, New York 10314,
as part of their communications apostolate.

ISBN: 0-8189-0729-0

Printing Information:

Current Printing - first digit   1   2   3   4   5   6   7   8   9   10

Year of Current Printing - first year shown

1997   1998   1999   2000   2001   2002   2003   2004   2005

TABLE OF CONTENTS

Introduction to Cycle C:
Ode to Joy

The Preface in Cycle A in this series, entitled *God Still Speaks: Listen!*, contains useful information on homilies. The Introduction to that volume deals with the fact that God is still speaking to us, that one of His ways is through homilies, that we ought to listen, that listening has its rewards as well as its price, and that we have a model for listening. The Introduction to Cycle B's *All Things Made New* deals with the newness of human life in Christianity. This introduction to Cycle C's *Ode to Joy* will emphasize the basic quality of Christianity, joy.

Twirling one's radio dial from one homily to another on Sunday mornings would give the impression that the Christian message is all seriousness. The truth is that it's not so important to be serious as it is to be serious about the right things. Although one might not know it from those radio homilies, permeating the Christian message is the value of joy.

Joy is contagious, but to communicate it homilists must first accept the gift and cultivate it within themselves. One needn't be a stand-up comedian to have a sense of humor. Extracting the humor from our own mistakes, idiosyncrasies, and faults builds the foundation for a healthy outlook toward ourselves and the world around us. Once we learn to take ourselves less seriously, chances are we will become more tolerant of the imperfections in others.

Those are among the reasons why the title of this volume is *Ode to Joy*. An elderly black woman, asked the secret of her happy face, had it right. She thought a long moment before answering, and then said, "Joy. Just that one word: J-O-Y. If people think of joy maybe they'd go around looking less glum. Folks don't smile enough."

She was right. About smiling, a poem by that omnipresent poet — "Anonymous" — said:

It costs nothing, but creates much.

It enriches those who receive, without impoverishing
those who give.

It happens in a flash, and the memory of it sometimes
lasts forever.

None are so rich they can get along without it, and none
so poor but are richer for its benefits.

It creates happiness in the home, fosters good will in a
business, and is the countersign of friends.

It is rest to the weary, daylight to the discouraged, sunshine
to the sad, and nature's best antidote for trouble.

Yet it cannot be bought, begged, borrowed, or stolen, for it
is something that is no earthly good to anyone until it is
given away.

And if in the course of the day some of your friends should
be too tired to give you a smile, why don't you give them
one of yours?

For nobody needs a smile so much as those who have none
left to give! Smile!

On the supposition that, of all the things we wear our expression
is the most important, a few years ago the sales head of one of America's
largest corporations assembled his sales force to meet a New York stage
director. The stage director was to teach them to smile. Many thought
they knew how to smile, but he convinced them that what they thought
were smiles turned out to be smirks. The difference, almost infinitesi-
mal, he said, lies in the eyes. In a true smile, the eyes also smile. After
two weeks' training, the sales force went out of the smile clinic and in
three months increased their sales fifteen percent. The most successful
leaders of people have nice smiles.

Why, then, don't we smile more? Perhaps because we're afraid
— afraid that others may think us simpletons, afraid that we may be
misunderstood. But why do we smile when we see a baby? Perhaps
it's because we see someone without all the defensive layers, someone whose smile for us we know to be fully genuine and without guile.
And that baby-soul inside us smiles wistfully in recognition.

The Old and New Testaments are full of expressions about joy
and laughter. As we illustrate in the homily for the Twenty-First Sunday in Ordinary Time in this C cycle, laughter goes all the way back to

the Book of Genesis. There it is recorded that three men, appearing before Abraham, prophesied that within one year Sarah would have a son. She, eavesdropping, had heard, and Genesis tells us (18:12) that Sarah laughed to herself and said, "Now that I am so withered and my husband is so old, am I still to have sexual pleasure?"

The story gets even funnier: after the Lord asked Abraham why Sarah laughed, Sarah, because she was afraid, dissembled, saying, "I didn't laugh." But God said, "Yes, you did" (v. 15). Then, when God directly promised Abraham that Sarah would give him a son, Abraham laughed as he said to himself, "Can a child be born to a man who is a hundred years old? Or can Sarah give birth at ninety?" (v. 17). Isaac was born of their union; after his birth, Sarah said, "God has given me cause to laugh, and all who hear of it will laugh with me" (Gn 21:6).

The Jewish Scriptures are full of other references to laughter. The Jewish law mandated that we rejoice before the Lord our God in all that we undertake (Dt 12:18). The Psalmist tells us that He who is throned in heaven laughs (Ps 2:4). The Book of Proverbs, purportedly an encapsulation of practical wisdom, said that a glad heart makes a cheerful countenance (15:13) and noted that, whereas it is slow death to be gloomy all the time, being cheerful keeps you healthy (17:22). Proverbs also says that the ideal wife is clothed with strength and dignity, and she laughs at the days to come (Pr 31:25).

Job motivates with the promise that God will fill your mouth with laughter, and your lips with rejoicing (Jb 8:20f.). Sirach, pointing out how to recognize true wisdom, tells us that a man's attire, his hearty laughter, and his gait proclaim him for what he is (Si 19:26).

On the very eve of his crucifixion, Jesus astonished his disciples by saying, "These things I have spoken to you that my joy may be in you and your joy may be full" (Jn 15:11). St. Paul's letters are full of joy. St. James wrote that we should consider it all joy when we encounter various trials (Jm 1:1). St. Peter observed that although you have not seen Jesus you love him; and you rejoice with an indescribable and glorious joy (1 P 1:8). And in two of his letters, St. John wrote that he was writing that our joy may be complete (1 Jn 1:4; 2 Jn 1:12).

The Christian tradition — even with a cross as its central symbol — continues the principle. In an Easter sermon, Saint John Chrysostom described a vision of Christ confronting the devil and laughing at him. St. Francis of Assisi said such things as, "I am God's clown; men come to me and laugh at me, and I laugh with them...

Spiritual joy fills our hearts... Be joyful in the Lord and be merry...
Go out happy, joyful, and praising God." Francis is thought of as
everybody's saint, not least because of his jollity. St. Thomas Aquinas,
knowing that sadness is a thing of the devil and an enemy of the spiritual life, proposed as a cure a good sleep and a bath. St. Thomas More
said, "It is possible to live for the next life and be merry in this."

Martin Luther once said: "God is not a God of sadness, but the
devil is. Christ is a God of joy, and so the Scriptures often say that we
should rejoice... A Christian should and must be a cheerful person."
Said John Wesley: "Sour godliness is the devil's religion." Even John
Calvin laughed: He wrote, "We are nowhere forbidden to laugh, or to
be satisfied with food... or to be delighted with music, or to drink wine."

Joy therefore pervades this volume as well as the others. Joy expresses itself in such three ways as laughter, dancing, and humor. The
ability to laugh is a need of our time as well of all time. During a laugh,
the throat goes into uncoordinated spasms, sending blasts of air out of
the mouth at 70 miles an hour. The body starts pumping adrenaline;
the heart rate increases; the brain releases endorphins and enkephalins
— natural painkillers. The lungs pump out carbon dioxide, the eyes
cleanse themselves with tears, and muscles relax and lose their tense-
ness. The exercise value of laughter is so great that a physician claims
that laughing 100 times a day is the equivalent of 10 minutes of strenu-
ous rowing.

The Book of Proverbs (17:22) said that a cheerful heart is a good
medicine. Perhaps the best known example of "laughter therapy" comes
from writer and editor Norman Cousins. Stricken with a crippling disease which doctors were unable to cure, Cousins turned to good food,
vitamins, and all the humorous movies, video cassettes, and comic strips
he could find. He claimed the mirth they generated not only alleviated
his pain, but led to a natural recovery.

Laughter lightens a heavy heart. In times of tragedy, nothing
seems funny. But humor can play an important role in preventing the
natural feelings of grief and sadness that occur from becoming larger
than the event itself. In some African cultures, tribes assign a "joking
partner" to people in mourning. Laughter in the face of tribulation
doesn't always indicate an attempt to deny, belittle, or cover up the pain.
Rather, the laughter says, "Yes, it hurts, but humor helps remind me
that this pain is only temporary."

Laughter gets the job done. Thomas Carlyle wrote: "The cheerful person will do more in the same time, will do it better, will perse-vere in it longer, than the sad or sullen person." And Michel de Montaigne said, "The plainest sign of wisdom is a continual cheerful-ness."

Indeed, the ability to laugh is one of the criteria that some people give for judging the human. A wise comedian said that laughter is the closest distance between two people. Many people claim that religion is our highest expression of ourselves; it follows that the ability to laugh and religion were made for each other. Many a good laugh can come from religious themes, like the youth who said, "Lot's wife was a pil-lar of salt by day, but a ball of fire by night." Or, on the same subject of Lot's wife turning into a pillar of salt, there was little Jimmie who interrupted the Sunday-school teacher to announce triumphantly, "My mother looked back once while she was driving, and she turned into a telephone pole!"

In the desert, two very different birds thrive. The vulture sees nothing but dead carcasses. The hummingbird seeks the lovely blos-soms of cacti. Each bird finds what it is looking for. So do people. In some parts of Greece, it's a very old custom to observe the Monday after Easter as a day of laughter — to celebrate the practical joke that God played on Satan by raising Jesus from the dead.

Dancing, too, is an instinctive activity of the joy of the Judeo-Christian tradition. After Pharaoh's horses and chariots and charioteers had drowned, the prophetess Miriam, Aaron's sister, took a tambou-rine in her hand, while all the women went out after her with tambou-rines, dancing (Ex 15:20). On David's return after slaying Goliath, at the approach of Saul and David women came out from each of the cit-ies of Israel to meet King Saul, singing and dancing, with tambourines, and joyful songs (1 S 18:6).

When the Israelites were bringing the Ark of the Covenant to Jerusalem, David came dancing before the Lord with abandon (2 S 6:14). Even the somber Jeremiah, presenting prophecies about the fu-ture of Jerusalem during bad times, promised Jerusalem that, carrying your festive tambourines, you shall go forth dancing with the merrymakers (31:4) and that the virgins shall make merry and dance, and young men and old as well (31:13).

Dancing is another instance where we have to understand the New Testament in terms of the Old. Although we have no instance of the Gospels explicitly saying that Jesus danced, his story of the party given the Prodigal Son by his happy father, speaking of the elder son coming in from the land, tells us that on his way back, as he neared the house, he heard the sound of music and dancing (Lk 15:25). It's hard not to imagine Jesus dancing at the wedding reception at Cana. And dancing has become part of our tradition, too, even at times in our liturgy — where it can be a prophetic sign, a way to express our hopes, our fears, and our faith. It's a sign that contradicts the cynicism and despair of such modern phenomena as consumerism, materialism, and militarism.

Humor, like laughter, is a resurrection. Both allow us to rise again and again. Humor opens lines of communication, eases tension, provides a much-needed safety valve for emotions in times of stress, and helps put life in perspective. Because of its liberating qualities, humor can free us to pursue our goals and fulfill our mission, enhance health, mend a broken spirit, lighten a heavy heart, relieve pressure in social and professional situations, get the job done faster, and tap the deepest human emotions.

Humor also serves as an outlet for irritation, aggravation, and frustration. That's reminiscent of Joe, Fred, and Charlie who, after having been out on the town and imbibed not wisely but well, after a bartender refused to serve them further got into an argument about the definitions of irritation, aggravation, and frustration. The argument went nowhere, but Charlie said he could demonstrate. Going to a phone at 1:30 a.m., he picked a number at random, dropped in a coin and dialed. When a sleepy voice answered he said, "Hello, is Charlie there?" "No, Charlie isn't here and this is a hell of a time to get a wrong number!" said the voice, and bang went the phone. Charlie turned to his buddies and said, "That was irritation." After a few minutes he dialed the same number and, when the same voice answered, repeated, "Hello, is Charlie there?" This time he was really read off; at the conclusion he said to his friends, "That was aggravation. Now I'll show you frustration." He dialed the number again, and when the same voice answered, he said, "Hello, this is Charlie. Have you had any calls for me?"

People with a sense of humor encourage others to be optimistic in times of trial by pointing out the bright side of a given situation. They recognize the comic side of the hassles and situations we encounter every day. If we choose laughter over irritation, we will feel better. So will those around us.

Jesus' message is, after all, one of hope. Although hope entertains the idea that one may expect what one desires, it isn't optimism; optimism usually implies a temperamental confidence that all will turn out for the best, often suggesting a failure to consider things closely. The Gospel is hope, not optimism. (We should, however, be mindful that the optimist is as often wrong as the pessimist, but is far happier.) Hope means treating the future as really future — that is, unknowable; and treating the present as really present — that is, as inescapable. None of Jesus' message is born of eagerness for resolutions born out of fantasy.

Jesus never intended us to be somber and morose in our pursuit of God's will. St. Thomas More's last letter to his daughter Meg before his execution for his faith is an example: "Mine own good daughter, never trouble thy mind for anything that shall ever keep me in this world. Nothing can come but that which God wills. And I make myself very sure that whatever that be, seem it ever so bad in sight, it shall in deed be best."

Politicians use humor to get a point across and make it stick. They make critical statements safely by masking them in comedy. In the business world, laughter is an ideal tension breaker; an apt joke can give everyone involved enough time to draw back, rethink a position, or reconsider an action. Executives can reach co-workers more effectively through appropriate humor. Humor is an idea solidly based on communications theory: It gets attention and achieves retention. More important for Christians, though, are the sentiments expressed by Blessed Julian of Norwich, who wrote: "The greatest honor you can give to Almighty God is to live gladly, joyfully, because of the knowledge of His love."

ODE TO JOY

FEAST OF THE IMMACULATE CONCEPTION
Gn 3:9-15, 20   Eph 1:3-6, 11f.   Lk 1:26-38

Mary's Life: Springtime of Grace
Original Sin and God's Mother; The Perfection of God's
Saving Power; The First Committed Christian; Full of Grace

In prison, reality is so unpleasant that convicts at every opportunity withdraw into realms of make-believe. One day, five convicts were sitting in the prison yard when one of them looked at an ad in a magazine. "Wish my mother had a home like that," he said, pointing at a little red brick bungalow with a green roof and shutters. One of the others took the magazine and flipped the pages. "That's what I wish my ma had. A car, so she could come and see me once in a while." Then the magazine was passed to Bill. But Bill just sat there, musing. The others thought that strange, because they knew his mother didn't have anyone left in the world but him. And they knew she loved him — they'd seen some of her wonderful letters. Finally Bill spoke. "I wish" — and his voice sounded as if it were coming from the other side of the wall — "that my mother had a good son."

And that's what we can wish of ourselves with relation to our heavenly mother Mary.

In those places in the world that have changes of seasons, there can be little doubt that one of the most beautiful seasons of all is Spring. Winter's gone with its coldness and barren earth, and Spring brings songbirds, bright green sprouts of all kinds shooting out of the ground, buds on flowers and trees, a refreshing warmth to the air, and all kinds of new beginnings to life.

Today, though not many parts of the earth have the warmth of Spring, we celebrate the first moment of Mary's existence as a wonderful springtime of grace. One feels the need for this in the Book of Genesis, which describes the wintry effects of the sin of the first Eve. One feels it even more in the temper of today's Gospel, in which Mary changes the course of the world by her free consent to God's request

---

Note: This homily is mostly on Ephesians; Cycle A is on Luke, Cycle B mostly on
    Genesis.

1

for her cooperation in sending the Messiah to free the world from its
sins.

But one is simply overwhelmed with this springtime of grace in
today's majestic portion of the letter to the Ephesians, which is the theological basis for the tradition of the immaculate conception of Mary.
Had the history of humankind ended with the story of Adam and Eve
in the Book of Genesis, look at what we would have had: disobedience to God, division, disarray, sexual innocence lost, man blaming
woman and woman blaming man and both blaming an outside force,
harmony shattered, an unending and irresolvable struggle, and no sense
of final victory. What Ephesians tells us brings light into this war-with-
out-end scenario. The hopeless struggle of Genesis is overcome by the
experience of grace lavished on a frail young girl.

Though most New Testament letters begin with giving thanks to
the community addressed, the writer of Ephesians goes directly to the
praise of God for revealing His plan of salvation. It continues in a way
that shows gift after gift and wonder after wonder from God. The hymn
— for that's what it is — in its triumph and joy refers to those things
Mary's consent made possible: God's adoption of us as His children,
forgiveness of sins, incorporation into Christ, and the seal of the Holy
Spirit. It is, in short, a springtime of grace. We can find some things by
ourselves: skill in work, position in the world, some of this world's
goods, or a spouse. Other things, however, are at least in part beyond
the unaided efforts of the self: goodness, for example, and peace of
mind.

God chose to give us these spiritual gifts. He has bestowed them
on us "in Christ," an expression which is repeated in various forms over
thirty times in this letter, emphasizing the unity of persons in Christ
through their incorporation into a visible community under his leadership. The letter says "in the heavens," which is to say that God is now
bringing His ordered plan into human activity. God made His choices
before the world began (v. 4) — that is, from the very beginning. On
this feast of the Immaculate Conception, we think of Mary, the first
Christian, and all other Christians whom she made possible by her
consent to God's plan as told in today's Gospel.

His purpose was to make Mary and all of us "holy and without
blemish in his sight." Although we don't often think about being holy,
the Christian should nevertheless be identifiable as such in the world.
Our having been chosen by God makes us different — not so much

that we're taken out of the world, but that we remain true to Jesus while being very much in the world and its concerns.

That God's chosen be without blemish is a concept taken from the sacrificial animals of the Jews: The animals offered were to be the best. As applied to God's chosen, like Mary and other Christians, this means that we abolish self-satisfaction or any notion of being second-best, and strive to be perfect. Like Mary confronted with the agony of decision in her delicate situation related in today's Gospel, we must place no store on human standards, but on God's.

Because Mary was selfless and sinless enough to consent to God, she put into place God's plan to make us His adopted children (v. 5). This beautiful image was more meaningful in the Roman world, where there held sway the *patria potestas*, wherein the father of a family had absolute power over his children as long as they and he both lived. Adoption was a very serious step: It took children out of one *patria potestas* and put them into another. After adoption, all debts, obligations, and rights connected with the previous family were canceled as though they never existed; the adoptee became a new person and had all the rights of a legitimate child, usually a son, in the new family.

This portion of Ephesians applies this procedure from the family of the world to the family of God. All is for the praise of the glory of His grace that He granted us in the beloved (v. 6). It concludes that we were chosen (v. 11), referring to the purpose of God, who accomplishes all things effectively and surely. We're the first to hope in Christ (v. 12) because of God's chosen people of old, particularly the Jewish maid of Nazareth whose purity enabled her to cooperate eagerly with God's plan and resulted in a springtime of grace.

Each individual has his own work to do: soldier, tailor, tinker, or whatever. It's the same with nations: the Romans contributed to the world law and administration; the ancient Greeks, beauty of thought and form; the Jews, religion; and so on. The greatest privilege of the Jews was to have been the first nation to await the coming of the Anointed One of God and, through the goodness and strength of their daughter Mary, to have witnessed his arrival. That brought about a springtime of grace which we, if we choose, are privileged to share. Mary shows what's possible when human life chooses to allow the grace of God to touch it.

FIRST SUNDAY OF ADVENT
Jr 33:14-16   1 Th 3:12-4:2   Lk 21:25-28, 34-36

Preparing for the Coming of One Who Has Already Come
Jesus is Coming: Prepare!; Eternal Vigilance; Waiting

"I can't wait" is an expression parents hear often from their young children before Christmas. Yet waiting patiently is a lesson everybody should learn as early as possible, or life can be very disagreeable. But there's no reason that developing patience need be unpleasant. Every adult as well as every child knows the joys as well as the pangs of waiting. We wait at terminals for loved ones, on street corners to meet friends, and in our homes to entertain. The expectant mother waits for the birth of her baby. In each case, as the time draws near we become more anxious. Will our friend be on time? Will our dinner please our guests? Will the mother safely have a healthy baby?

Today, the First Sunday of Advent, the beginning of the Church year, we begin a period of waiting — waiting for the Lord's other comings as we remember with joy his First Coming as the baby of Bethlehem. St. Bernard speaks about three comings of Jesus. "In the First Coming which we celebrate at Christmas," he says, "the Lord was seen on earth and lived among people. In his last coming, 'all flesh shall see the salvation of God.' The other coming (a third kind) is hidden. In it, only the chosen ones see him within themselves, and they receive fulfillment. In brief, his First Coming was in the flesh and in weakness, this intermediary coming is in the spirit and in power, the last coming will be in glory and majesty."

Advent commemorates a joyful kind of waiting, a waiting for Jesus that contains promise, love, preparation, alertness, reflectiveness, prayer, new beginnings, and fulfillment. It's a special kind of waiting for the God who has come, does come, and will come. It's a waiting for Jesus the savior, the Christ, the only son of God, the Lord (*Catechism of the Catholic Church*, nos. 430-451). It has both a penitential and a hopeful, expectant character.

It's not the first period of waiting in religion. In the seventh century B.C., Jeremiah the prophet waited. The moral life of the southern kingdom of Judah in his time was corrupt, characterized by sham, injustice, and dishonesty. In the midst of all that, today's reading from the Book of Jeremiah, part of his "Book of Consolation," a joyful part of the book, is full of hope. He promises a new branch of Judaism from the tree of David that won't be the same as the old one, and will sprout into new life.

The prophecy is a strange one, in view of the fact that the kings who had followed David were such a sorry lot — most (with two exceptions) being corrupt as well as unjust. David's dynasty was, to all practical purposes, dead. Nevertheless, this new branch would have many fresh characteristics. It will, for example, be virtuous — specifically through the practice of integrity over the dishonesty of the past. This promised branch finds its fulfillment in Jesus of Nazareth.

When Jesus came, some of his disciples' misunderstandings involved the idea of waiting. When, they wanted to know, was the end of the world coming? And what about Jesus' Second Coming? Their questions were legitimate. Throughout the Jews' history, their world had ended frequently. As a people, they'd lived through the Babylonian captivity, when all had seemed finished, and invasion and occupation by many foreign powers.

We all experience the end of our world often enough to understand our final end: when a parent, spouse, or child dies, or when a marriage breaks down, or when a job has gone. In all such cases, we say that our world has come tumbling down. With Jesus and his Apostles, he, knowing that their anxiety was misplaced, answered by addressing the destruction of Jerusalem and the end of the world at the same time. The terror involved in the destruction of Jerusalem would be a lesson about the end of the world.

Jesus, like everyone else, had his ideas of what's important. (A farmer once ran an ad that said, "Wanted: young woman who owns tractor. Send photo... of tractor." He had his own ideas of what was important.) Jesus highlighted a few points that he wanted his followers to remember. For one thing, the timing of the end events is unpredictable. For another, the Second Coming will in due time be known to the whole universe. Jesus' expression "Son of Man" (v. 27) refers to his Second Coming in glory. The fact that he would come in a cloud links this coming with Jesus' transfiguration and with his ascension, both of which involved clouds. Lastly, Jesus tells us that we must be on the alert: beware, be vigilant, and pray.

The last, to pray, befits the Gospel of St. Luke, our special evangelist during this coming Church year, whose Gospel is called, among other things, a "Gospel of Prayer." The only non-Jewish writer of the New Testament, Luke is also the most educated and most literate of the authors of all the books of the Bible.

Luke, the refined Gentile, warns us to be ready and not to become bloated with the pleasures of this world. Living in the Roman Empire had become completely decadent with sexual corruption, hedonism, gluttony, and barbaric cruelty. Luke was saddened that what was called "civilization" had sunk so low.

Despite Jesus' teaching about the unpredictability of the timing of the end, people never stopped speculating about it. In St. Paul's time, Christians thought that Jesus' Second Coming was going to happen in their lifetime. In probably the first New Testament book to be written, and thus the oldest of Christian writings, Paul's letter to the Thessalonians, reflecting that belief, concentrates on those things that Paul thought to be important. One of these is the Gospel value of love (3:12). Also, like everyone who believes the end to be near, he fully expresses his emotions, telling the Thessalonians how much they mean to him. That alone is a lesson in preparing for Jesus' Second Coming.

A modern lesson in preparing for Jesus' coming is the story of a junior executive who approached his grouchy boss to tell him how deeply he admired his creative genius. The boss was very surprised, and also deeply impressed. That night the boss came home to his 14-year-old son and sat him down. He said, "The most incredible thing happened to me today," and told him the story.

Then he continued, "As I was coming home tonight, I thought about you. When I come home I don't pay a lot of attention to you. Sometimes I scream at you for not getting good enough grades in school and for your bedroom being a mess. But somehow tonight I just wanted to sit here and, well, just let you know that, besides your mother, you're the most important person in my life. You're a great kid and I love you!"

The startled boy started to sob and sob, and he couldn't stop crying. His whole body shook. At last, he looked up at his father and said through his tears, "I was planning on running away tomorrow, Dad, because I didn't think you loved me. Now I don't need to."

Perhaps the idea may be summed up in an unknown author's poem entitled *The Time Is Now*:

> If you are ever going to love me,
> Love me now, while I can know

The sweet and tender feelings
Which from true affection flow.
Love me now
While I am living.
Do not wait until I'm gone
And then have it chiseled in marble,
Sweet words on ice-cold stone.
If you have tender thoughts of me,
Please tell me now.
If you wait until I am sleeping,
Never to awaken,
There will be death between us,
And I won't hear you then.
So, if you love me, even a little bit,
Let me know it while I am living
So I can treasure it.

With the Thessalonians Paul, like Jesus, in a positive and affirming way encourages them to avoid unethical conduct (3:13) and to keep their fervor alive. He reminds them of the instructions that were handed down from Jesus through the Apostles (4:1). These were practical principles that Paul worked out in accordance with his understanding of the role of the Spirit (4:2).

How would we live this Advent if we knew it was going to be our last? We would certainly focus our life on what we think matters. What mattered to Jeremiah was to make all virtue, especially integrity and justice, the centerpiece of people's relationship with God and others. Paul's focus was to pray for an increase of love, to fully express our emotions in telling others how much they mean to us and how much we love them. Jesus adds to all this to beware, be vigilant, and pray.

Now's the time to prepare: to watch and wait for Jesus. There will be some anxiety, surely. But mostly there will be eagerness, as there is when we go to meet a loved one. There will be a glow of expectancy that's similar to that of a woman awaiting the birth of her baby, or to that of children before a Christmas crèche.

We meet Jesus not only historically at Christmas, or at our death, or at the end of the world. We meet him every day of our lives, through all the graces of our friendships and the opportunities he gives us. We must watch for him. To watch for Jesus means — as Cardinal Newman said (*Parochial and Plain Sermons*) — to be awake, alive, quick-sighted, zealous in honoring him; to look out for him in all that happens; to be detached from what is present, and to live in what is unseen; to live in the thought of Christ as he came once, and as he will come again; to desire his Second Coming, from our affectionate and grateful remembrance of his first.

Let our preparation for this Christmas be a test. Are we willing to forget what we've done for other people, and to remember what other people have done for us; to ignore what the world owes us and to think of what we owe the world; to put our rights in the background, our duties in the middle distance, and our chances to do a little more than our duty in the foreground; to look behind the faces of our fellow human beings to their hearts, hungry for joy; to admit that probably the only good reason for our existence is not what we're going to get out of life, but what we're going to give to life; to close our book of complaints against the management of the universe and look around for a place where we can sow a few seeds of happiness? Are we willing to do these things even for a day? If so, we're ready to keep Christmas. If not, let's do something about it, starting with this Advent period of waiting.

SECOND SUNDAY OF ADVENT
Ba 5:1-9   Ph 1:3-6, 8-11   Lk 3:1-6

Getting Ready: Removing Obstacles to Complete Joy
Coming Events Cast their Shadows; Prepare the Way of the Lord;
We Are Filled with Joy; Optimism

Attempts to make sense of life are universal. A famous poet (T.S. Eliot) expressed the wish to have carved on his gravestone about life: "I've had the experience, but I've missed the meaning." Viktor Frankl, an Austrian Jewish psychiatrist who was thrown into the concentration camp of Auschwitz during World War II, addressed his fellow prisoners as they were lying motionless in despair-filled silence with only an occasional sigh in the darkness of their cell.

He told them that whoever is still alive has reason for hope; that whatever they were going through could still be an asset to them in the future; that the meaning of human life includes privation, suffering, and dying; that someone was looking down on each of them with love — friend, wife, somebody else alive or dead, or God — and wouldn't want to be disappointed. They should courageously integrate their life into a worldview that has a meaning beyond immediate self-grasping, and know how to die.

Does your acquaintance with life find this optimism and hope remote? Does your experience make you dwell upon the shadow side of life, the many ways in which we suffer, fail, lose heart, or feel that nothing's worthwhile? Are you as unimaginatively pessimistic as the old lady who was taken to see the beautiful ballet "Swan Lake"? Later, when asked how she liked the story, she said to her friend: "He fell in love with a duck. So what good could come of it?"

Today's liturgy constitutes a vision of optimism and hope that can sing of the Lord's wonders and recognize His providence at work in everything that happens. Today's portion of the Book of Baruch was written by an anonymous author around 200 B.C., probably at Alexandria for the Jews living there who had a problem keeping their faith: The Temple was far away, they were living in a culture which was completely opposed to the heritage of Judaism, and some were finding local prosperity very attractive, to the detriment of their faith. Significantly telling the Jews to "look to the east," today's passage personifies Jerusalem as a mother about to receive back her exiled children.

In a broader sense, the passage urges all who are struggling with faith in an alien culture to stand up, to have confidence, to be strong. The mood of the passage is full of celebration. Inasmuch as it directs our attention toward how expectation and anticipation of the Messiah find fulfillment in the birth of the child in Bethlehem, it's good Advent reading. Baruch's image of flattening the high mountains and filling out the valleys was frequent in First Testament times. It derived from the custom of having a herald precede a king when the king was going on a journey, to forewarn the inhabitants of his arrival so that they could repair their ill-kept roads.

St. Luke begins his narrative of Jesus' public ministry with John the Baptist, who was straightening out the crooked paths of human hearts and leveling the valleys and hills of people's selfishness to prepare them for Jesus. The Baptist was also trying to straighten out the calf-paths of the human mind — those paths into which human minds, like some modern roads, continue to follow primitive trails made by calves for their own reasons, but which reasons are no longer valid for people. John's personality, conviction, and enthusiasm for his message caused people to overlook his odd dress and come to him.

Luke provides a roll-call of who held power at the time. Five of his seven historical figures are secular, two religious. Among the secular figures, all of the individuals mentioned were corrupt, cruel, lecherous, barbaric, and depraved, and provide a great contrast for the righteousness of John the Baptist's message.

The religious leadership links the story of salvation history to events in contemporary Palestinian and world history. Luke reserves the place of honor for the high priest. Annas had occupied that post from A.D. 6 to 15, when he was deposed by the Romans. For three years he was succeeded by various members of his family and then, from A.D. 18 to 36, by his son-in-law, Caiaphas. Though Caiaphas was the actual high priest, it was to the more powerful and influential Annas that everyone, including Caiaphas, paid honor.

From this background of intrigue and power emerged, as if from a polluted fog, the solitary figure of John the Baptist, with a message of optimism. He preached in the desert. The ancient Israelites often romanticized the desert: There they wandered as a rebellious people and in later centuries came to idealize the desert as being the time and place when they were closest to the Lord. John's prayer to Jesus was, in the words of St. Richard of Chichester adopted by "Jesus Christ, Superstar," "to see you more clearly, to love you more dearly, to follow you more nearly." That invitation was depicted in a painting done by the artist Holman Hunt in 1854 entitled "The Light of the World." It portrays the Christ, crowned with thorns, carrying a lantern, knocking at a closed door. When the artist's friends pointed out that he had put no handle on the door, he replied, "We must ourselves open the door to the light; the handle is on the inside."

Luke associates the preaching of John with a call from God (v. 2), thereby identifying him with the prophets whose ministries began with similar calls. John preached repentance. Repentance signifies not regret for the past or the performance of "penance," but rather a new outlook on life in keeping with the will of God. This was to be a heightening of the Jews' response to deliverance from captivity: an attitude of gladness, joy, laughter, song, and — above all — grateful recognition of the God responsible for effecting their deliverance. In the words of today's Responsorial Psalm, "The Lord has done great things for us; we are filled with joy."

To perform his mission well, John went about the entire region of the Jordan. This makes sense. Since John wished to encounter, sermonize, and baptize people, he would naturally have sought an audience among the people traveling the main trade routes. The roads leading from Jerusalem, Bethel, and Bethlehem met in that area before continuing into Perea on the eastern shore.

All of that was the attitude of St. Paul when he wrote one of his loveliest letters, the letter to the Philippians, "The Epistle of Joy." Although Paul was in prison while writing this letter, he was completely taken up with the optimism of the day of Christ Jesus (v. 6). The Son of God had become a human being, true God and true man (*Catechism of the Catholic Church*, 456-470), and will come again. That will be a glorious day that will mean the general resurrection and unending happiness for all who are faithful to Jesus. With that before him, Paul underscored his concern for ethical growth, reminding us all to discern what is of value (v. 10) in life. He was not unlike the British writer G.K. Chesterton, for whom the possibility of enjoying anything at all must be based on a kind of humility and wonder that takes nothing for granted, but lives in a state of continual surprise. That's like the best of Christmases.

Paul in Philippians shows a great ability to let go and surrender, without becoming passive: With prison chains hanging from his wrists, he writes of great joy and love. This kind of surrender involves a growth in freedom — not the freedom to be whoever we want, but the ability freely to become who God is calling us to be; not the freedom to do whatever we want, but the freedom to love others, in ever-widening circles, as we've been loved.

Some people look back to the "good old days" for better opportunities for hope. But what was life really like in the past? For most of human history, the worker was considered a cross between a rodent and a beast of burden. In the "golden age" of the British Queen Elizabeth I, flowering around 1600, human conduct was a brutish, nasty spectacle. When Shakespeare wrote and Drake sailed, every man carried a lethal weapon and went about prepared to kill or be killed. Nobles sported three-foot swords, the lesser gentry 12-inch daggers or ponderous clubs. Cut-throats roamed through London, plundering and killing with impunity.

Care of the insane, the crippled, and the blind was unknown. Lunatics were chained in dungeons or exposed in cages for public view; sometimes they were thrown into a pit of snakes "to bring them back to their senses." Sadism disfigured the games of the day; unless a sport was cruel, spectators were bored. At local fairs men fought each other with heavy clubs, the combat ending when one was beaten to insensibility. In the England of Charles Dickens, who died in 1870, the treatment of children — a sure index of human progress — was brutal.

And in the United States? As late as 1820 indentured servants were virtual slaves. The master could beat them, systematically starve them, and shoot them if they tried to escape. Popular punishments for minor offenses were the clipping of ears, maiming, and branding. The fight for the 12-hour day was violent. And 150 years ago life expectancy was a grueling 38 years for males. The work week was 72 hours. Women had it worse: Housewives worked 98 hours a week. Chances are that in your entire lifetime then you would never hear the sound of an orchestra or travel more than 20 miles from your birthplace.

In New York during Theodore Roosevelt's early manhood unscrupulous men sent small boys into the streets as bootblacks and peddlers, then collected their small earnings and herded the children into a filthy pen for the night. Imprisonment for debt — even for $5 — was universal in the United States until 1820. In foul prisons debtors were locked in the same cell with murderers, thieves, and degenerates; together they starved, froze, and rotted — unless they could purchase favors from the warden.

The cruelties of previous times were nowhere better exhibited than on the high seas. Herman Melville's *White Jacket*, published in 1850, describes how in the United States Navy a man could be flogged till his bones gleamed white. Records show that the merchant marine continued that practice as late as 1870. More murderous yet was the practice of keelhauling, common among American whaling ships during the first half of the nineteenth century. To keelhaul a man, you tied him to a rope that had been passed under the ship's bottom. His shipmates pulled at the other end of the rope, dragging him overboard, under the keel and up the other side of the hull, while the barnacles lacerated him to ribbons. Sometimes, mercifully, he was drowned.

Let's rather root ourselves in the present, with all its difficulties, and in the tradition of today's liturgy. Let's pray that we may be willing to have the crooked paths in our lives straightened and the valleys and hills of our selfish desires leveled. Let's join more fervently in the prayer after the Lord's Prayer that we say with optimism at every Eucharist — that "we wait in joyful hope for the coming of our Savior, Jesus Christ."

That Advent optimism should be realistic. We're not like the little boy who was overheard talking to himself as he strode through his back yard, baseball cap on sideways and toting ball and bat. "I'm the greatest baseball player in the world," he said proudly. Then he tossed the ball into the air, swung and missed. Undaunted, he picked up the ball, threw it into the air and repeated to himself, "I'm the greatest player ever!" He swung at the ball again, and again he missed. He paused a moment to examine bat and ball carefully. Then once again he threw the ball into the air and said, "I'm the greatest baseball player who ever lived." He swung the bat hard and again missed the ball. "Wow" he exclaimed. "What a pitcher!"

Rather, we ought to be like David of the Older Covenant. When Goliath came against the Israelites, the soldiers all thought, "He's so big we can never kill him." David looked at the same giant and thought, "He's so big I can't miss." In our reflections, we ought to take into account not only our major sins, but also our personal dispositions that may be causing them: the laziness that prevents us from doing kind acts, the resentment towards another that blocks communication, the fear that forces us to compromise our principles, the pride which precludes true regard for others, the social sins of prejudice and intolerance that can destroy a society.

If we take any other perspective, the epitaph for our life may be, "I've had the experience, but I've missed the meaning."

THIRD SUNDAY OF ADVENT
Zp 3:14-18   Ph 4:4-7   Lk 3:10-18

Ode to Joy
Waiting; Getting Ready to Shout with Joy; The Best Kind
of Rejoicing: in the Lord; Rejoice: God Is in our Midst

Folklore tells a story of followers of a Guru who sought to learn from
the Master the stages he had passed through in his quest for the divine.
He said, "God first led me by the hand into the Land of Action, where
I dwelt for several years. Then he returned and led me to the Land of
Sorrows; there I lived until my heart was purged of every inordinate
attachment. That's when I found myself in the Land of Love, whose
burning flames consumed whatever was left in me of self. This brought
me to the Land of Silence, where the mysteries of life and death were
bared before my wondering eyes."

"Was that the final stage of your quest?" they asked.

"No," the Master said. "One day God said, 'Today I shall take
you to the innermost sanctuary, to the heart of God Himself.' And I
was led to the Land of Laughter."

That story is somewhat like Dante's *Purgatory*, whose only exit
was passing through a wall of fire. Once the pain was burned away by
love, the other side was Paradise, sheer joy.

Life is full of both sadness and joy. Both can be opportunities
for growth, and joy can overcome sadness. An example is Beethoven,
whose deafness gradually became so profound that he shared in the
difficulties of many deaf people: He was unable to do such simple things
as join in group conversations, he felt embarrassed and then isolated;
eventually he felt it necessary to withdraw within himself. Conducting the first performance of his Ninth and last symphony, pathetically
he had to be told to turn around to face the audience to acknowledge
the waves of applause, because he couldn't hear them. Yet in the midst
of his deafness — a sadness unique for a musician — he composed his
beautiful, lilting "Ode to Joy."

Today has for many years been called, after its first words, "Rejoice Sunday." Today's liturgy is the Church's ode to joy and, while
shot through with sadness, as was last Sunday's, it's full of examples

of the triumph of joy. Today's Gospel is, as was last Sunday's, part of the story of John the Baptist. At this outset of Jesus' ministry, John was proclaiming Jesus as the Messiah. This led to the crowds asking, as we all must ask in facing Jesus, "What should we do?" (v. 10). The Baptist's answer (v. 11), as with his answers to the succeeding questions, was an initial announcement of a new world. Beyond that, he tailored his answers to his questioners.

John's answer to the crowds in general had to do with charity: that they share their food and clothing. In our day, with half the population of the world going to bed hungry every night, and even starving, and the "haves" sharing clothing with the "have nots" in a major way mostly only at Christmas, his answer still applies.

There's a relevant story about a salesman who dreamed that he had gone into the next life. There he found all former salesmen separated into two groups: the failures lodged in one place, the successes in another. He watched the failures — a thin, hungry-looking mob — while the waiters came in to serve dinner. A waiter went down one side of a table and up the other laying out great platters of delicious food, but — strangely enough — he was preceded by another waiter who affixed to each diner's arm a long iron spoon. This spoon rendered the arm absolutely rigid, so that it couldn't be bent at the elbow. As a result, the men couldn't eat.

The new arrival then went to see the successes, whose dwelling-place was that of a multitude of genial, well-fed, happy gentlemen. There he witnessed the same procedure he had seen in the other place. But here the long spoon rigidly fixed to the arm of each diner proved no impediment whatever. Each man dipped his spoon into the food and fed the man seated next to him! Returning to the first group, he asked one of the salesmen why they didn't do the same thing, and got the reply, "I'm starving, and I should feed that dirty crook next to me?"

The question from the tax collectors was the same: "What should we do?" (v. 12) The system made fraud easy for them, and so John's answer to them and to all politicians (v. 13) concerned social justice: they're to avoid dishonesty, greed, and ill-gotten riches. The third group asking the same question (v. 14) were the soldiers, or police agents — for the most part Jews who helped the extortions of the tax gatherers. John's answer is for the strong and powerful of all time: Stop shakedowns, bullying, strong-arming, and blackmail.

Among the people, there was a mood of anticipation of the new

age, and a wonderment (v. 15). They, in fact, had many reasons to think
John himself the Messiah: his remarkable austerity, which struck the
imagination; the suddenness of his appearance in the wilderness; and
his mighty voice, which jolted them from their listlessness. And there
had been no prophet for about 400 years! John, honest and direct as
always, quickly denied that he was the Messiah (v. 16). His baptism
was with water: It was preparatory, and only an external symbol of
internal repentance. The Messiah to come was so far above him that
John didn't consider himself fit to loosen his sandal straps, a job performed only by servants. But the baptism Jesus would use would be in
the Holy Spirit, and in fire — to John an image of a purifying force.

The last line of today's Gospel (v. 18) reminds us that John the
Baptist was preaching "the good news" — what we call the Gospel.
Within another few verses, this ascetical man, this humble man, this
man of courage will be arrested, to be removed from the stage of history. The one mightier than John (v. 16) was ready to appear, and the
human race would focus upon him. The joy of his coming would triumph over the sadness of John's loss.

Today's first reading contains essentially the same message: optimism over pessimism, joy over sadness. The Book of Zephaniah was
written in the age of King Josiah (640-609 B.C.), when Assyrian gods
were being worshiped even in Jerusalem, which was polluted by the
presence of pagan shrines everywhere, even in the Temple area. Although most of Zephaniah is gloomy, here he presented hope, to reside in the remnant of Jews that would remain faithful. The city and
the people are to rejoice because the Lord is coming to renew them.

Twice he states that, despite the sad things that are happening,
God is in their midst. That contributes to the mood of excitement, expectancy, and joy throughout this passage. God is in the midst of our
sad events, too, and, like the people of that time, we must remove our
arrogance and pride in order to receive Him.

Unfortunately, to be joyful is often seen as frivolous and to be
gloomy is to be serious. Seriousness isn't necessarily a virtue; it can
be a lapse into taking oneself gravely, because that's the easiest thing
to do. It's easy to be heavy, hard to be light. Public comedians often
have ten writers, dramatists far fewer. If we see all that in perspective,
then, as Zephaniah says, God will rejoice over us with gladness and
renew us in His love. Let's remember that as we sing the carols of
Christmas.

The original opening words of this section of Zephaniah — "Shout for joy" — are the same as the word used in the opening of today's reading from St. Paul's letter to the Philippians: Rejoice (v. 4). Joy is in the Jewish tradition: The Psalmist said that He who is throned in heaven laughs (Ps 2:4), and the Book of Proverbs (17:2) that a joyful heart is the health of the body, but a depressed spirit dries up the bones. And joy is a word Paul uses a dozen times in his beautiful letter.

All of this despite the fact that Paul is writing from jail at Ephesus! Elsewhere he says that in that jail he contended with deprivation, maltreatment, and other barbarity at the hands of his guards. He writes with almost certain death awaiting him, to people who are new to the Christian way and are going to face dark days. What a wonderful lesson for us: to allow God to be God, to realize that He's in charge, that even in the midst of trouble we need simply trust Him, and that perfect justice and peace will come only when Christ comes again in glory!

In this passage Paul mentions several reasons why he feels justified in calling for joy. One is the Philippians' unselfish kindness (v. 5). The follower of Jesus should likewise have gracious gentleness, patience, and forbearance because, Paul says, the Lord is near. "Near" doesn't mean being a short distance away, as in "outside the door" or "around the corner," or a short time away. It means that he's with us here and now, present in our midst, and closer to us than the person sitting next to us. He's close by grace. That grace comes in many ways: through liturgy, through Christian community, through the special presence of his Spirit. So we rejoice!

Finally, says Paul (v. 6), our joy should override our sorrow because God answers prayers. Remember that as you tell God what you want for Christmas. In every form of prayer, we come to God, for one thing, for ourselves — for forgiveness for the past, for the things we need in the present, and for help and guidance for the future. We also come to God for others. We petition God full of thanksgiving, because there should be thanks in everything — in tears as well as laughter. The result? The experience of Christ's unique peace that surpasses all understanding (v. 7) — and his joy.

These days, even though merchants and advertisers give the impression that joy is the equivalent of pleasure and can be bought, at their best the songs and sentiments of this season tell us that joy is found in relationships, especially with family and friends. We most often find joy in all the loving things we do for others in this or any other season: in the helpfulness we extend to those in pain; in the thoughtfulness we give to the deprived, especially the hungry, the homeless, and the elderly; in the understanding we give to those who are bereaved; and in our overall efforts to make our lives together more loving. "Grief can take care of itself," Mark Twain once noted, "but to get the full value of a joy, you have to have someone to divide it with." Another (Rousseau) has said: "When a person dies, he clutches in his hand only that which he has given away in his lifetime."

Joy is a gift of the Holy Spirit that is one of the marks of being a faithful Christian. If we truly believe that the Good News is really good news, we must be a people of joy! In the words of Hilaire Belloc, many people think they're being religious, whereas they're really only being uncomfortable.

But our expectations and efforts often disappoint. And so the advice of today's readings is a tremendous help: Zephaniah tells us to keep God as our light, Paul tells us to be of a generous spirit, and John the Baptist — despite his austerity — is a model of joy in spreading the Good News. As important for us as trying to bring more good into the world is our duty to recognize and be joyous over the good that's here. For that, we give glory and thanks to our God. The same joy of Zephaniah, Paul, and John the Baptist that was too intense to keep to themselves is here today. It waits to be shared. To have it, recognize it, and share it is our "Ode to Joy."

FOURTH SUNDAY OF ADVENT
Mi 5:1-4   Heb 10:5-10   Lk 1:39-44

Preparing for the Blessed Event: Obedience
Opening our Lives for the Coming; Caroling;
Opening the Way to God; Obedience and Surprise

In his *Divine Comedy*, Dante pictured Purgatory as a seven-story mountain. On each level, those guilty of one of the Deadly Sins were condemned to stay. Where Dante located the slothful, he sculpted the scene of the Visitation, to force the guilty to face and consider Mary's haste to go to Elizabeth (today's Gospel, v. 39). Perhaps Mary was doing the natural thing in wanting to stay with an understanding elderly relative until she'd had time to come to terms with what was happening to herself, but mostly she went as an act of charity to her cousin in need.

Mary's beautiful charity is the antithesis of a story from the brothers Grimm. It tells us of a feeble old woman whose husband died and left her all alone. She went to live with her son and his wife and their little daughter. Every day the old woman's sight dimmed and her hearing grew worse, and sometimes at dinner her hands trembled so badly the peas rolled off her spoon or the soup ran from her cup. The son and his wife were annoyed and one day, after she knocked over a glass of milk, they told each other enough was enough.

They set up a small table for her in the corner next to the broom closet and made the old woman eat her meals there. She sat all alone, looking with tear-filled eyes across the room at the others. Sometimes they spoke to her while they ate, but usually it was to scold her for dropping a bowl or a fork.

One evening just before dinner, their little daughter was busy playing on the floor with her building blocks, and her father asked her what she was making. "I'm building a little table for you and mother," she smiled innocently, "so you can eat by yourselves in the corner someday when I get big."

Her parents sat staring at her for some time and they suddenly both began to cry. That night they led the old woman back to her place at the big table. From then on she ate with the rest of the family.

From Nazareth in Galilee, where Mary lived, to Ain Karem, about five miles west of Jerusalem, where Elizabeth lived, was about ninety miles, more than a tough four-day journey on foot. The roads and paths were full of landslides, rocks, cloudbursts, brooks without bridges, holes, snakes, scorpions, and robbers — and, of course, there were no hotels. Mary showed her unselfishness not only by quickly facing that trip with eagerness to be of help: She was also willing to stay in the background, loyal to God's wishes, obediently accepting all the uncertainties without asking why.

When these two mothers-to-be visited (v. 40), two worlds met — not worlds of space, but of time. Elizabeth, advanced in years, symbolized the approaching end of the Age of the Law and Prophets. Her son John the Baptist would herald the new age of salvation which Israel had long awaited and which Mary now represented. Their sons' careers would be as collaborators, not competitors. In the Visitation, Promise greeted Fulfillment, and both Mary and Elizabeth responded to the Holy Spirit.

Though it was Elizabeth's husband Zechariah's house where they met, and Mary's dignity was the greater, it was Mary who greeted Elizabeth. Her greeting was with all the warmth of a kinswoman's affection as well as a deference to the aged that is so becoming for a young lady. When the angel Gabriel had come from God to Zechariah with the news of Elizabeth's impending pregnancy, Zechariah had doubted, giving reasons why it would all be impossible. As a result, the angel had given Zechariah a sign: He would be mute until the events would take place. In contrast, at the same angel's Annunciation to Mary that she was to become the mother of Jesus, Mary had simply questioned "how" the birth of her child would take place: At the time, she wasn't married. The "divine moment" happened at the instant when Mary proclaimed "I am the maidservant of the Lord."

Mary had uttered her consent, and arrived to visit the aged Elizabeth a picture of radiant joy. Under the special inspiration of God, the Holy Spirit spoke through Elizabeth, and she gave high praise to Mary. Her praises showed an easy familiarity with the Jewish sacred writings and echoed the praises given to Israel's heroines of old.

Then Elizabeth gave voice to her awareness that the infant in her womb leaped for joy (v. 44). Later, when a woman in a crowd would be so overjoyed by Jesus' words that she would cry out, "Blessed is the womb that carried you" (Lk 11:27), Jesus would reply, "Rather, blessed are those who hear the word of God and observe it" (Lk 11:28). On that future occasion, Jesus was doing essentially what Elizabeth was doing now: praising Mary for her faith obedience. As St. Augustine said of Mary, "It's a greater thing for her that she was Christ's disciple than that she was his mother." Mary, the poor girl of little consequence, had in her prayerful heart truly heard God's word and kept it. She was to be surprised by what God would do with her obedience. Elizabeth couldn't resist the temptation to contrast this with her husband's doubt.

A profound vision of Jesus' destiny as a leader came from the prophet Micah, from whom today's First Reading comes. He lived at the same time as Isaiah, Amos, and Hosea, and had the usual message of prophets: Repent and turn to God from your disobedience.

Micah would have understood the connotations of "little town" in the words of the Christmas carol that sings, "O Little Town of Bethlehem." He came from a village about 25 miles southwest of Jerusalem. Coming from "the sticks" to the "big city" of Jerusalem, he spoke out against the evils he saw with all the bluntness we attribute to "country bumpkins," and he blamed the leaders, because they should have known what God wanted for His people.

In today's passage, Micah asserts straightforwardly that any hope for the leadership of their people couldn't come from sophisticated Jerusalem. The people there were too hardened, the kings there had often oppressed the people, and the current kings, Ahaz and Hezekiah, though descendants of King David, weren't much. Whatever hope there was would have to come from elsewhere. Micah looked to the small town of Bethlehem, about five miles south of Jerusalem. He called it also Ephrathah (v. 1), because when the Jews had come from Egypt and conquered Canaan, Bethlehem had been settled by the Ephrathah clan of the tribe of Judah. The name Bethlehem itself means "house of bread." Its important origins were from ancient times (v. 1) — that is, from the ancient dynasty of Jesse and his son David.

Micah saw a ruler coming from this town who would be worthy of David. Just as David had been a shepherd, so too this coming leader: His leadership would be pastoral. But this man would be as unlike the descendants of David as David was. Unlike the weak, vacillating kings then ruling, this man would be firm; unlike their smallness, he would possess a greatness which the whole world would acknowledge. Again the Christmas carol sums it up:

> The hopes and fears
> of all the years
> are met in thee tonight!

In our joy-filled Advent preparations for Christmas, when we might overlook the why of Jesus' appearance in human form, today's passage from the letter to the Hebrews sets us straight. It's been one of the constant preoccupations of humankind all over the world to take away sin. Under the former covenant — before Jesus — this was done by sacrifices: animals slaughtered in a precise ritual. Blood was considered to be the life of the animal, and sacrificing it a sign that the giver was willing to give his or her life to God.

First Testament sacrifices were, however, only a pale copy of what true worship ought to be. In itself, sacrifice is a noble thing but, human beings being what they are, it's easy for the practice of sacrifice to degenerate. Whereas sacrifice ought to be a token of love and a pledge of devotion, it's understandable that some people think of it as a way of buying God's forgiveness. Putting into the mouth of Jesus the words of a Psalm (40:6-9), the letter to the Hebrews says that God no longer wants animal sacrifices. What He really wants is our obedience so that our sins can be forgiven and the way to Him opened up. As we look at Christmas as reflected in today's liturgy, we have a sense of the past as well as the present. Sometimes that sense of the past can be merely nostalgic: over the meadows and through the woods to grandmother's house, or dreaming of a white Christmas, or fantasizing about Christmas-card illustrations. A realistic sense of the past, though, includes an obedient response to God's leadership in the present. Opposing obedience with prideful and slothful self-will sets up a barrier to our relationship with God.

The persons in today's liturgy show that God often surprises the obedient with what He will do. If we follow their example, we can show our worthiness of God's coming to us in Christ at Christmas by arising from our sloth and becoming, like Micah, Mary, and Elizabeth, each in our different ways as they were different in theirs, Godbearers in our world that needs God so much.

CHRISTMAS MASS AT DAWN
Is 62:11-12   Tt 3:4-7   Lk 2:15-20

Christmas Past, Present, and Future

The essence of the "straight man" in film or on stage is that he gives. He gives the best lines, the stage, the spotlight. Carl Reiner did that to coax the hilarity out of Sid Caesar on *Your Show of Shows*. Dean Martin possessed that rare straight comic gift as Jerry Lewis's partner.

Note: This homily is for the Mass at Dawn; for the Mass during the day, see the
    following. For the Vigil Mass, see Cycle A; for the Night Mass, Cycle B.

George Burns had it with his wife Gracie Allen. In one scene, for example, George and Gracie were holding hands. A man stepped out of the wings and kissed Gracie, who kissed him back.

Then she turned to George and asked, "Who was that?"

George: "You don't know?"

Gracie: "No. My mother told me never to talk to strangers."

George: "That makes sense."

The world from which we come tells us that at Christmas we're expected to give gifts and to receive them, leaving open the question of whether it's better to give than receive. In show business, by giving the straight man creates the show. And he gets by giving.

So it is with us and God, especially with regard to attendance at Sunday Mass. We're God's straight men, and we get by giving. We give our presence every Sunday, even though we take a risk that the homily won't be any good, we'd rather sleep, and we don't want to be bothered with the crowd who go to our church.

With apologies to Charles Dickens' *Christmas Carol*, I expect that we're here to commemorate Christmas past, Christmas present, and Christmas future.

Christmas past tells us, as our Responsorial Psalm reminds, that Jesus came to be people's light and to give that light to everyone who comes into the world. Just fantasize about that for a moment! A beam of light traveling at the rate of 186,000 miles per second (which is the way God created it) in less than two seconds passes the moon; in eight minutes it reaches the sun; in six hours, it leaves our solar system; in four light-years it touches the nearest star; in 32 thousand light-years it breaks free of this galaxy; in 170,000 light-years it arrives at the next nearest galaxy. In view of the fact that there are millions of galaxies, one can see that the Creator of the universe is indescribably awesome.

Why, then, did the Creator of the universe choose, in that first Christmas past, to come in the way He did: in a smelly, cold stable in a little town, in an out-of-the-way country, appearing first to insignificant people? I would suggest that it was to teach many lessons for which we need not a far-off, majestic, awesome God, but Emmanuel, God-with-us. Among those lessons are humility for everyone in our world who subscribes to the popular idea of being his own king or her own queen. As our Gospel reminds, there's the lesson from Mary of being attentive to God's word and pondering it in our hearts. For all time, when people look upon work as a chore to be avoided, the worker's son and his foster-father teach us to work diligently. He who grew from this place in wisdom, age, and grace before God and people, teaches us to grow in all things toward him, our head.

There are many other lessons from Christmas past. Jesus comes in a lowly estate — in the form of a poor man born of a simple maiden — so that he might gently attract and bring humankind to salvation. If he had been born amid the splendor of a rich family, people could have said that the face of the world had been changed, once again, by the power of wealth. If he had chosen to be born in Rome, then the greatest of cities, they would have ascribed the same change to the power of her citizens. If he had been the son of an emperor, many would have been afraid to approach and would have pointed to the advantage of authority. If his father had been a legislator, their cry would have been, "See what can be brought about by the law."

As God arranged it, though, it was the Godhead alone that transformed the world. The lack of the necessities of life was the best way of proclaiming the will of God. As he lay in the manger surrounded by poverty, the divine Word, the son of God, drew to himself both rich and poor, the eloquent and the inarticulate, the powerful and the powerless — all who would accept his invitation. Motivating it all is the lesson of God's unfathomable love for us.

Contemplating the lessons of Christmas present, we see around us a great deal of confusion about the feast's meaning. Up to about a hundred and fifty years ago, where reformers and nonconformists held sway Christmas wasn't permitted to be celebrated more than any other day: They wanted to do away with anything that derogated from the purity of the Gospels. And they wanted to get away from anything that in any way smacked of "papists" (Roman Catholics).

From that time to our own, Christmas has gradually taken on the character of a grand commercial bazaar. The confusion of today was aptly put by a little Catholic-school girl, who said, "I've been taught in school that the meaning of Christmas is giving, but when I see the store windows and watch TV I can't help thinking of all the stuff I'll be getting."

The lessons of the Scripture readings of today's Mass are no less true today than when they were written. From Isaiah we learn that the new Israel, the Christian community, is the recipient of God's Good News. The letter to Titus rejoices in the sheer undeservedness of our salvation, made available to us when the grace of God was made visible in Jesus Christ. And the Gospel of this Mass has all the essential elements of what we celebrate today.

For the lessons of Christmas future, let's remember one essential difference about time between God and us. For us, time is always horizontal: our watches tell us that one minute follows the previous one and precedes the following one; our calendars tell us that one day follows another, and each month does the same. For God, however, time is vertical: that is to say, there are no minutes, no days; all time is always present to Him. That means that the Christmas that took place two thousand years ago is still with Him, as much as the Christmas of today and the Christmas of next year or a thousand years from now.

That means, moreover, that every act we do to bring God's light further into the world is another small Christmas. And the way God's light comes into the world today is through us. A missioner in Japan tells the story of being called to minister to a Catholic lady who lay dying at her home. Her son, a medical doctor, although not a Christian, always greeted him respectfully when he brought the Eucharist to his dying mother and eventually anointed her, but was always formal and distant. A few months after the death of his mother, the physician appeared on the missioner's doorstep. After an exchange of social amenities, he came to explain that he wanted to go to confession. He had heard his mother speak of the inner peace she had experienced in the Sacrament of Reconciliation and had seen that for himself, and he wanted to try it for himself: There were things weighing heavily on his mind. The priest called down God's blessing on him; evidencing peace, he thanked the priest and left. Six months later, the doctor took instructions and was happily baptized. His mother had brought him the light of the world. And, in a country where only 0.3% of the people are Catholic, where conformity is cultivated and where individuality isn't admired, the doctor himself thereafter provided the light of the world, too, to all around him.

Every time we do a good deed, in God's sight we're creating some of the joy that Jesus came to bring. Every time we go to church when we don't feel like it, we're giving rather than getting and adding to the world's welfare. Every time we act as peacemakers, every time we go against the grain to help another, every time we try to be understanding, every time we meditate on the spiritual life, God sees us as continuing the delight that we robustly celebrate today. Even though God created light to travel at 186,000 miles per second, for the traveling of

His special light He has chosen to have us bring it — a slower process, of course, but blessing both the one who brings His light as well as the one who receives it.

Remembering the enchantment of Christmas past, the joy of Christmas present, and the attractiveness of Christmas future, may you have a Merry Christmas, may its bliss be with you into the new year and always, may you remember how to achieve it, and may you bring some of His divine light into the world.

CHRISTMAS MASS DURING THE DAY
Is 52:7-10   Heb 1:1-6   Jn 1:1-18 (or 1-5, 9-14)

Jesus the Life and Light of the World
A Contribution to the Meaning of Life

Because so much depends on an author capturing the attention of the reader as soon as possible, one author (Donald Newlove, *First Paragraphs* [New York: St. Martin's Press, 1992]) searched through the very best first paragraphs he could find in famous writers of all time. He went through a panoply of such authors as Ernest Hemingway, Charles Dickens, Herman Melville, F. Scott Fitzgerald, Edgar Allan Poe, James Joyce, Flannery O'Connor, William Faulkner, Norman Mailer, John Updike, Eudora Welty, and many others. He concluded that the greatest first paragraph ever written is the beginning of St. John's Gospel that we just heard. He spoke of John's great canvas of eternity and his getting down to earth with the coming of Christ. He said that John must certainly have read Homer and the Book of Genesis, and comments that John's first paragraph is bigger than both of them.

In the first words of his Gospel — "In the beginning" — John echoes the very first words of the Bible. In the very beginning, God's creative words gave life and light. From the very beginning was the one whom John calls "the Word." "Word" in Greek (the language John

---

Note: This homily is for the Mass during the Day. For the Vigil Mass, see Cycle A; for the Midnight Mass, Cycle B; for the Mass at Dawn, see immediately above.

was using, for his non-Jewish audience) is *Logos*, which to those schooled in philosophy meant much more than "word." It meant everything from "word" to "intellect" all the way to "the meaning of existence." So John was announcing that in Jesus we find the ultimate explanation of the meaning of life.

Our use of the word "word" still shows its importance. In praise of an upright man we say, "He's a man of his word." Children, imitating the nobility of old, say, "Word of honor." When we're after some deep information, we ask, "What's the word?", and there are few condemnations worse than "You can't take his word for anything."

In the Jewish Scriptures, a word was far more than just a sound. It was something that was alive, charged with power. The Jewish Scriptures are full of examples of that. In the creation story, for example, at every stage we read "And God said... ," and an aspect of creation came into being. Isaac, having been deceived into giving his words of blessing to Jacob instead of Esau, couldn't take the blessing back (Gn 27). And the Jews had in their Wisdom literature the concentrated presentations of the words of wise men. Wisdom and the Word are the same: God's agent for enlightenment.

John saw that "the Word was with God" — not as a single action of the past, but in a continuous, timeless existence. But not only "with God": "the Word was God" — so that the Word, Jesus, is in the best position to reveal who God is. Sometimes we think that, when Jesus came, he changed God — from angry into loving. But God has always been like Jesus. It isn't God who's changed; it's humankind's understanding of Him that has changed.

Then (v. 4) John, like a composing artist, enunciates the two themes of his work: life and light. The life is the life of God: the eternal life that God lives, the opposite of destruction, condemnation, and death. Life for human beings isn't mere existence — even inanimate things exist — but a sharing in the being of God.

The word "life" is frequently on the lips of Jesus. Jesus regrets that people won't come to him that they might have life (5:40); he asserts that he came that humankind might have life and have it more abundantly (10:10); he says that he's the way, the truth, and the life (14:6). In John's Gospel, the word "life" occurs more than 35 times, and the verb "to live" or "to have life" more than 15 times more. At the very end of his Gospel, John says that he has written that through belief in Jesus we may have life in his name (20:31).

John's light is the everlasting light, the timeless light revealed in time, the light manifested in the flesh although hidden by nature, the light that shone around the shepherds and guided the Magi. It's that light which came into its own people, and they didn't receive it.

The word "light" occurs in John's Gospel no fewer than 21 times. He says that Jesus' light is that which puts the darkness of disorder to flight, like God moving upon the dark chaos and replacing it with the creation of light. Darkness, the antithesis of light, means whatever is in opposition to God. It stands for life without Christ. One of humankind's oldest fears is fear of the dark — still present in children, but even for adults the world is full of forebodings and threats. No matter how hard the darkness has tried, it hasn't overcome the light.

Jesus is the true light (v. 9) — different from the lights of the deceptions and illusions that people have followed. Some are only flickers of the truth, others will-o'-the-wisps. Jesus the true light dissipated the shadows of doubt, the blackness of despair, the starkness of death. When the star brought the wise men to the humble cave instead of to a regal palace, God was making a statement about our value system: that it wasn't His. The tragedy is that, though "the world came to be through him" (v. 10), he came to people who were his own, but they didn't accept him (v. 11).

The phenomena apply to people of all time. It applied to the Israelites of Isaiah's time. Isaiah visualized the lonely task of the watchmen of Jerusalem looking out hour after hour, day after day for the least sign on the horizon of the return of their king. He imagined them seeing God Himself returning to the city to save it and to once again make His people great. He saw the messengers shouting along the mountain ridges, "peace... salvation... Your God is King!" (v. 7), the watchmen repeating the messengers' cry (v. 8), and all the people breaking out in song (vv. 9f.). All of that resounds in other First Testament texts and echoes in the New Testament. God prepares not only the Jewish people for His coming, but every person in this world in one way or another. And to those who accept Him and His values He gives the power to become His children (v. 12).

That brings John to the climax of his hymn, what we celebrate today: the Word made flesh (v. 14). Flesh is all that's transitory, mortal, imperfect, and at first sight seemingly incompatible with God. This is the tremendous mystery of the incarnation, the story that brings the infinite one, the creator, the divine, to the insignificant town of

Bethlehem, where in a smelly stable He became one of us in every-thing but sin.

Man's maker was truly made man — so that the Ruler of the stars was in the thick of life. He came in the most unlikely circumstances. A helpless baby, the child of a poor family, in a subjugated country — all of it doesn't seem a hopeful seedbed for liberation, redemption, and freedom. He could be hungry and tired from his journeys, and he was accused by false witnesses, evaluated by a mortal judge, beaten with whips, crowned with thorns, suffered, and died. It's the stuff of life as it's lived around us.

That's the depth of the Christmas story. People who don't understand that don't understand the goodness of humanity. When God created us, He saw all that He had made and found it very good. Yet down through the centuries there have been those who claimed that one aspect of God's creation, humanity, is bad. Their position is summed up in the ditty, "Had I been the Deity's adviser, methinks I might have planned it wiser."

At the same time as he is human, Jesus is God. The early Christians realized that they couldn't think of God without thinking of Jesus, that all that the word "God" conveyed found adequate expression in Jesus Christ.

For a time, Jesus "made his dwelling" — literally, "pitched his tent" — with humankind. And we saw his glory: Jesus' whole life was a manifestation of the glory of God as spoken of in the Jewish Scriptures, which indicated the presence of God in the desert during the Exodus, on Mt. Sinai at the giving of the Commandments, over the Tabernacle, and above the Temple. Now this glory was uniquely Jesus' own. By living among us, Jesus enables us to come to the heart of God. That's the message of Christmas.

The letter to the Hebrews ratifies John's ideas. Today's portion is a splendid summary of the history of salvation, and a condensed treatment of the mystery of incarnation and redemption. It also makes clear that Jesus alone brings to humankind the full revelation of God. It says that Jesus is superior to the prophets (vv. 1-3) and over the angels (vv. 4-6). He's the new place where the spoken Word, the dynamic activity of God, is to be found. He's God's ikon, the light of God reflected in our world. God spoke through the prophets only in fragmentary and varied ways (v. 1). Often the prophets were characterized by one idea: Amos for social justice, Isaiah for the holiness of God, Hosea for the forgiving love of God. But no prophet had grasped the entire truth.

Jesus did, and in our time, the final period of humankind's religious history, he's the one through whom God preeminently speaks. Since Jesus' redemptive sacrifice, God spoke to us through a Son (v. 2). With thoughts similar to John's Prologue, the letter to the Hebrews reminds us that this Son existed before he appeared as man. No creature, not even an angel, can match the unique dignity of his person (v. 4).

Today, we've split the atom, conquered a portion of space, and harnessed nuclear energy, and we play with new kinds of life in test tubes. Yet many people don't realize our need for the revelation of Jesus. Christ is born to us today in order that he may appear to the whole world through us. The mystery of Christmas lays upon us all a debt to God and an obligation to the rest of humankind. Bethlehem is no longer a hillside cave. It is, rather, every place where we create justice, freedom, and love. We do this not only by preaching the Good News, but by living it and thus revealing Jesus. May your living Jesus and revealing him to those around you through your love give you and yours a blessed Christmas!

HOLY FAMILY
Si 3:2-6, 12-14 (A, B, & C)   Col 3:12-21 (A, B, & C)   Lk 2:41-52

Family Life: Dream and Reality
Good Family Relationships

The author of an essay called "What Is A Boy?" writes that all boys have the same creed: to enjoy every second of every minute of every hour of every day and to protest with noise (their only weapon) when their last minute is finished and the adults pack them off to bed at night.

The essay says that a boy is a composite — he has the appetite of a horse, the digestion of a sword swallower, the energy of a pocket-size nuclear bomb, the curiosity of a cat, the lungs of a dictator, the

---

Note: Today's homily is on all the readings. For a homily mostly on Matthew, see Cycle
A; on Luke 2:22-40, Cycle B.

imagination of a Paul Bunyan, the shyness of a violet, the audacity of a steel trap, and the enthusiasm of a firecracker.

Today's Gospel episode is the story of the finding of the child Jesus in the Temple — a story that makes us question whether Jesus was like other boys. That Jesus' parents every year went to Jerusalem for the feast of Passover (v. 41) showed them to be deeply pious. They trained their son to be the same. At this time, only the Jewish men who lived in Judea, and were thus close by, were obliged to go to Jerusalem for the great feasts. Women weren't obliged at all. But many who weren't strictly obliged often attended out of devotion.

On his twelfth birthday, a young Jewish male became Bar Mitzvah, "a son of the Law," and assumed the obligations of the Mosaic Code. It was the age when a boy began the practice of his chosen trade. We can well imagine how the Holy City, the Temple precincts, and the sacred ritual fascinated the boy Jesus.

When an Eastern caravan like the one for a Passover celebration got under way, all was noise, confusion, and excitement. Usually the women started earlier than the men each day, because their travel was slower. The two sections wouldn't meet until both had reached the evening encampment. It wasn't through carelessness, then, that Mary and Joseph didn't miss Jesus: No doubt Joseph thought he was with Mary and Mary thought he was with Joseph (v. 43).

During the Passover season, it was the custom of the Sanhedrin to meet publicly to discuss religious questions for all who were interested. The Rabbis sat on a chair with their pupils sitting on the ground at their feet. Jesus, searching for knowledge like an eager student, was listening to them and asking them questions (v. 46).

Upon finding the child Jesus, Mary, like any mother finding a lost child, was probably torn between hugging and spanking him. She informed the young Jesus that Joseph and she had been looking for him with great anxiety (v. 48). Jesus deftly took the name "father" from Mary's imputation of it to Joseph and gave it to God: "Did you not know I must be in my Father's house (namely, the Temple)?" (v. 49).

This was Jesus' first recorded public utterance, and it reveals that his reflections had led him to knowing something of who he was. When did that moment arrive that he knew himself to be different — unique? As Jesus grew older, he continually manifested greater graciousness (v. 52) because, like all thinking people, he grew in wisdom. As God, Jesus had infinite knowledge. As man, his mind could advance in experiential knowledge. And God intended many lessons from Jesus' "hidden life" in Nazareth — for one, the lesson that prominent and brilliant successes aren't essential elements of a noble life: Millions of the beloved of God are to be found among the obscure. But, as Luke's Gospel says, he grew. Growth is a part of human existence, and Jesus realized its fullest possibilities.

Lest we think that Jesus' words to his parents showed undue independence, Luke stresses Jesus' obedience toward them (v. 51). Whatever he knew of his special relationship to God, it didn't cause him to look down on his parents, the gentle Mary and the hard-working Joseph.

All of that accords with the best of Jewish teaching. About two hundred years before Christ, when the book called Sirach put together wise counsels on how to lead a life pleasing to God, it contained today's section on the relationships between parents and children. This passage is a detailed commentary on the only scriptural command that has a reward attached: Honor your father and your mother, that you may have a long life (Ex 20:12). Sirach adds the religious motivation that those who honor their parents atone for sins (vv. 3 and 14). That's a reward more amazing than "long life": In fact, it suggests the substitution of "full life." Jesus, for example, didn't have a long life. But his life was certainly full.

Sirach, though, seems to be talking not so much about young children as about the duties of adult children toward their aging parents. With people living longer in our society, those duties are today very complex. There's a cult of youth and beauty in our society and an often barely veiled intolerance of the old.

A story's told of an old man who had lost his wife and lived all alone. He had worked hard as a tailor all his life, but misfortunes had left him penniless, and now he was so old he could no longer work for himself. His hands trembled too much to thread a needle, and his vision had blurred too much for him to make a straight stitch. He had three sons but, all grown and married now, they were so busy with their own lives that they only had time to visit their father once a week.

Gradually the old man grew more and more feeble, and his sons came by to see him less and less. "They don't want to be around me at all now," he realized, "because they're afraid I'll become a burden." He stayed up all night worrying what would become of him, until at last he thought of a plan.

The next morning he went to see his friend the carpenter, and asked him to make a large chest. Then he went to see his friend the locksmith, and asked him to give him an old lock. Lastly he went to see his friend the glassblower, and asked for all the old broken pieces of glass he had.

The old man took the chest home, filled it to the top with broken glass, locked it, and put it beneath his kitchen table. The next time his sons came for dinner, they bumped their feet against it.

"What's in this chest?" they asked, looking under the table.

"Oh, nothing," the old man replied, "just some things I've been saving."

His sons nudged it and felt how heavy it was. They kicked it and heard a rattling inside. "It must be full of all the gold he's saved over the years," they whispered to one another.

They decided to take turns living with the old man. So the first week the youngest son moved in with his father, and cared and cooked for him. The next week the middle son took his turn, and the week after that the eldest son. This went on for some time.

At last the old father grew sick and died. The sons gave him a nice funeral, mindful of the fortune they thought was sitting beneath the kitchen table; they felt they could afford to splurge a little.

When the funeral was over, they hunted through the house until they found the key to the chest, and unlocked it. Of course, they found it full of broken glass.

"What a rotten trick!" yelled the eldest son. "What a cruel thing to do to your own sons!"

"But what else could he have done?" asked the middle son sadly. "To be honest with ourselves, if it weren't for this chest, we would have neglected him until the end of his days."

The eldest son tipped the chest over to make sure there was nothing valuable hidden there. The three brothers stared silently at the bottom, where they saw an inscription that read, "Honor thy father and mother."

Along with Sirach, today's passage from the letter to the Colossians shows the shape of a happy home. It's from a section that exhorts Christians to live their baptismal life. During the ceremonies of baptism, the candidates took off their old clothing, a sign of their former way of life, and put on a white garment, a sign of Christ's life. The letter lists the garments that must be put on for the Christian to

live a life in community with others. The beautiful advice on the social virtues that should characterize our response to God through Christ
is especially applicable to family life.

To the letter's list of "Household Rules" of ethics, there might
today be other applications and tomorrow still others, as needed, but
for all time the key phrase is "in the Lord." Pictures like submissive
wives (v. 18) and nagging fathers (v. 21) may need explanation, but
"in the Lord" never changes.

Those who don't like the advice given — about submissive wives,
for instance — should look at the passage carefully. What's presented
here is something new in all the world up to that time: an ethic of re-
ciprocal duties. The words "one another," for example, are repeated
three times (vv. 9, 13, 16). Remember that at that time under Jewish
law a woman was a thing, the possession of her husband: A man could
divorce his wife for any or no reason. In Greek society — the society
of the culture of the time — a respectable woman had to lead a life of
seclusion: She was never to be seen on the streets alone, even for mar-
keting, and she was in complete servitude to her man. Under both so-
cieties' double standard there was no reciprocity: All the privileges
belonged to the husband, all the duties to the wife.

For the Christian, the wife is to be a support to her husband (v.
18), yes, but the husband is to love his wife (v. 19). Therefore the husband is to practice the virtues of those who share Christ's life (v. 12):
heartfelt compassion, kindness, humility, gentleness, patience, and
forgiveness (v. 13) — all of them essential for family life. Over all of
them the Christian should wear the most important garment of all, love
(v. 14). Christianity is, above all, community: togetherness in the body
of Christ (v. 15).

The same reciprocity applied to children. Under the Roman law
of the time the parents were dominant, especially the father, whose
patria potestas gave him the power to make his child work like a slave,
or to sell his child into slavery, or to condemn his child to death, or to
do whatever else he wished. Under the new dispensation, children are
to obey their parents (v. 20), yes, but the duties are in both directions,
and in the Lord. These brand new precepts mean an awareness that Jesus
is always an unseen presence in the family.

May God teach us the sanctity of human love, show us the value
of family life, and help us to live in peace with all the human family.

SOLEMNITY OF MARY THE MOTHER OF GOD
Nb 6:22-27   Gal 4:4-7   Lk 2:16-21 (All A, B, & C)

Christian Freedom
Growth in Maturity

Lest the celebration of Christmas lose its luster, St. Paul reminds us in today's portion of his letter to the Galatians that Jesus' birth will continue to have meaning. Paul is saying that in the childhood of the world the tutelage of the Mosaic Law was necessary, but with the coming of Jesus the world advanced to a new status of maturity. We've experienced the power of the Holy Spirit, who has re-created us as God's children and enabled us to live our lives according to the sense and spirit of this new relationship. When Paul speaks of the coming of the fullness of time (v. 4), he refers to the phenomenon of the human race's rite of passage from childhood to adulthood.

With individuals, this growth into maturity usually referred, in a double standard, to males rather than females (who, it was probably thought, never matured). In the Jewish world, after a boy completed his twelfth year he underwent the ceremony called "Bar Mitzvah" in which he became a "son of the Law," which is what "Bar Mitzvah" means. Then — as with Jews still today — he's considered mature, a man. For him, the fullness of time has come. In the Greek world of Paul's time, the boy was under his father's care from ages seven to eighteen, whereupon he became an *ephebe* — what we might call a cadet — and for two years was under the care of the State, receiving military and gymnastic training. That meant arrival at manhood. In the Roman world of that time, somewhere between the ages of fourteen and seventeen the young man, after exchanging the purple-striped *toga pretexta* of youth for the plain white *toga virilis* of manhood, was taken to the forum for his introduction to public life and manhood.

Paul is comparing these practices to the point in history when God's saving intervention in the growth in maturity of the human race took place. It was at that point that God sent His Son (v. 4). That Jesus was "born of a woman" emphasizes his taking onto himself the human condition for his mission.

Note: This homily is on Galatians. For homily on Luke, see Cycle A; on Numbers, Cycle B.

Mary's role is central. She's an example of mature, joyful, spontaneous faith in action. As Jesus is true man, Mary is true woman. As with us, she journeyed in faith. Today we celebrate her as the Mother of God. In this feast, once the only Marian feast in Rome, we recall the part she played in the fulfillment of the ancient blessing promised to Israel and we give thanks for that blessing which has been bestowed upon us all.

Mary is a model for us also in the way she exercised her freedom and maturity. By accepting God's call to be the mother of Jesus, she also became the mother of all the redeemed. Just as she chose to be the mother of Jesus, in our freedom we're challenged to bring him forth in our own private and public worlds in this new year.

Many people think of freedom solely in terms of being able to do what they feel like doing. They think that the free-est people live with no obligations or commitments. People who have no regard for rules are sometimes referred to as "free spirits." Some celebrities, appearing to be very free, joke about the numbers of marriages or affairs they've had. But such people aren't really free. The deepest kind of freedom involves the ability to love and make commitments. St. Augustine said, "Love God and do what you want." Our temptation is to do what we want without any concern for deeply loving God or anyone else.

Some choices deepen our freedom and our humanity; others make us less free and diminish our humanity. Sins make us the least free. Sinners have weakened their capacity to love. Sinners are choosing for themselves at the expense of others. The liar is more harmed than the person lied to, the thief more than the person stolen from, the adulterer or adulteress more than the partner sinned against.

We're born free in the sense that we're born with the power to make free choices: We're born to be free. But that power must be developed and strengthened. Nothing frees us more than loving and being loved. Loving touches the deepest level of our personhood, and being loved frees us more than any other experience.

We have the freedom to receive the status of God's adopted children and enter into our inheritance. That adoption isn't by natural birth, of course, but by God's action — that is, by grace. The call to grace in its ultimate form is a summons to be one with God, to assume peership with God. Hence it is a call to total adulthood, in which both spiritual growth and the process of psychological maturation are inseparable.

After Jesus' birth God now looks upon each of us and sees the likeness of His only-begotten child. The human countenance is forever altered.

The proof that we're literally God's children comes from the instinctive cry of our heart whereby we want to be intimate with God. This cry is to call God *Abba*. This is the Aramaic word for father; the sound of it is so sacred and intimate to Paul that he keeps it in the original tongue. The Aramaic here means "my Father" rather than "the father," and has overtones in English of "daddy."

It's an extremely exalted privilege that the Christian, by virtue of being God's child and thus a brother or sister of Jesus, is entitled to pray to the Father with the same formula that was used by Jesus himself. All of this empowers the Christian's inmost conviction as she or he exclaims lovingly of God, "Father!", rejoicing to be no longer a slave but a child, and an heir (v. 7).

We're called to be mature, full-grown people. To grow from the simple trust of early childhood into a personal, reflective, integrated, truly committed, and mature faith is possible for most people only after they've passed through the turmoil of adolescence. Growing up is the act of stepping from childhood into adulthood — actually, more of a fearful leap than a step, a leap that many people never really take. Though they may outwardly appear to be adults, even successful adults, many "grown-ups" remain until their death psychological children who have never truly separated themselves from their parents and the power that their parents have over them.

In the first half of our life our main task is trying to become the person we want to be and building up our ego, and in the second half to let it go. Ultimately, the prospect of death leaves us no choice but to give thought to our level of maturity in faith. But it's not death itself, but letting go of self, that's difficult.

Today is January First, the beginning of a new calendar year. January got its name from the Roman god Janus. Janus had two faces, one looking back and the other forward. Today we look back upon our record during the past year in order to come up with accurate appraisals of ourselves in trying to be better in the new year.

We, too, can be two-faced — not in an evil sense, but in the sense of blindness. Consider, as just one example of our blindness, our relationship to our own face. It's very dependent on mediation: reflection in mirrors, for instance, or the eyes of others. Even our idioms fall on either side of a doubleness. We use the word "face" to mean appearance, outward show, or a surface or facade, as in "on the face of it, it seems thus and so," or "putting the best face on" a failure. We also use "face" to stand for the reality, dignity, integrity, or even the inmost essential aspect, of a person or thing. We speak of looking the evidence in the face, of saving or losing face, of being faceless, of now seeing through a glass darkly but at the end face to face with God. Do we really know our own face, the substance of what we're really like?

Every January First, we're presented with a handsome sum (more than a half million) which is ours to spend during the next 12 months. Each of us is given, not the dollars we fantasize about, but 525,600 minutes with which to build a life. We do think about time like money sometimes: We speak of "spending time" doing this or that.

To get as much out of time as we can, we talk faster, walk faster. A psychologist who compared several countries found the pace of public life to be fastest in Japan, followed by the United States, England, Taiwan, Italy, and Indonesia, in that order. In each country, the pace in larger cities was faster than in smaller ones. In the United States, Boston turned out to be the fastest-paced city of those studied (perhaps because of the number of colleges and universities there, with so many young people), Los Angeles the slowest. Chicago fell in the middle, while Salt Lake City was right behind New York. Answering why it's so isn't easy.

We think much more about the use of our money, which is renewable, than we do about the use of our time, which is irreplaceable. If we had to make a choice of handing over to someone else our checkbook or our datebook, it would be much wiser to hand over our checkbook. Everyone in the world — poor as well as rich — has exactly the same amount of time, even though it may seem different. We, too, experience "different" times: It's one thing on our wedding night, another if our fingers are caught in the car door. In the use of all our time for the coming year, one of our emphases should be growth in the Lord's freedom and maturity.

Let's take with us some of the lessons of today's liturgy: from the First Reading's Book of Numbers, to live in joy because the Father blesses us; from the Second Reading's letter to the Galatians, to live in mature freedom because the Son redeems us; and from Luke's Gospel, to live reflectively, like Mary. That's the way to fulfill the heartfelt wishes we extend to you for a Happy New Year.

SOLEMNITY OF THE EPIPHANY OF THE LORD
Is 60:1-6   Eph 3:2f., 5f.   Mt 2:1-12 (All A, B, & C)

Having a Star
Light to the World; The Appearances of God;
Light and Darkness; The Universality of God's Message

Goals determine strategy. In the United States Civil War, the goals of
Union General George McClellan were completely different from those
of President Abraham Lincoln. Lincoln's goal was to win the war and
thereby crush any possibility of secession. McClellan's goal was to deny
victory to the South, and then settle. McClellan's goal of peace with
or without union led to his slow-downs and permeated his strategy of
fighting to compromise. McClellan fought not to lose and Lincoln
wanted to fight to win. Because their goals were irreconcilable, Lincoln had to fire McClellan.

Goals make a big difference in life, too. Most people without
goals want more. When that's not enough, they want better, and when
better's not enough, they want different. When different is not enough,
they become sad, their life becomes meaningless, and they become
alienated. All the while, what they need is goals.

People's goals are like the star of the magi in our Gospel of
today's Solemnity of the Epiphany, the end of the Christmas season.
The star is an apt symbol of the attraction of light in darkness. The moth
is attracted to the flame, the voyager to the lighted window, the nations
to the light of the Lord in Jerusalem, and the magi to the star of
Bethlehem. That star can sometimes mean trouble, but trouble is far
easier to deal with than meaninglessness. Those who have died for
something are far better off than those who live for nothing.

Darkness, or black, on the other hand, is the color of night, the
color of melancholy, grief, and loss. It's also the color of death, the
color worn by Lucifer, Nazi storm troopers, Italian Fascists, bad guys
in the old westerns, Darth Vader, the Wicked Witch of the West, motorcycle gangs, and Dracula.

We don't know much about the visitors to the infant Jesus mentioned in St. Matthew's Gospel. Because Matthew is the only Gospel

---

Note: Today's homily is on Matthew.

that speaks of the magi, and that with only the few words we have here, over the centuries Christians have added all kinds of details. For example, they made them three in number, after the number of their gifts. They gave them names: Gaspar, Balthazar, and Melchior. They made one young, one middle-aged, and one old. They posited that the magi came from all over the world, including black Africa. As a matter of fact, some scholars think that their story is in a literary type called midrash, which is a poetic and mystical meditation on a mystery in the light of the Sacred Scriptures. The rabbis loved midrash, and the Talmud is filled with it. In it, though, it's often impossible to tell what is fact and what is meditation.

Midrash or not, Matthew might have had purposes in using the story here. A Jew writing for Jews, he wants to show a deep contrast between the Jewish and the non-Jewish worlds: Non-Jewish leaders traveled hundreds of miles to honor Jesus; Jewish leaders who were five miles away couldn't be bothered! Matthew wants us to think of the magi in terms of Isaiah 60, which is today's First Reading. His message is the Good News that God loves all people — non-Jews as well as Jews — and invites all to salvation.

The fact is that we don't know the magi's names, where they came from, or how many there were. The Greek word *magoi* is difficult to translate. The magi have been erroneously called both kings and astrologers. They weren't kings; nor were they astrologers in any sense that connotes superstition, but only in the sense that they saw in the stars the order of the universe and, not unreasonably, believed that the stars had something to do with the destiny of those born under them. The magi were the sages of their people, whose profession was the propagation of wisdom.

It appears that they had first seen the star two years before their arrival. There are many scientific theories to explain what the star might have been: Halley's comet, for example, or a brilliant conjunction of the planets Saturn and Jupiter, or a special position of Venus. But the action of the star implies that, in the evangelist Matthew's mind at least, it was a supernatural phenomenon. That the star could point out an individual place shows that it must have been some luminous object very near the earth; it also moved from east to west, which stars don't ordinarily do. The star must have disappeared during the magi's encounter with Herod, for upon the resumption of their journey the magi were exhilarated at seeing the star (v. 10).

Why did the magi conclude from the appearance of the star to the birth of the "king of the Jews"? Perhaps they had acquired some background from the Jews dispersed throughout the world. Immediately before Jesus' time particularly, expectation was in the air: not only among the Jews in Palestine, but with people all over the Roman Empire. Unlike some Utopian schemes of our time, many people of experience had come to the opinion that they couldn't build the golden age without God. So it wasn't strange that the magi should search.

More numerous and more serious difficulties than their two-year journey stood in the way of their following the star to its destination. A major one was a man whose story is interwoven with theirs and with Jesus': Herod, called "the Great" because of his political astuteness. He had made himself useful to Rome, so Rome used him. In 40 B.C. the Roman senate had appointed him king of Judea, where he remained for 43 long years. He was the only ruler in that area who had ever succeeded in keeping the peace. And he had other good points. There were, for example, his achievements in building, which included the Temple in Jerusalem. He could also be generous. When financial times were especially bad, he remitted taxes. In the famine of 25 B.C. he even melted down his own gold plate to buy food for the starving.

But there was another side to Herod. Because he was only half Jew, the other half being Idumaean, the Jews despised him as one who didn't observe the Law. So Herod felt insecure, which fertilized one of his dominant faults: suspicion. This grew as he became older. That deep fault often caused Herod to murder, his favorite methods being strangling, burning alive, drowning, poisoning, and the sword. If he suspected anyone as a rival, that person was as good as dead.

Perhaps his greatest tragedy was that he'd murdered his first wife Mariamne, whom he had loved very much. Unjustly suspecting Mariamne of infidelity, he became stark mad and, in his ungovernable jealousy and rage, ordered Mariamne and her alleged lover slain immediately. As soon as his passion subsided, his affection for Mariamne returned, and he spent the rest of his life lamenting her; he often appeared to talk to her as if making love to her ghost, though he had nine other wives.

He'd also murdered many other relatives, including his sons Alexander and Aristobolus. Even as the magi were visiting him, he was awaiting permission from Rome to execute another son, Antipater. When Matthew writes that King Herod was greatly troubled (v. 3) at the magi's news of the newborn king, it's easy to understand why all Jerusalem was disturbed as well. Everybody knew what Herod was capable of, and shivered.

Motivated by reports from his notorious spies as well as his news from the magi, this psychotically suspicious individual assembled all the chief priests and the scribes (v. 4) for details from the prophets about where the Messiah would be born. Their considered answer (vv. 5f.) was Bethlehem. That was the popular opinion, too: When some in a crowd following Jesus later on thought him the Messiah, others, thinking he came from Galilee, asked, "Doesn't Scripture say that the Messiah will come from Bethlehem?" (Jn 7:42). Herod's chicanery (vv. 7f.) of ascertaining from the magi the exact time of the star's appearance and instructing them to report back was typical. But had Herod, the consummate politician, taken this business really seriously, he would have sent a few horsemen in their tracks.

On entering the house and finding the child with Mary his mother (v. 11), the magi's faith was again put to the test: Accustomed to court splendor and cultured surroundings, they saw no servants or other trappings they were used to associating with royalty. They obeyed a divine message to leave for their own country by another route (v. 12). The magi had kept faith with their star.

As for Herod, toward the end of his life he was reined in more closely by the Roman Emperor Augustus, himself not a scrupulous man. Augustus, in fact, said that it was safer to be Herod's pig (*hus*) than his son (*huios*). The Jewish historian Josephus relates that when Herod at age 70 knew the end wasn't far off, the bloody tyrant retired to Jericho, the loveliest of the cities he had built; there he locked in the theater 5,000 prominent men of Jerusalem, giving orders to kill them as soon as he himself should die, in order to forestall the general rejoicing he knew would follow upon his death.

Herod's death followed five days after he had acted upon Augustus' permission to execute the death sentence against his son Antipater. It was a horrible death, his body by that time like a putrefying corpse. He had well prefigured his son Antipas who had John the Baptist murdered and would reign during Jesus' crucifixion. Herod's massacre of the Holy Innocents is easy to believe.

The magi had come because God calls all people, of every race and nation, to recognize Jesus as their Lord and do him homage. Through the shepherds and the magi at the beginning of Jesus' life, our Lord's kingdom broke into the world. At Jesus' death, above his head would appear the title which the magi used in asking for him: "the King of the Jews."

God calls us, too. On our journey through life, we're to search for a goal that gives meaning to life and try to acquire the qualities it takes to stay with that goal through thick and thin. Our goal has to have meaning, purpose, and commitment — all of which are inseparable. The activity of a beehive or assembly line may be purposeful, but it's not meaningful. A life without meaning, purpose, and commitment together, in Shakespeare's words "is a tale told by an idiot, full of sound and fury, signifying nothing."

One source of meaning, purpose, and commitment in our lives is to be instruments of Jesus' epiphany (showing) in the world — like the magi, though not necessarily in such dramatic fashion. We make the prayer of the Solemn Blessing at the end of this Mass determine the major goal of our life: "The wise men followed the star, and found Christ.... May you too find the Lord when your pilgrimage is ended."

THE FEAST OF THE BAPTISM OF THE LORD
Is 42:1-4, 6f.   Ac 10:34-38 (both A, B, & C)   Lk 3:15f., 21f.

Wind, Fire, and Us
Beginnings; Well Begun Is Half Done;
Faithfulness to Baptism; Jesus' Baptism and Ours

We've just celebrated some great Christmas feasts: the Solemnities of the Holy Family, Mary the Mother of God, and Epiphany. With today's Feast of the Baptism of the Lord and the beginning of commemorating Jesus' adulthood, some may think we're in a time of lesser importance. The truth is that today isn't just a great feast, but a very great one. Here, the Holy Trinity is manifested for the first time: The Father speaks from heaven, the Son is present, and the Holy Spirit descends.

St. Luke presents the psychological setting by saying that the

---

Note: This homily is mostly on Luke.

people were filled with expectation (v. 15). The people were wondering whether John the Baptist might be the Messiah, a misconception
they pursued time and time again. To the people's constant questions,
John was always honest in his answers — here saying that one mightier
than he is coming (v. 16). In the Jewish Scriptures, the word "mighty"
was used often for the leader of the final struggle against evil: So John
was portraying Jesus as the great liberator in the war against Satan.

We can appreciate John's selfless other-directedness toward Jesus
if we apply it to ourselves and imagine ourselves in a world without
mirrors. Eliminate as well from that imaginary world reflecting pools,
polished silver, bright store windows, and any other place where we
might catch a glimpse of ourselves. Although this might wreak havoc
with the cosmetics industry, it would encourage us to see beyond ourselves to a world that badly needs us: a world of sin, of unrelieved suffering, of addictions, of strife, of diseases such as AIDS and
Alzheimer's. It would also help us to understand the selfless and other-
directed nature of John the Baptist.

John said of Jesus that he would baptize with the Holy Spirit and
fire. As for the Spirit, John was again speaking in the context of the
Jewish Scriptures, which frequently attribute messianic achievement
to the Spirit. Throughout the Bible many extraordinary accomplishments reveal the presence of the Spirit (the life-power) of God, from
creation to the appearance of the messianic king.

John's image of fire may seem strange at first. Reflection reveals
a deeper meaning. In the Jewish Scriptures, great appearances of God
often surround Him with fire. When God was making His covenant with
Abraham, there appeared in the post-sunset darkness a smoking brazier and a flaming torch (Gn 15:17). An angel of the Lord appeared to
Moses in fire flaming out of a bush (Ex 3:2). The Lord preceded the
Israelites through the desert from Egypt as a column of cloud by day
and a column of fire by night (Ex 13:21f.). Ezekiel described his vision of God in terms of a huge cloud with flashing fire (Ezk 1:4ff.).

Fire had a prominent place also in liturgical services, where
people met their savior. God gave Aaron and his descendants, the
priests, directions on how to put burning embers on the altar and how
to place the meat-offerings there (Lv 1:7ff.). And the Lord instructed
Moses that the fire was to be kept burning on the altar (Lv 6:2, 6).

Like fire and the Spirit, Jesus' baptized followers are to be dynamic and active: "fired up" with the Holy Spirit to proclaim God's

Good News to all the world. In today's Gospel, when all the people were baptized (v. 21), John had fulfilled the mission confided by the angel to his father Zechariah before his birth: to prepare a people fit for the Lord (Lk 1:17).

That Jesus was at prayer indicates again the importance of the event: Luke often portrays Jesus at prayer on crucial occasions — at his election of the Twelve (6:12), during his Transfiguration, at Peter's confession that he was the Anointed of God (9:18); Jesus prayed that the faith of the chief of the Apostles may not fail when tempted (6:12; 9:18-20; 22:32); he prayed before his fulfillment of the Father's plan of love by his passion (22:41), and on his cross (23:46).

At Jesus' baptism, the skies opened — imagery frequently implying a vision of heavenly secrets. Jesus' baptism is a promise to be fulfilled at Pentecost, when the heavens will be open again and the Spirit will descend upon the community (Ac 2). The fact that the Holy Spirit descended on him in bodily form like a dove (v. 22) refers to many things. One is the Messianic gift to be bestowed on the Church at Pentecost. More pertinent to our beginning of the Church year, though, is the picture in the first pages of the Bible of the morning of the first creation, when the breath of God (*ruah elohim*) flew to and fro like a bird above the primordial waters as a power of fruitfulness and life. Now, at the beginning of the New Testament, with Jesus' baptism heralding a new creation, we see the Spirit coming upon Jesus.

The God who revealed Himself at Jesus' baptism is one who shatters the categories within which we try to contain Him. He's a God Who's to be found in the wilderness of our lives and Who aligns Himself with the poor. His voice here in the wilderness where John was baptizing may have been an epiphany even for Jesus. For the first time in his humanity, Jesus may have realized the unique relationship that he had with the heavenly Father.

For the other hearers, the voice of the Father brought recognition that Jesus is the beloved of God who not only bears the sins of the world, but will also take them away. Jesus is the Servant of the Lord of whom Isaiah spoke in today's First Reading (42:1). The opening of the eyes of the blind foretold in Isaiah represents an end to suffering that's due to humankind's creaturely status, whereas the setting free of captives marks an end to people's suffering at the hands of other human beings.

Judaism never considered that the role of Suffering Servant and of Messiah would be combined in one person. Yet the words of the voice from heaven at Jesus' baptism are the same as the first words of the Suffering Servant passage in Isaiah, some of which was today's First Reading. (Isaiah's "chosen one" [v. 1] is the same as Luke's "beloved Son" [v. 22].) Because the Servant is an ideal individual as well as the representative of the final community of the Lord, through his baptism Jesus is declared to be thoroughly human. Because of his total union with all human weakness, the Servant Jesus must descend into human death, so as to infuse a new life into every area of humankind's existence.

St. Peter was sufficiently impressed by the awe of this occasion that he later wrote of that unique declaration that came to Jesus out of the majestic splendor: "This is my Son, my beloved, with whom I am well pleased" (2 P 1:17). Peter preached that message over and over again. The last recorded time was his preaching to the Gentiles in today's Second Reading. His message on this occasion was, first, that Jesus was the fulfillment of the words from heaven at Jesus' baptism. Secondly, God shows no partiality (v. 34) for Jews over non-Jews: Rather, all over the world whoever acts uprightly out of her or his respect for God is acceptable to God (v. 35).

Peter preached that what had been reported about Jesus of Nazareth (v. 37), beginning with the marvels of his baptism, shows that God's revelation of His plan for the destiny of humankind culminated in Jesus. Jesus' whole ministry and message are integral parts of God's revelation. And the Spirit of God is with him: "God anointed Jesus of Nazareth with the Holy Spirit and power" (v. 38). By Jesus' being "anointed," Peter means his baptism.

Jesus' baptism is one of the four parts of the Church's primitive religious instructions (the other parts being his death, resurrection, and ascension). When the Gospel message was standardized around 50 A.D., Jesus' baptism was, indeed, the first part of the message. Perhaps one reason for this was to reach the unconverted followers of John the Baptist. Another purpose was to show who Jesus is. We're the heirs of 2,000 years of Christian reflection that lead us to know that Jesus is the divine Son of God, but that was not so clear in Jesus' time.

Our baptism is as awe-inspiring a phenomenon as was Jesus'. Through baptism, we've become branches of Jesus the vine (Jn 15:1-17). Through baptism, we've achieved death to sin and life in God (Rm 6:1-23). Through baptism, we became members of the body of Christ

— part of the People of God. Through baptism, we're incorporated into the death and resurrection of Christ. Through baptism, we're adopted as children of God, having the Spirit dwell within us. We must be open to the Spirit and remain faithful to our calling.

SECOND SUNDAY IN ORDINARY TIME
Is 62:1-5   1 Cor 12:4-11   Jn 2:1-11

There's More to Life than Meets the Eye
God's Signs and Gifts; Looking beneath the Surface of Things;
Symbols of Deep Meanings

At least one modern camera is named after Argus, a monster in Greek mythology who had a hundred eyes. It was said that only two of his eyes slept at any one time. So to be Argus-eyed came to mean to see a great deal, including what lies beneath the surface. Apropos of looking into the depths, Gilbert and Sullivan in their comic operetta *H.M.S. Pinafore* said humorously, "Things are seldom what they seem, / Skim milk masquerades as cream."

The Gospels see Jesus' stories on many levels of depth. The first is the facts level, which in today's Gospel is easy. Jesus, his mother, and five of his disciples were at a wedding in the little town of Cana. In a place and time of much hardship and poverty, everyone in town looked forward to a wedding as one of the relieving joys of life. The wedding took place in the evening after a feast. By that time it would be dark and, with a canopy over their heads, the newly-married couple would be conducted through the village streets in the light of torches to their new home. They were taken by the longest route, to be seen and wished well by as many people as possible. They couldn't manage a honeymoon, so they stayed at home and for a week held open house.

On a deeper level, Judaism saw in the joy of the wedding feast a figure of the Messianic age. Wine was, then as now, a bond of friendship when used in moderation to rejoice the heart of people. To run out of wine at a wedding was more of a humiliation for the couple than it would be today. For one thing, hospitality in the East was a sacred duty; for another, running out of wine would show poor planning, or — worse — the couple's lack of prosperity, which would mean the absence of God's blessing.

Some cynics have humorously commented that Mary's pointing out that they had no wine (v. 3) was really saying, "The wine's finished — let's go home." More seriously, her observation wasn't a request exactly, but a mother's indirect expression of caring. By arriving with an uninvited band of fishermen in tow, Jesus may have contributed to the wine shortage. Jesus' answer began with a word that our idiom may sometimes consider discourteous: Woman (v. 4). On a deeper level, the word looks back to Genesis (3:15), which said that God would put enmity between Satan and "the woman," and forward to Jesus' words to his mother from the cross about John that she was to behold her son (Jn 19:26). In all cases, it was the same message: a declaration of spiritual relationship. Obviously from what followed, Jesus' reply wasn't an outright refusal. On a deep level Jesus added something he mentioned frequently: "My hour has not yet come." This meant the hour of his passion, death, resurrection, and ascension — the time of his glorification, the way in which he achieved our salvation.

Mary, knowing she hadn't been repulsed, instructed the waiters to do whatever he told them (v. 5). At the Annunciation scene, Mary wanted everything done according to the word of the Lord. Now, she wanted to see to it that others, too, would act according to that same word. She didn't know what Jesus would do, but she believed in him, and — unlike many of us — could trust even when she didn't understand. Mary was a signpost to Jesus.

The water jars were there because Jewish custom demanded many washings. These were practical for sandal-clad feet tracking into the house dust and mud from unsurfaced dirt roads. There were also ceremonial hand washings before, during, and after eating. The jars were stone because stone couldn't contract ritual uncleanness. Altogether they contained approximately 120 gallons — about half an oil barrel.

At Jesus' order, the waiters filled the water jars to the brim (v. 7). On the ordinary level, this would prove that nothing but water was in them. On a deeper level, there are many meanings. The jars are as with everyone's life: If we put in less than the full amount, we profit less. Then, too, the water changed into wine meant a lot of wine — but, on a deeper level, the amount of wine suggests the lavish generosity of God's grace. And the change mirrored the Genesis story of creation, in which God's word alone sufficed to bring about change.

For Jesus, this was the beginning of his signs (v. 11). Whereas the other Gospels call them miracles, St. John calls them signs because they point to who Jesus really is: They're sign-ificant. There's more to Jesus than meets the eye. In him, the new covenant is at hand, and it's superior to the old: The wine kept till last proves best. On the Feast of the Epiphany, we commemorated the showing of Jesus to the magi, and on the feast of his Baptism a further showing of Jesus, when the Father proclaimed Jesus as His son. Now, at Cana, Jesus himself manifested his glory.

While the miracle may have had other motives, such as regard for his mother, kindness to his host, caring for people, approval of happy occasions, or insinuation of the Eucharist, the Evangelist implies that the first motive was the confirmation of the incipient faith of the disciples: His disciples began to believe in him. And that may be the deepest part: not the transformation of water into wine, but of the disciples into believers.

The whole affair caused a new exhilaration, as had today's prophecy of Isaiah, which serves as a helpful background to today's Gospel. In Isaiah's time, the Temple had been lying in ruins for generations after the exile; it seemed that the Holy City was forsaken, abandoned by a silent God. Seeing only the surface level, the people had become small-minded, jealous, miserable — and mindful of the warnings of previous prophets that destruction is exactly what the Israelites' infidelity to God would bring on them.

Isaiah saw a deeper level. He broke into a love song over the messianic Jerusalem that would come with the suddenness of the desert dawn (v. 1) — the moment that God's people would become fully obedient and trustful. Jerusalem's victory will be "like a burning torch," reminiscent of the Feast of Lights and witnessed by nations from all over the world. To a caring God Who has a tender love for His people, Jerusalem will be given a new name (v. 2): it will no longer be *apsibah*, "forsaken," but Hepsibah, "My Delight" (v. 4).

The Bible has many different metaphors for the relationship of intimate love between God and His people. Covenant is one. Father and children is another. In the New Testament, vine and branches is another, the Body of Christ still another. Beginning with Hosea, one of the most beautiful ways of describing the relationship is that of marriage. A lyrical description of marriage is the best image Isaiah can come up with in today's passage: As the bridegroom rejoices in his bride, so God rejoices in His people (v. 5). An ancient rabbi wrote, "Anyone who has never seen the joy of [a wedding] feast has never known joy at all." And the New Testament uses the image often — speaking, in addition to the marriage feast at Cana, of marriage as paralleling the mission of Jesus, of the wedding as a powerful symbol of our own baptismal journey, of the Church as the bride of Christ, and of heaven as a wedding feast.

The message of seeing beneath the surface is presented also in today's Second Reading. The people of Corinth to whom St. Paul wrote believed myopically that whatever gifts they had, including the spiritual, were due to their own merits. The recipients of God's gifts were "lording it over" the less fortunate. Paul says that, diverse though all the gifts are, they all come from the one God. In nature, because each being has its own gifts from God, fish can't drown in the water, birds can't sink in the air, gold can't perish in the refiner's fire. It's the same with us. All of us have our own distinct abilities. And we should use them to complement one another, for the good of the whole community, for building up God's kingdom on earth.

As we might, the Corinthians fought over which gifts were better. Paul's priorities came up with a different list than theirs. Miracles and the gift of tongues, which the Corinthians put first because they were spectacular, Paul put at the end of his list, because they have dangers of delusion, self-hypnotism, and hysteria. First on Paul's list is the expression of wisdom (v. 8), a gift which contains such ingredients as the Argus-eyed ability to see deep and far.

On a very deep level, we can apply today's lessons to the wedding party that is our life because Jesus cared about people and wanted them to enjoy themselves and be happy. He wasn't a killjoy: He made people feel good, as though they were bathed in sunshine. The people who crucified Jesus never accused him of being a bore. To the contrary, they thought him too dynamic to be safe. It has been later generations that muffled up Jesus' personality and surround him with an atmosphere of tedium, recommended him as a fitting household pet for the insecure, vulnerable, and retiring.

But the party entails work that's serious. We should work for justice, because without justice there can be no party. We should feed the hungry, because without feeding the hungry there can be no party.

We should respond to God's invitations as the ongoing way of the life of love of a bride and groom, or there can be no party.

THIRD SUNDAY IN ORDINARY TIME
Ne 8:2-4, 5f., 8-10   1 Cor 12:12-30 (or 12-14, 27)   Lk 1:1-4; 4:14-21

Christ, the Principle of Life and of Unity
Jesus, the Fulfillment of Joy; Witnessing to the Son of God;
Religious Unity; Where to Go for Spirit and Life

St. Luke's Gospel, our major Gospel for this liturgical year, has been called "the loveliest book in the world." Today's excerpt contains two introductions: one to Luke's Gospel, the other to Jesus. Both introductions are solemn, both speak of what has been "fulfilled," and both represent a beginning. Luke writes his introduction as though he thought that he was going to write the greatest story ever told, and nothing but the best was good enough for it.

He acknowledges that many had undertaken before to write the facts of Jesus' life and indicates that his eye-witness sources (v. 2) would help a third-generation Christian, "Theophilus," arrange accounts in order. "Theophilus" means "Lover of God," and stands for each of us.

Today's Gospel excerpt then skips to Luke's introduction of the beginnings of Jesus' ministry. He's careful to begin with Judaism: Jesus was in the habit of teaching in the synagogues (v. 15). The synagogue was an institution begun during the exile as a place to help the Jews retain their identity as Jews. Now the central age of history was beginning, the prophets fulfilled, all eyes fixed on Jesus: Jesus, the hometown boy who had become a rabbi, who was now prompted by the Holy Spirit to return to Galilee (4:14). Galilee, the little agricultural garden province in the north of Palestine, had many towns and villages, a wonderful climate, and a great water supply. It was the least conservative province of the nation.

From the tops of some of the hills into which Nazareth was built, which Jesus had probably climbed as a boy, there stretched a panorama of important reminders of the history of Israel: the plain of Esdraelon to the south, which had been a constant battlefield and had many other scriptural memories; Carmel to the west, where Elijah had fought and won his epic battle with the priests of the pagan god Baal; and the blue Mediterranean in the distance. Three great roads skirted Nazareth: the road from Jerusalem in the south, the Way of the Sea between Egypt and Damascus with its many caravans, and the great road to the east, with convoys from Arabia and the Roman legions marching to and from the Empire's eastern frontiers.

The synagogue at Nazareth would have been the same as all others in essential respects, but this town of perhaps as many as 2,000 inhabitants might have been more cosmopolitan than most. The Sabbath synagogue services in Jesus' time consisted at least of prayers, readings, a homily, and the priestly blessing. It had its origins in the long history of the Jews, not least of which was the book from which today's First Reading comes: Nehemiah.

Nehemiah lived in those sad days after the Exile when the Jews had returned home — or what was left of home. They had before them the enormous task of rebuilding — not only physically rebuilding the Temple and the city of Jerusalem, but also the far more difficult task of rebuilding the nation. Nothing seemed to go right.

A good layman, Nehemiah worked with the priest Ezra to restore both the government and religion. Society and religion were considered inseparable, as in truth they are — no matter what position one takes on the separation of Church and State, which is an entirely different matter. Together, Nehemiah and Ezra laid the foundations of Judaism.

The ceremony in today's section was basically a Fourth-of-July kind of "Declaration of Dependence" on God. The ceremony, with special rostrums set up so that all could see and hear, was a Liturgy of the Word, which became the first half of the Christian Mass. We, like those people of 2500 years ago, stand when the Gospel is read. Then their assembly, hands raised high (v. 6), answered "Amen, amen!" — an exclamation, then as now, of total commitment. At that time the people came to listen to God's Word, tried to understand it, internalized it, and left in joy. So should we.

In Jesus' time, the ruler of the synagogue could invite any adult Jewish man to read the Scripture of the day and deliver a homily on it. He often called upon visitors for this, and Jesus and the Apostles made frequent use of this opportunity to preach the Good News. The book to be read and commented upon was determined by the season, the particular passage left to the choice of the preacher. Today the book was Isaiah, and Jesus combined passages (61:1f. and 58:6) that were originally addressed to Jews looking forward to a nation rebuilt and restored. For Luke, the words were prophetic, because Jesus was about to usher in the true restoration.

As was the custom, Jesus stood to do the reading (v. 16), and sat down to deliver the homily (v. 20). His homily began with his simple but dramatic statement, delivered with quiet authority, that this Scripture passage was now being fulfilled (v. 21). He said that he had arrived as the special one sent by God to bring God's Good News to the poor. Although Jesus intended this to be nothing less than the beginning of a revolutionary new social order, the people promptly misunderstood it to mean that the Jews would now be masters and not slaves in their country. When he spoke of the release of prisoners, they misunderstood him to mean release from the Roman yoke. But Jesus' mission in life was solely to do the will of his heavenly Father.

That mission was what also motivated St. Paul's first letter to the Corinthians, from which today's passage continues from last week. Among the many problems of the Corinthian Church — not too different from ours — were immorality, irreverent behavior in church, drinking, discrimination, denial of authority, and doubts about the Resurrection. Despite all that, today's reading gives one of the most famous pictures of the unity of the Church ever written.

In using the cooperating members of the human body to teach the need for unity and communal effort (v. 12), Paul was possibly adapting a common story of classical antiquity. The metaphor of a group as a body isn't strange to us, either: We speak of "the body politic," "a legislative body," and our own physical body. As with the physical body, diversity among people doesn't imply disunity. Paul speaks not only metaphor, but reality: The Church is Christ's body. Lest anyone draw a wrong conclusion, such as the members of the Church being equal to Christ, Paul makes the basic point that the members are always subordinate to Christ. As members of Christ's body in the Church, all must be concerned for one another (v. 25). That's still true. Every one of us is precious in God's sight.

Someone has calculated that every human body, on average, has some medical problem every three days. To resolve it, usually an aspirin will do, or a bandaid, or a good night's sleep. Sometimes, though, our more serious conditions require batteries of therapies. Our "vessels of clay," as Paul called our bodies, have other limits: Without food, they last only weeks; without water, only days; without air, but a few minutes. Does this mean that our almighty Creator's design is fraught with flaws, such that God has to depend on the medical establishment to undo His blunders? No, God had a better idea. He sees weakness not necessarily as an absence of strength, but rather the means to strength.

Has Jesus failed, then? In today's Gospel, he cited himself as having fulfilled the prophecy of Isaiah to help the poor, release prisoners, heal the sick — yet homeless poor remain in our streets, our prisons are overcrowded, and everyone of us will eventually succumb to physical death. No, he has elected that, he being no longer present among us in the flesh, we are to be his hands to do his work, the feet to run his errands, the voice to speak in his behalf. If Jesus wants someone sent, he depends on apostles; if he wants to be spoken for, prophets; if he wants people taught, teachers; if he wants aid given the unfortunate, administrators (v. 28).

We all have our own gifts. With a diversity in our unity, not all of us serve on the same basis. Yet each of us is called to personal holiness and a sharing of our talents with others. We saw in today's Gospel that at the beginning of his public life the Son of God stood alone in Nazareth to boldly proclaim God's message in the face of members of his own faith. At the end he stood alone before Roman authorities like Pilate and Herod. And at the hour of his death he hung on the cross alone.

We, too, have issues on which we may have to stand alone. We have definite vocational decisions to make: whether to be clergy like Ezra, or lay people like Nehemiah, or missioners like Paul.

More specifically, we live in a time that witnesses many terrible attacks on human life. Warfare and genocide have accounted for the deaths of millions of human beings. Abortion attacks human life itself: eliminating the unborn infant only because it's alive.

Who, after all, deserves to be born? Would-be parents are using genetic screening for what they consider a clearly responsible purpose: insuring the birth of healthy children. These tests ultimately pose the most complex problems of all: What constitutes health? And who bears the responsibility for decisions affecting unborn children?

Genetic histories can indicate the probability of Fragile X syndrome, which indicates that a person can give birth to a child who will be defective in some way — deaf, for example, or retarded. Increasingly sophisticated genetic tests have prompted some women to request amniocentesis to screen for Alzheimer's, for example, even though the disease generally does not manifest itself until old age. Some parents use these procedures to insure the birth of children who are not "healthy" in the conventional sense. More than "perfect" children, some parents hope for children who resemble themselves: One doctor reports a call from a dwarf couple wanting to abort a child of normal height; a bioethicist has puzzled over the case of a deaf couple who didn't want a hearing child.

Abortion is resulting in over 4,300 deaths in this country alone every day, day in and day out. It has led to a coarsening of our entire culture's respect for life: the increasing acceptance of assisted suicide for the elderly and ill; experiments on living human embryos; the abuse of women, children, and the elderly; irresponsible sexual license; the weakening of families; and the further victimization of the poor to whom society is willing to give abortion rights in place of real justice.

In a more simple time, our materialistic society estimated that a human being weighing 140 pounds contained enough fat for seven cakes of soap, carbon for 9,000 pencils, phosphorous to make 2,200 match heads, magnesium for one dose of salts, iron to make one medium-sized nail, sufficient lime to whitewash a chicken coop, enough sulphur to rid one dog of fleas, and water to fill a ten-gallon barrel. All was valued at 98 cents.

Then, when a more sophisticated analysis became possible, it was discovered that the average human also has more than a pound of nucleic acids and enzymes, valued at about $800 a pound. Still later, a scientist estimated that the human body is actually worth more than $6 million, and that price covers only the raw materials; the intricate work of fashioning the materials into human cells, if it could be done, might cost six thousand trillion dollars.

In all cases, we're to be real people — not like a Hollywood set with all front and nothing in back — and, fulfilled and fully human, imitators of Christ our principle of life and of unity.

FOURTH SUNDAY IN ORDINARY TIME
Jr 1:4f., 17-19   1 Cor 12:31-13:13 (or 13:4-13)   Lk 4:21-30

The Largeness of Love
Who Is Jesus?; Open vs. Closed Persons; Love Must Be Broad as Well as Deep

In choosing readings for their wedding Mass, young couples often pick today's section of St. Paul's letter to the Corinthians. This is Paul's "Hymn to Love," beautiful as well as instructive, sublime in tone yet practical in application. It reminds us of what married love, and all love, should be. Paul wrote it, though, specifically to the people of Corinth. Wise in the ways of the world, they preferred seductive gifts that were the most sensational.

In informing them that the most important gift of all is love, Paul first contrasted love with the more spectacular gifts, the possession of which, if love is absent, is useless. Speaking in tongues was a characteristic of pagan worship of the time, accompanied by a clashing and clanging of cymbals and the blasting of trumpets to make the show alluring. And what they liked about prophecy was especially the power that accompanied it — an attraction that's still with us, as witnessed by our fondness for magic and spellbinding speeches.

Even those who boast a strong faith, if they lack love, can be cruel. Those who "give everything" and are thus adjudged by their neighbors to be "charitable" can in reality, if they are without love, be prideful, contemptuous, and humiliating to the people who are objects of their largess. And, says Paul, even if I hand my body over, if I don't have love, it can put me on the borders of dangerous display in religion.

Then Paul outlines what love does and doesn't do. It's Paul's idea of the life-giving qualities that love ought to have — not a complete list, but addressing what he saw among the Corinthians. He says, for example, that love is patient, and that's obvious. It's kind, a quality which, I'm afraid, isn't always true of Christians — as those Christians who have persecuted in Christ's gentle name bear witness. A good example of loving kindness is Jesus' conduct with the woman taken in adultery.

Love isn't jealous — it doesn't begrudge the beloved all good fortune. It isn't pompous — it is, rather, self-effacing. It isn't inflated with its own importance. It's never rude, but is tactful, polite, and — very important — gracious. It's not self-seeking: Rather than lining up with those litigious people who seem in our time to seek the last pound of the flesh of their rights, lovers think first rather of their duties. Love isn't prone to anger: Concerned about the other, it doesn't go into self-centered bursts of temper or exasperation. It doesn't brood, keeping records like an accountant. It doesn't rejoice over hardship, but does what's more difficult: It rejoices with those who are happy.

Full of forbearance, love can gloss over whatever human faults are present in the beloved. It's trusting, believing the best of others. Full of hope, it realizes that, despite our imperfections, God isn't finished with us yet. And it has the power to endure: It can conquer all defects, and can transform with a Cinderella-like wonder.

Lastly, Paul goes back to considering love in the light of the other gifts. Whereas all else will fail — all else, even knowledge with its power — our love shall still be there. It's complete: Though we now see the world distortedly as through an imperfect mirror, when we see things as they are we shall realize that love is what counts. And it's supreme, reigning over even the considerable virtues of faith and hope, which it will outlast.

Thinking about this passage and, here as always with the Sacred Scriptures, applying them to ourselves, we should ask if we can add other characteristics of Christian love to Paul's list. Some people have done that, and come up with cute sayings like "Love is… a warm puppy." If I were asked to complete a statement that began "Love is…" I would say that a description that would have to be added in our time would contain "largeness": "Love is… large."

Largeness is always present in great love. Take, for instance, from today's First Reading, the example of Jeremiah, born around 645 B.C. When he received God's call to be His prophet, he was a generous youth of about nineteen or twenty. His country, Judah, was a puppet in the hands of Assyria. Contrary to what the Israelites thought — those who liked to consider themselves alone as God's "chosen people" — God was calling Jeremiah to be a prophet not only to the people of Israel, but to all the nations (v. 5).

God told him (v. 19) that the people would fight against him. And Jeremiah was by inclination unskilled in confronting hardened opponents, the entrenched "city hall" of political and religious leaders. Reacting to Jeremiah's hesitancy, God presented him with images of

strength into which God had made him (v. 18): a fortified city, a pillar
of iron, a wall of brass. Because Jeremiah's love was large, he generously accepted God's call, and gave himself completely to his searing
assignment.

The preeminent example of one whose love was large enough to
match his mission is, of course, Jesus. Today's passage from St. Luke
is a continuation from last week's scene of Jesus in the synagogue, and
it presents the other half of that story. Although Jesus had to disagree
with some of the things that were taught and done in the synagogue,
he, unlike many modern Church critics, nevertheless faithfully attended
the synagogue Sabbath services.

He began by stating the theme of his sermon (v. 21): that very
day this Scripture passage was being fulfilled in the villagers' hearing.
Initially it didn't sink in that Jesus was talking about himself. The group
listening to our Lord that day were, after all, many of the people who
had known him when he was growing up: his teachers, the cobbler who
repaired the family sandals, storekeepers who sold them food, childhood companions who ran with him through the city's streets.

We can imagine them remembering the young boy who'd come
to the synagogue with his parents. So nice to have him back, and so
good to know he hadn't forgotten his religious training! Religion can
be like a hometown: familiar, unchanging, a constant in a chaotic world.
We want to wrap religion around us like a security blanket and often
to stay the same — and Jesus didn't provide that. So — ominously —
they also asked each other, "Isn't this Joseph's son?" (v. 22).

Knowing their quandary, Jesus tried (vv. 23f.) to broaden their
understanding of his role. First he mentioned obliquely his awareness
of the jealousy of the people of Nazareth over what he'd done at
Capernaum (v. 23). Then (vv. 25-27) he interpreted the Scriptures —
verses they probably knew by heart. He said that two of their favorite
prophets, Elijah and Elisha, had worked many miracles among some
non-Jews and were more favorably received by them than by some
Jews.

The implication was that Jesus' mission can't be limited to one
people or to one social and religious group, any more than God's love
can. The people of Nazareth failed to understand that with God love
begins wherever human need is found. No one was going to tell them
that religion had to go so far as Elijah traveling to Sidon, or Elisha

cleansing a Syrian, or even Isaiah teaching good news for the poor and liberty for the oppressed.

Besides, Jesus was a bundle of contradictions: His mission was weighted in favor of the poor, yet he dined with the wealthy; he reprimanded his disciples for their ambition, and yet constantly called on the rich and powerful to be, like himself, of service to the poor and powerless; and he made it clear that all people from all walks of life and from all nations will receive his saving message.

For Israelites, these were fighting words! The people in the synagogue thought Jesus blasphemous in identifying himself with Elijah and Elisha, arrogant in thinking himself better than they, insulted if foreigners would heed a prophet better than they would. They asked the question often asked of anyone who dares to speak out for God: "Who do you think you are?"

At the beginning of the episode, the eyes of all in the synagogue looked intently at him (v. 20). By the end of the episode, they looked no farther than their eyes could see, and showed fierce hatred: They led him to the brow of the hill on which their town had been built, intending to hurl him down headlong over its edge to his death (v. 29). But because his time had not yet come, he walked through them and went away (v. 30). When in the Father's wisdom the time for the end of Jesus' ministry would arrive, Jesus would be led to another hill, Calvary, outside another city, Jerusalem, there to be put to death for all the human race.

Jesus' sacrifice became possible because of the largeness of divine love. We ought to practice this kind of love by word and example — in prophetically speaking out God's truth, and in honoring others who do. Prophecy isn't so much picturing the future as it is challenging us to return to faithful observance of our obligations. We're reminded of Nathaniel Hawthorne's short story, "The Great Stone Face," in which a small town in New England waited for the coming of a prophet and holy man who would look like the features of a stone outcropping in a local hillside. They waited, but no one ever seemed to come, and the village lost hope and spirit. One day an old man of the town died and, as he was laid out, someone noticed that he did look like the face in the hill. He had been with them all the time and they never recognized him until it was too late!

FIFTH SUNDAY IN ORDINARY TIME
Is 6:1-8   1 Cor 15:1-11   Lk 5:1-11

Put Out into Deep Water
The Fisherman's Net; The Awesomeness of God;
The Holiness of God; God's Call

Henry Thoreau, of Walden fame, said that the mass of people lead lives of quiet desperation. While that may be true of the mass of people, it's certainly not true of those who involve themselves in causes greater than themselves. Such are the people in today's liturgy.

At this point in St. Luke's story of Jesus' life, Jesus' pulpit for a while will be the outdoors: the hillside, the boat, the open road. Right now the crowd was pressing in on Jesus (v. 1) at the shore of the Lake of Galilee. The fishermen who owned the two boats alongside the lake had disembarked and were washing their nets (v. 2). Jesus got into the boat that was Simon Peter's and asked him to put out a short distance from the shore (v. 3). In that position, which prevented the crowds from crushing in too close, Jesus taught them. When he finished, he gave Simon Peter that meaningful command that takes away quiet desperation and is applicable to the lives of all of us: "Put out into deep water" (v. 4).

St. Peter had many reasons against this disturbance to his routine. He knew that night-time was the best time for fishing, and this was morning. He knew tides and times as only long-time fishermen do, and this wasn't the right moment. He had worked hard all night and caught nothing (v. 5), and he was tired. But he gave an admirable response, which amounted to saying, "If you say so, I'll do it." And he did. The result? They caught such a great number of fish that their nets were tearing (v. 6).

Peter had witnessed miracles of Jesus before: healings, including the cure of his mother-in-law, but he didn't know medicine; the changing of water into wine, but he wasn't a physicist. But those miracles didn't reach him as much as this one did: He did know fishing, and he could testify that what he had just experienced was extremely unusual. To recognize a miracle — or a person — one must have an eye that really sees. Many people had seen apples fall before Isaac

Newton did, but Newton saw it and came up with the law of gravity; many people had seen kettles of water boil before James Watt did, but Watt saw it and came up with the steam engine.

Peter was so overwhelmed that he fell at Jesus' knees and asked the Lord to leave him, for he was a sinful man (v. 8). When at the beginning Jesus had told him to put out into deep water, Peter had called him "Master." Now, reflecting his awe, he called him "Lord."

Peter's sense of God's awesome presence was intimate — as intimate as the call of Isaiah in today's First Reading. Isaiah's summons had all the elements of a vocation: God's call, the individual's misgivings, God's reassurance, the commission for a task, and the individual's faith acceptance of the call. Isaiah, terrified when he remembered the sinfulness of himself and his people, dreamed of six-winged celestial beings called Seraphim singing before God, "Holy, holy, holy" (v. 3).

Holiness is the essential quality of God. The word indicates God's utter transcendence, His complete apartness from anything sinful, and the mystery which belongs to God alone. The threefold repetition stresses the superlative. We repeat these words before the Eucharistic Prayer of the Mass as a reminder that we're about to experience the awesome presence of the all-holy God.

The Seraphim's song concluded, "the earth is filled with His glory!" — God's glory being the radiation of His holiness upon the world, especially people. As St. Irenaeus said, "The glory of God is people fully alive." Isaiah showed the impressiveness of it all by speaking of the place shaking and the house being filled with smoke (v. 4). The smoke, a sign of the divine presence, was reminiscent of the clouds which surrounded God on Mount Sinai.

Popular belief had it that to see God would lead to one's death: A person couldn't see God and live (Ex 33:20). So the reaction of Isaiah, who was overwhelmed by his personal unworthiness, was almost humorous: "I'm doomed!" (v. 5). Then God took the initiative, as He does with all unworthiness. He had one of the Seraphim take one of the coals burning for the incense at the altar (v. 6) and touch Isaiah's mouth with it (v. 7). Isaiah was thus symbolically purified to be worthy of his calling to speak as God's prophet. Finally, in the ancient imagery of God enthroned above the firmament and holding court with His heavenly advisors, God asked, "Whom shall I send? Who will go for us?" (v. 8). And Isaiah, now readied, answered with wholehearted generosity, "Here I am, send me!"

That vision is aptly modernized in a poem that updates God's call
to all of us (from Marriage Encounter, Fond du Lac, Wis.):

> And I said who me?
> And He said yes, you.
> And I said
> But I'm not ready yet
> And there is company coming
> And I can't leave the kids
> And you know there's no one to take my place.
> And He said you're stalling.
> And the Lord said go
> And I said but I don't want to
> And He said I didn't ask if you wanted to
> And I said
> Listen I'm not the kind of person
> To get involved in controversy
> Besides my father won't like it
> And what will my neighbors think?
> And He said baloney.
> And yet a third time the Lord said go
> And I said do I have to?
> And He said do you love Me?
> And I said
> Look, I'm scared people are going to hate me
> And cut me up in little pieces.
> I can't take it all by myself.
> And He said where do you think I'll be?
> And the Lord said go
> And I sighed
> Here I am, send me.

There's another commemoration of Isaiah's impressive reverie
at Mass. The minister, just before he reads the Gospel, prays quietly:
"Almighty God, cleanse my heart and my lips that I may worthily proclaim your Gospel." And when the Gospel is announced we all trace
the cross upon our forehead, lips, and heart, asking that our thoughts
and feelings be cleansed and made worthy to receive God's word and
our lips able to proclaim it.

As with Isaiah, God took the initiative with Peter. Seeing that Peter's feeling of unworthiness was not unwillingness, Jesus advised him not to be afraid, and added that from now on he as a fisherman would have the lifelong vocation of catching people (v. 10). No matter what Peter's life had been up to this point, God could make all things new, even to change unworthiness. Then, in contrast to the beginning when Jesus asked Simon to go a short distance from the shore and then into deep water, the elegant conclusion tells us that they brought their boats back to the shore (v. 11). The disciples now left everything and became Jesus' full-time followers — a brief summary of what must have been a long and gradual process.

Like Isaiah and Peter, St. Paul also had a sense of awe and of unworthiness before God, for having hated Jesus and his Church. In fact, when we look at the Apostles, we find that none of them had much native talent or ability — with the possible exception of Judas Iscariot. But God often chooses the foolish to put to shame the so-called "worldly wise." He called a great sinner, Augustine, to be a bishop, doctor of the Church, and saint; he called an adversary of Augustine, a razor-penned intellectual, to be the great Saint Jerome; he called Thomas Aquinas, judged by his peers to be a "dumb ox," to be a great theologian and saint; he called a simple man like St. John Vianney to be the patron of the diocesan clergy; and he called a relatively unintelligent man like Joseph of Cupertino to be a saintly priest.

Today's section of Paul's letter to the Corinthians was prompted by the belief among some Corinthians that the resurrection of the body is impossible. In today's passage, Paul appeals to the testimony of those who saw the risen Christ, mentioning only the appearances to those persons whom Jewish law would accept as witnesses.

As in the Gospel, Paul makes Peter preeminent by saying that Jesus had appeared to him before he came to the rest of the Apostles (v. 5). Thus did Jesus extend his love and graciousness toward one who had denied him in his greatest need. But Peter in his regret had also cried his heart out. And Jesus' great wish was to comfort Peter in his pain. A love is truly outstanding if it thinks more of the heartbreak of one who has hurt than of the hurt that the other has inflicted.

And the more than five hundred to whom the risen Jesus appeared — can you imagine their reaction to an appearance by the one who had been crucified and buried but who was now risen and standing in their midst? These people, who had been crushed by his death, would be thunderstruck. They would greet him not by polite applause, but with a standing ovation. They would have jumped for joy, hugged their neighbor, and broken out in laughter.

Isaiah, Peter, and Paul were all called by God to put out into the deep waters of life. Through our baptismal charge, so are we. They proclaimed their unworthiness in the presence of the Holy One. So should we.

Perhaps we're most like Peter, and perhaps our call is most like his. He blew hot and cold, was sometimes insightful and sometimes obtuse, sometimes brave and at other times weak. Like Peter, let's accept the risk of casting off from our shore — secure, sheltered, and comfortable — to go wherever the Spirit blows, and set out on the adventure of faith. The philosopher Nietzsche said, "Build your houses on the rim of Mt. Vesuvius." By that he meant that it's desirable to live dangerously. In our case, supreme love can't exist without supreme daring.

When we wonder why somebody doesn't do something, let's realize that I am somebody. With our whole lives, let's risk putting out into deep water. Thus we never need to lead lives of quiet desperation.

SIXTH SUNDAY IN ORDINARY TIME
Jr 17:5-8   1 Cor 15:12, 16-20   Lk 6:17, 20-26

Choice of Christ's Values over the World's
Trust in God; Happy Are They Who Hope in the Lord; Our Fundamental
Option between Good and Evil; The Meaning of Jesus' Resurrection

In the city, frequently light interference at night makes it impossible to see the stars. In the country, you can see the stars clearly, especially on a moonless, cold night in winter. We often take the fixed stars for granted, because they're always the same at the same time of the year from the same observation post. What easily catch our attention and our awe, however, are shooting stars and falling stars. So do lightning and thunder. They're out of the usual, and give magnificent displays.

We often think of Christ's words as stable stars, and we've heard them so often that we sometimes take them for granted. We have to stop and think to realize that Christ's words are shooting stars or flashing lightning and rolling thunder as well, all calling for our attention.

Such are the beatitudes in today's Gospel. Each of them cuts across the sky of our attention like shooting stars on a clear night. Jesus mentions four beatitudes here, and four woes, but there are many more. Each of them goes against the world's wisdom. To the crowd that came to him from all Judea in the south and from as far north as the coast of Tyre and Sidon, and to us, Jesus contrasts two expressions of hearts. He says that the happy people are the poor, the hungry, the sad, and those who are hated because of him. And the truly unhappy people are the rich, the full, the laughing, and those who have successfully curried the favor of the world.

Did you ever hear such nonsense? Our radios, our television sets, and our newspapers and magazines all scream the contrary. Advertising defines reality for us, telling us what it means to "be real" and identifying persons as — and in terms of — objects: the big, the expensive, and the showy; gourmet foods, relaxation, and social respectability.

For them, lust replaces chastity, power replaces obedience, and money replaces poverty. Models' faces reflect self-absorption, their individuality isolated from relationships with others. Advertising advocates that you get what you can while the getting's good, eat in the best restaurants, and patronize the best in entertainment to keep you laughing. Jesus' basic thought, on the other hand, is that, like those who have nothing, we must put all our trust in God.

A true story is told of an old man who moved from a quiet rural farm to the fast-moving New York City. He never really adjusted to the roads moving in all directions. One day, late in the evening, he traveled into the heart of the city to do some shopping, but when walking back to catch his bus everything went pitch black. It took him a few moments to realize that there had been a power failure. There he was, surrounded by children wailing, women crying, horns blowing — a torrent of chaos. The old man stood trembling. How could he possibly cross a road safely without the help of traffic lights? How long would it be before someone attacked him?

It was then that someone took his arm and asked where he lived. The old man gave the name of the street. The other began to lead him into the chaos. They safely crossed streets, passed by all signs of danger. When at last they arrived at the old man's quarters, the old man said: "I don't understand. How were you able to walk through all this?"

"But this is what I do every night," the other man replied. "You see, I'm blind."

We can apply that story to say that Jesus is the blind man, leading the despairing from their situation of chaos and fright to their home — which is a place of peace, happiness, and fulfillment in knowing him. We're to trust, grope about in the dark, and continue to hope, even when there seems to be no hope. Following a crucified Messiah, the lowest of the low, may seem incredible — but it's no more incredible than following a blind man.

According to G.K. Chesterton, a wise Christian, Jesus promised his people three things: that they would be absolutely fearless, greatly happy, and in constant trouble. That master of paradox added the thought, "I like getting into hot water — it keeps me clean!" That's close to the unworldly inner peace Jesus is talking about — a happiness that can't be destroyed by changes in fortune, or our current mood, or the circumstances that touch our lives.

There's an inner unhappiness from denying the spiritual, the noble, and the meaningful in behalf of physical fulfillment only. This is the state of "woe" of which Jesus speaks. It describes the smug who've climbed to the top after all kinds of compromises, only to discover that there's nothing there.

Jeremiah in today's First Reading has a similar notion, setting forth the two directions for the journey of the heart, the "seat of moral personality" (*Catechism of the Catholic Church*, #2517). Like Jesus, he gives his message twice over: in the language of a curse and in the language of a blessing. And like Jesus, he states his values in the present tense, meaning now: Blessed is the one who trusts in the Lord, and cursed is the one whose heart turns away from the Lord. Adversity, like being poor, or hungry, or sad, while to be avoided, can, if we handle it right, be useful for our spiritual growth.

Jeremiah compares those who draw their life's inspiration from God to a tree near the water's edge, whose roots drink in the life-giving water, and those who trust only in humankind to a barren bush in the desert, growing in a lava waste, a salt and empty earth (v. 6). In Jeremiah's parched, arid land, where a person was always in danger of starvation because of drought, his metaphors were meaningful. Today's Responsorial Psalm carries the same message: "Happy are they who hope in the Lord."

To come to that stalwart position requires daily effort, constant struggle, and patience. The tree by running waters had to grow little by little, while the bush in the desert, being shallow, gave up. The righteous person is wise enough to seek good models for his life, smart enough to avoid what will likely lead him to spiritual death, and insightful enough to use the opportunities of grace. The person whose hope is anywhere but in the Lord is insolent, unconcerned about occasions of sin, and reckless of his company. Most people are a combination of both the good and the bad.

Why should we look for happiness in Christ's way rather than in the world's? We get part of the answer in today's portion of St. Paul's first letter to the Corinthians, in which he speaks of immortality, eternal life, and resurrection. Paul says that if our hopes in Christ are limited to this life only, we're the most pitiable of people (v. 19).

People have pondered the meaning of life and death since prehistoric days, from the unlit cave to the palatial desks of contemporary philosophers and the cells of mystics. The preponderant belief is that people don't die, that there's life after life, and that our souls will live on in some form. The greatest minds through the centuries have believed that we're immortal: Socrates, Plato, Kant, Spinoza, Goethe, Darwin, Schweitzer, William James, and hundreds more.

Blaise Pascal asks, "Which is the more difficult — to be born or to rise again: That what has never been, should be, or that what has been, should be again? Is it more difficult to come into being than to return to it?" When Thomas A. Edison, one of the greatest intuitive geniuses, was dying, his doctor leaned over to hear him whisper, "It is very beautiful over there." Rabindranath Tagore, renowned Indian philosopher and poet, said: "Death is not extinguishing the light, it is putting out the lamp because the dawn has come." William James, the eminent Harvard psychologist, declared that as he grew older his belief in immortality increased. Why? "Because as I get older I am just getting fit to live."

Our true existence is beyond both space and time. The resurrection of Jesus is the guarantee of our own resurrection and is what puts sense into choosing Christ's way. The fact that Jesus rose from death proves that truth is stranger than fiction, that love is stronger than hatred, that good is stronger than evil, and that life is stronger than death. Paul calls Jesus' resurrection from the dead "the firstfruits of those who have fallen asleep" (v. 20). Every Jew in Paul's audience would understand that the "firstfruits" referred to that part of the harvest which was the first and the best to ripen, a sign of the harvest to come. They were brought to the Temple to be offered to God. Jesus' resurrection, too, was a sign of the harvest of resurrections of all believers to come. The resurrection is so fundamental to Christian belief that it, along with the cross, stands at the center of our teaching.

In our search for happiness and inner peace, we can't live schizophrenic lives with one foot in this world and the other foot in the next. Even though ours is an era in which there's little concept of personal morality, we can't avoid making a choice between the two ways: the way to heaven or the way to hell.

Is there a hell? At its simplest, hell is the inevitable outcome of a failure to choose and live by the values of the Kingdom of Heaven. The Kingdom of Heaven is the place into which Jesus says his followers are welcomed by his heavenly Father; hell is living with the consequences of ultimate evil. Images of hell in the New Testament are fire (Mt 13:50), outer darkness, loss, and remorse (Mt 8:12; 22:13; 25:30); none of these is absolutely adequate to capture the sense of hell. The affirmations of Sacred Scripture and the teaching of the Church on the subject of hell are a call to the responsibility incumbent upon persons to make use of their freedom in view of their eternal destiny (*Catechism of the Catholic Church*, #1036).

And yet we can't make heaven and hell the sole motivation for our lives. An old Irish tale tells of Paddy walking along a country road and meeting an angel. The angel had a firebrand in one hand and a pail of water in the other. In answer to Paddy's question about the angel's baggage, the angel answered, "With the pail of water I'm going to put out the fires of hell, and with the firebrand I'm going to set fire to all the mansions of heaven. Then we'll see whose life motivations are proper!"

We can't be blind to all of the stars and the spectacular displays in the heavens. But, as C.S. Lewis said (*The Four Loves* [New York: Harcourt, Brace, Jovanovich, 1960]), to follow the stars that challenge us to love means that we shall be vulnerable. Love anything, says Lewis, and your heart will be tugged, and maybe broken. If you want to avoid that, you should give your heart to no one, not even a pet. You shall have to wrap it up with luxuries, avoid entanglements, and lock it up safe in the coffin of your selfishness. But in that coffin — dark, motionless, silent, airless — your heart will change. It won't be broken;

indeed, it will become unbreakable — and impenetrable, and irredeemable. And you'll find that the only place outside heaven where you can be perfectly safe from all the dangers of love is hell. We don't know if stars shine there, but if they do, it will be too late for them to do any good.

SEVENTH SUNDAY IN ORDINARY TIME
1 S 26: 2, 7-9, 12f., 22f.   1 Cor 15:45-49   Lk 6:27-38

Noble Forgiveness of Others
Imitating God in His Mercy; Nobility of Character;
Going Beyond the Golden Rule; Loving Enemies

Suppose you found out from incontrovertible evidence that your next-door neighbor was telling lies about you — not to only one or two people, but to many; not once, but often; not only in the past, but today; and not in little items, but in matters so important that they affect your livelihood. In fact, you've sadly come to realize that your neighbor is an enemy. What do you do? Confront your neighbor? Retaliate? Take your neighbor to court?

Hardly anyone would immediately think of loving such a one. In the Older Covenant, even good people assumed that hatred of evil persons is right. David's action toward Saul in today's First Reading was a bit different, involving as it did David's king. In modern terms, a good case could be made that King Saul was psychotic: paranoid in his constant suspicion that David was plotting against him, jealous of David's popularity, and schizoid in being pleasant at one time and filled with anger and hatred at another. So he sought to kill David.

David, along with his nephew Abishai, had the opportunity to turn the tables when they discovered Saul asleep. Abishai, a volatile youth, wanted to take advantage of the opportunity to thrust his spear into the sleeping Saul. After all, in those days one always killed one's enemies if one had the chance. But because of David's respect for the sacred aspect of kingship (v. 9), he chose the daring act of removing the king's spear and water jug from their place at Saul's head (v. 12). To taunt

Saul's army with the knowledge that he had pierced their defenses, David invited Saul's general to come and pick them up. David's last sentence, that although the Lord had put Saul in his power he wouldn't harm him, contains the link of this reading with today's Gospel.

Jesus extended the love commandment from being not only toward God's anointed, or even only toward one's countrymen, but to the whole world, even to one's enemy and persecutor. Of all the words he could have used for love of our enemy, the word he used doesn't mean the love of a man for a maid, or the love we have for our friends. His word means an active feeling of benevolence for another person, wanting the highest good for that person — and even a going out to that person. As a poet (Edwin Markham) wrote of an enemy:

> He drew a circle that shut me out —
> Heretic, rebel, a thing to flout.
> But Love and I had the wit to win;
> We drew a circle that took him in!

In spite of our founder's admonition to love our enemies, Christianity often fell victim to the temper of its time and circumstance. Because it's so difficult to overcome difference with kindness, even the Church chose instead (for purity of faith) for centuries to ostracize, excommunicate, imprison, torture, and execute. Opposed with benevolence, "often, errors vanish as quickly as they rise, like fog before the sun" (Pope John XXIII).

Jesus doesn't expect us to do the impossible and feel the same for our enemy as we would for the dearest objects of our love. We speak of falling in love with our dear ones — a feeling of the heart such as on Valentine's day. For our enemies we must use our willpower and deliberateness. Jesus' life gives the supreme example of it.

Among enemies Jesus knowingly includes those who curse you (v. 28), people like the hypothetical neighbor whose bad will we described at the beginning. Jesus' kind of love for them means that, if anyone strikes you on one cheek (v. 29) — verbally or physically — you're to turn the other. If that seems difficult, think about it: The wise person finds enemies more useful than the fool does friends. Many owe their greatness to their enemies. The flattery of friends can be more hostile than hatred, for hatred corrects the faults flattery had disguised.

Jesus enunciates the Golden Rule: "Do to others as you would have them do to you" (v. 31). This isn't a *quid pro quo* ethic, whereby one who receives good is obliged to reciprocate. And, rather than being reactive, whereby we do good for people who have previously done good for us, it's pro-active, whereby we do good for people who have not done good for us, and from whom we don't expect good in return. Pro-active love is fundamental to Christian living.

Not everyone is happy with that. A mother happened to overhear a group of little girls concocting a scheme of revenge against another little girl who had apparently done something mean. She took the children aside and said, "It seems to me you're doing to her what you don't want her to do to you. I don't think this is the Golden Rule, is it?" "Well," replied one little girl, "The Golden Rule is all right for Sunday, but for every other day, I'd rather have an eye for an eye and a tooth for a tooth!"

Some may be surprised to learn that the Golden Rule is a heartpiece of other religions, too. Buddhism says, "Hurt not others in ways that you yourself would find hurtful" (*Udana-Varga* 5, 18). Confucius, the Chinese philosopher, about 500 years before Christ said, "Do not unto others what you would not have them do unto you" (*Analects* 15, 23). Hinduism says, "do naught unto others which would cause you pain if done to you" (*Mahabharata* 5, 1517). Taoism says, "Regard your neighbor's gain as your own, and your neighbor's loss as your own loss" (*Tai Shang Kan Ying P'ien*). Islam says, "No one of you is a believer until he desires for his brother that which he desires for himself" (*Sunnah*). The Jewish Talmud says, "What is hateful to you, do not to your fellow man" (*Shabbat* 32id).

It's also in Isocrates, the Greek orator, about 400 years before Christ; in the early Stoic philosophers of Greece and Rome, beginning about 300 years before Christ; in the Book of Tobit (4:15), about 200 years before Christ; in Hillel, one of the great Jewish rabbis, who was born shortly before Christ; and in Philo, the Jewish thinker from Alexandria who lived roughly the same time as Jesus.

But Jesus is unique in teaching that "others" includes everyone created by God, including enemies. Here (vv. 32-34), Jesus lists common ways that people think is sensible conduct toward our neighbor — loving those who love you, doing good to those who do good to you, lending money to those from whom you expect to be repaid. But Jesus says that's not enough: In each case he concludes by asking, "what credit is that to you?" As a poet (Jane Merchant) wrote:

> If I forgive an injury
> Because resenting would poison me —
> I may feel noble, I may feel splendid,
> But it isn't exactly what Christ intended.

Jesus' standard of comparison is God. His followers must become children of the Most High (v. 35), manifesting the life of God among humankind.

Only if we love our enemies and expect nothing back will we be acting like God. When we've purified ourselves, by the grace of God, to the point at which we can truly love our enemies, a beautiful thing happens. It's as if the boundaries of the soul become so clean as to be transparent, and a unique light then shines forth from the individual. We're then acting like God. And, as God's conduct shows, there's nothing inconsistent between the Golden Rule and the Iron Rule, which — an aspect of "tough love" — is never to do for others what they can do for themselves. Difficult? Indeed it is. That's why Chesterton said, "Christianity has not been tried and found wanting; it has been found difficult and not tried."

And that's why our liturgy reminds us of today's portion of St. Paul's first letter to the Corinthians. Paul, simultaneously the rabbi and the Christian preacher, in good rabbinic style presents as the summary of our life that it consists of choosing between two Adams. Just as the first Adam is the source of natural life, so the Risen Christ, "the heavenly man," "the last Adam" (v. 45), is the source — and also the model — of spiritual life. Most of us can identify with both figures battling for supremacy within our own personalities. If we adhere solely to the first Adam within us, we can't aspire to the Christian life. If we nurse grudges, we will be consumed by them. If we hold on to our hatreds, they will destroy us.

Jesus isn't just alive, like the first Adam, but life-giving, a source of life for others. He teaches values that aren't earthbound — values, indeed, that can't even be understood when seen only in the context of this life. It's only through sharing in the risen, glorified life of Christ, the prime image of God, that we're renewed according to the image of the Creator.

Paul exhorts us to grow into the image of the heavenly person by transforming ourselves. Paul's advice follows the example of David in being influenced by heavenly considerations over such natural responses as the destruction of a threatening mortal enemy. Jesus advises difficult practices like turning the other cheek, loving our enemies, and nobly forgiving others, when the natural response might demand vengeance and self-protection. Let's think about how we may follow this difficult advice in our lives.

EIGHTH SUNDAY IN ORDINARY TIME
Si 27:4-7   1 Cor 15:54-58   Lk 6:39-45

Integrity
Positive Judgments of Others; Our Call to New Life in the
Risen Lord; Mind Your Tongue!

People in the world of business used to be proud to have the motto, "My word is my bond." Once one's word was given on a deal, it was considered binding. A transaction worth millions could be completed by a few words or the shake of a hand. That action of a few moments would receive written confirmation a day or even weeks later. Today, unfortunately, one's word is frequently not trusted as one's bond.

What seems to be missing is personal integrity. That's one of the qualities we should want to carry with us always in this life; it's surely one of the criteria on which we shall be judged. Integrity means wholeness, being complete and not divided in any way: physically, spiritually, or esthetically. It means that you have every quality that you should have, and nothing in the wrong place. It means being well-rounded: that you're as poetic as you are rational, as visionary as practical, as imaginative as realistic, as artistic as hardheaded, as magnanimous as sturdy.

It's an uncompromising adherence to a code of moral or other values: utter sincerity, incorruptibility, honesty, and candor. Integrity of character avoids any and all kinds of duplicity, deception, artificiality, or shallowness. One of the difficulties with developing integrity is that that's most easily done in reflective silence. That doesn't mean we can't publicly talk about it. Today's liturgy does.

Today's Gospel is a series of three unrelated separate sayings of

Jesus harvested into one place, either because St. Luke strung them together that way or because Jesus had adapted himself to the Jewish way of preaching. The three sayings have to do with the blind leading the blind, the splinter in a companion's eye, and a good tree and its fruits. The sayings are part of Luke's "Sermon on the Plain," the charter of Christianity, perennially meaningful. Shorter than Matthew's "Sermon on the Mount," the sayings are a short list of absolutely essential components of authentic Christianity: "one-liners" such as modern comedians use, like "take my wife — please!" Jesus' one-liners here are about being a true follower of Jesus, mostly in the area of integrity within oneself and having positive judgments of others.

Jesus applies these principles to several areas. For one thing (vv. 39f.), there isn't much sense to leaders trying to guide others until and unless the leaders have been there themselves. For another thing (v. 41f.), we ought to have enough integrity to see both ourselves and others honestly. Jesus must have been exercising his sense of humor when he compared a splinter in a neighbor's eye with a whole wooden beam in one's own. His idea can be encapsulated in the old saying that there's so much bad in the best of us and so much good in the worst of us that it hardly behooves any of us to talk about the rest of us. To the Christian disciple who's concerned with the faults of another and ignores his own, Jesus applies the word "hypocrite," a designation he had previously given only to the scribes and Pharisees.

Lastly a good tree doesn't bear rotten fruit, nor a rotten tree good fruit (vv. 43f.). While this isn't scientifically true, Jesus' meaning is that internal dispositions reveal themselves in external actions — something like today's aphorism to the effect that "if you give them enough rope they'll hang themselves." Someone once said to a teacher, "I can't hear what you say for listening to what you are." People show their true condition best when they're being themselves. If a person's speech is profane or crude, we have a right to conclude that there's something wrong with the person inside: He's insecure, or weak, or ignorant, or doesn't like himself very much.

The portion of the Book of Sirach in today's First Reading uses the same approach. Written almost 200 years before Christ, early on this long book of 51 chapters was called "Wisdom of the Son of Sirach"; then it came to be also called *Liber Ecclesiasticus*, "Church Book," because the Church made extensive use of it in presenting moral teachings. It's a collection of helpful, holy teachings. Today's excerpt is a very good example of the widespread emphasis on speech in the Wisdom literature of the Ancient Near East, as well as in the Jewish Scriptures. This emphasis on speech was carried forth by the teaching of Jesus and other New Testament passages, especially the Epistle of St. James.

Sirach says that people's faults appear when they speak, especially when they speak and aren't considering their words. We often hide behind masks — but conversation reveals our inner thoughts no matter how careful we are to dissemble. Speech is a means of testing the inner character of a person, because what comes out in speech betrays what's in our heart. The climax of the reading is the last line (v. 7), saying that what a person says is clearly the test of that person. Sirach's teaching is very relevant for human integrity in today's world of public relations and image-making, the soundbite and the slogan.

Through speech God gave human beings the ability to communicate in greater detail than any other animal, and yet some people are so gross in its use! Speech is mightier than fighting, speech can be poetry, speech is civilization itself, speech was made to open person to person, but we allow our use of speech to degrade our integrity. We allow our art forms to take advantage of the fact that nowhere in the world is speech freer than that given us by our Constitution's First Amendment, to produce dialogue that's brutally vulgar. From the speech we hear in the streets, we wonder how much of our speech is the improvement on silence that it's supposed to be. We even desecrate the reverential silence we're supposed to respect at church on Sunday. The maids in the courtyard the night Jesus was being condemned told St. Peter, who at the time was denying Jesus, that his speech gave him away (Mt 26:73), and the same is true of us: Speech is a mirror of the soul; as a person speaks, so he is.

If we need motivation toward integrity, today's reading from St. Paul gives it. In this chapter, Paul asserts that belief in the resurrection of the Lord implies belief in the resurrection of the faithful. In today's passage, Paul's own experience of the Risen Lord and his life of hardship focussed his attention on the life beyond the present world. Our new life in Jesus renders insignificant the physical death that appears so final and complete to those who don't see life in terms of the eternal risen life of Jesus.

Sin, scorpion-like, contains a sting, by which it injects a poison (v. 56). That poison is death, moral if not physical. Being so personally self-satisfied as to be constantly criticizing others and lacking true integrity is one result of that poison. As the poet (Anonymous, *The Man in the Glass*, adapted) wrote:

> When you get what you want in your struggle for self
> And the world makes you king for a day,
> Just go to a mirror and look at yourself,
> And see what THAT one has to say.
> For it isn't your father or mother or spouse
> Who judgment upon you must pass;
> The person whose verdict counts most in your life
> Is the one staring back from the glass.

* * * * *

> That's the person to please, never mind all the rest
> For he's with you clear up to the end.
> And you've passed your most dangerous, difficult test
> If the one in the glass is your friend.
> You may fool the whole world down the pathway of years
> And get pats on the back as you pass.
> But your final reward will be heartaches and tears
> If you've cheated the one in the glass.

Paul ends the chapter, as he often does, by making his teachings a challenge. In this case, it's a demand for action: be firm, steadfast, always fully devoted to the work of the Lord (v. 58), knowing that we have all the glory of our resurrection to look forward to.

Even so-called educated and highly successful people often appear to lack the integrity to find meaning, direction, and contentment in life. Our entire goal is to respond to God's call to new life with the risen Lord, a life that results both from his gift and our efforts. Fulfillment of that goal is infinitely worth the struggle involved in retaining our integrity. Our children are often the best judges of integrity versus phoniness. They're not impressed by false fronts of even their parents. We can't fake integrity or hide it, so let's try deliberately to develop it.

NINTH SUNDAY IN ORDINARY TIME
1 K 8:41-43   Gal 1:1f., 6-10   Lk 7:1-10

Faith and "Outsiders"
Against Exclusivism and Elitism; The Gospel Is for Everyone;
Openness; What Kind of Person is the Person of Faith?

What did you have for breakfast today? Cereal? Toast? Eggs? No matter in what form, you literally ate a piece of a star. It consisted mostly of carbon, nitrogen, oxygen, and hydrogen, with a sprinkling of other elements. Except for the hydrogen, those atoms had been forged in a star that exploded, left its remnants in the universe, and died long before our sun and solar system were born. The hydrogen was made in the big bang that allegedly began our universe. Some astronomers think that it was on dust grains floating in interstellar space that these atoms first assembled themselves into the organic molecules that are the forerunners of life, and that the water that's three-quarters of our body came from a comet. So our breakfast and we are stardust.

In light of all that, it doesn't become us to be small-minded. Especially abhorrent is small-mindedness in religion. Did Jesus save people on other planets, if they exist? We can be sure that God has made provisions for all people, no matter where. On earth, is salvation for all people linked to our Judeo-Christian tradition? Today's Gospel tells the story of a man who was outside that tradition. The story's from St. Luke's Gospel, which pays special attention to non-Jews, avoids Hebrew terminology, and rarely quotes the Jewish Scriptures.

On the face of the Roman centurion's situation, the prospects for an intervention by Jesus weren't good. The petitioner was a military officer in command of a "century," a company of 100 soldiers. But because the Roman legions were seldom kept at the maximum strength of 6,000 men, the century often consisted of only 50 to 60 men. The centurion, a company commander, was probably the equivalent of a captain today, though he rose from the ranks and would be considered a non-commissioned officer.

The centurion was to the Roman legion what a mainspring is to a watch: The whole army depended on him. Circumstances suggest that this particular centurion was probably in the service of Herod Antipas, tetrarch of Galilee. In addition to the centurion being a representative of the hated occupying army, this incident took place in Jesus' adopted town of Capernaum, which is in Galilee, where the memories of Roman cruelty were fresh.

The centurion sought a cure for his dying servant, very probably a poor Jew and possibly the reason behind his master's faith. Knowing the way things work in the military and politics, the centurion enlisted the help of Jewish elders to present his credentials to Jesus. They in turn presented the best-case scenario to Jesus: that the centurion was racially open-minded and a philanthropist.

The centurion was a person of faith. He was an honest and generous man, well-disposed and even loving toward the Jews. He had built a synagogue for them. And now he showed his sensitivity toward the Jewish custom of not entering the home of a Gentile, which would make the Jew ritually unclean: In words we paraphrase just before we receive Holy Communion, he said, "I am not worthy to have you enter under my roof" (v. 6). That's the cry of every honest person before God. We hear its echo in the voices of many who lament, "I'm not strong enough in my faith. Help me!" Jesus marveled at the centurion — marveled at him — and expressed surprise and delight at the centurion's request. But that was nothing compared to the excitement and joy of the centurion's messengers when they returned home and found the slave in good health (v. 10).

The centurion was the kind of open person King Solomon had in mind when he voiced the prayer in today's First Reading as he solemnly dedicated the Temple in Jerusalem. Solomon prayed that God's house would be open to non-Israelites and that they, too, would be able to be heard within its precincts. For Solomon, coming to know God's name and dedicating the Temple in that name was a way of expressing the tension between God's nearness and His utter transcendence. Earlier in this same prayer (8:27), Solomon had told God that if the highest heavens couldn't contain Him, how much less the Temple which Solomon had built. Solomon knew that the largeness of God is unfathomable. But adherents of a faith can become more rigid than its founders. Despite Solomon's prayers, the Jerusalem Temple had become a place strictly for Jews.

So, too, some early Christians very much wanted things to go their own way rather than God's. After St. Paul had converted the Galatians, for example, some teachers attacked Paul's standing as an apostle and told the Galatians to follow First Testament rules. The agitators seem to be avid Jewish Christians from Jerusalem who insisted on the absolute necessity of circumcision and Jewish dietary laws for acceptance into the Christian community. They seem to operate on two diametrically opposed fronts. On the one side, they rejected Paul's authority to preach because he wasn't a member of the Twelve who knew Jesus intimately and didn't have the Gospel first-hand. At the same time, they seem to be members of some pre-Gnostic sect who worshipped angels or gods who they thought inhabited the stars and saw themselves as a new race, a bit better than anyone else.

Paul looked for a larger-minded view. He asserted (v. 1) that he wasn't an apostle commissioned by a congregation, or even by prophets, but an apostle through Jesus Christ and God the Father. Instead of the thanksgiving that he usually placed at the beginning of his letters, Paul, with little to be thankful for in the Galatian situation, expressed amazement at the way his converts were deserting the Gospel of Christ for a perverted message. He reasserted the one Gospel he had preached (vv. 7-9). Against opponents' charges that he had sought to conciliate people with flattery and to curry favor with God, Paul began a vigorous defense of himself (v. 10).

In the Christian view of people, there's no room for isolationism, or provincialism. In God's eyes, there are no "foreigners": All are equal and are called to become His children. Solomon saw, however vaguely, God's plan to reveal Himself to all nations. Paul saw that all human beings, of whatever culture, nation, or race, could belong to God, through Christ. The moral conversion that Jesus' Good News demands is profound and far-reaching; it makes for the development of all persons as full human beings. Nothing truly human is alien to the Good News, and all people, of whatever culture, color, or race, can accept it.

What kind of person is the person of faith? At the very least, not bigoted, biased, or prejudiced (a humorous but accurate graffito reads, "If I didn't believe it with my own mind, I never would have seen it"). The person of faith is, rather, welcoming, hospitable, and friendly, open to God and to others. Solomon's prayer in the Temple is a reflection of that spirit. Paul's response to the Galatians pleaded against a closed-in type of faith that could be measured only by living up to legal prescriptions. And the centurion's servant was healed against all odds because of the centurion's faith.

In the centurion and his faith, there are further lessons for us.

Concerned over his servant, the centurion was a man of compassion. He was a humble man, sending others to plead his cause. He was ego-free, and so was able to recognize authority in Jesus. He was vulnerable in the face of Jesus' power, open to what he needed but knew he didn't deserve, and he reached out to what can only be called grace. He was sensitive, not asking Jesus, a Jew, into his Gentile home. He's a great example of the discerning heart which we all need.

The centurion showed spiritual growth, which is the evolution of an individual. An individual's body may undergo the changes of the life cycle, but it doesn't evolve. Within a person's lifetime, however, the human spirit may evolve dramatically. New patterns may be forged, spiritual competence take advantage of unlimited opportunities for growth to increase until the moment of death in advanced old age. The centurion represents, by far, most of the people in the world today. The faith of the true Christian should go out to his like, and should be as great as the stardust from which all of us came.

FIRST SUNDAY OF LENT
Dt 26:4-10   Rm 10:8-13   Lk 4:1-13

Life Is a Journey
Spiritual Renewal; Prayer, Charity, and Asceticism;
Holiness True and False; Jesus Is Lord

Statements of philosophers about life are interesting. Life is a sexually transmitted disease. You're a puff of smoke that appears briefly and then disappears (Jm 4:14). Life is a quarry, out of which we're to mold and chisel character. Life is a cabaret. But for us on this first Sunday of Lent, it's important to know that life is a journey — a journey that consists in our becoming, a journey toward God, an inner journey. That, and our being pilgrims on this journey, is what Lent is all about. Every Lent is a milestone for us on that journey.

Jesus' temptations were a milestone for him; they're narrated in each of the three liturgical cycles on the First Sunday of Lent. His temptations make it clear that he was fully human as well as divine: Temptation is a part of human life. With Jesus as with all of us, temptations are also tailored to our personal condition. His in particular at this time were appeals to the basic drives within all of us: for security (bread), for power (kingdoms), and for recognition and fame (the Temple).

Today's Gospel scene is bursting with drama as well as meaning, with the full force of the godhead confronting the world of diabolical power in a battle of cosmic proportions. Human refusal to respond to God's invitation is described in biblical terms as sin, the misuse of human freedom. One of the ironies about belief in the reality of sin is that it's tied in with belief in human dignity. For to believe in sin is to believe in human freedom and personal responsibility. Whenever we seek to avoid responsibility for our behavior, we're trying to give away our power to some other entity, be it a person, or "fate," or society, or the government, or our boss.

In Aldous Huxley's novel *Brave New World* there are only a few so-called savages who still profess belief in human freedom. They're quarantined away from the rest of society until they're willing to adjust to the new order of things. At one point the one in control says to one of the savages, "We prefer to make things comfortable. We give you Christianity without tears." The savage replies, "But I don't want comfort. I want God. I want poetry. I want goodness. I want freedom. And I will accept along with these the possibilities of evil, heartbreak and tragedy." The one in control says, "In fact you're claiming the right to be unhappy." The savage replies, "Yes. I'm claiming the right to be unhappy."

Contrary to portrayals of the Devil-tempter as a grotesque figure in red leotards or as an almost comical businessman wearing a mafia-like hat and dark glasses, the Devil is the serious personification of the evil in the world. In bringing him to the fore, the early Christians were attempting the extraordinary and noble enterprise of trying to make sense of good and evil: a subject of crucial importance to human society. When we speak of the Devil, what there is no doubt about is the power that evil — the abuse of power, cruelty, greed, contempt, malice, envy, and the desire to humiliate and destroy others — holds in the human psyche, and how important it is to deal with that. There, the early Church Fathers thought, is where the Devil enters in: as the antithesis of love. And the Devil is a regular visitor to our world: Auschwitz, the Falls Road, pedophiliac adults, animal torturers, school bullies, youth who burn down churches "for fun" all show how possible it is to lose touch with love.

The Scriptures give the Devil three precise names and functions. He is the one who divides and separates (*dia-bolos*); he is the one who accuses (Satan); and he is the one whom Jesus calls the father of lies (Jn 8:44). The Evil One surely enters our lives in these three ways, splitting us into warring parts, filling us with negative and accusatory voices, and telling us lies about who we are and who God is. And, for some unexplainable reason, it's usually easier to do his evil thing than the right thing. Why, for example, didn't they put the vitamins in ice cream instead of in spinach?

Jesus is led by the Spirit into the desert (v. 1) not primarily to be tempted, but for prayerful communion with his heavenly Father. The desert had a strong attraction for the Israelites. They'd been close to God when they'd wandered through the desert during the Exodus. They'd encountered God in the desert around Mt. Sinai, where God had given them their revered Torah. In the desert the prophet Elijah had renewed his faith when he was discouraged. The prophet Amos had never wanted to leave the desert, for he was close to God there. In the desert Isaiah had advised to prepare the way of the Lord. John the Baptist was baptizing in the desert.

And Jesus was "closer" to his heavenly Father in the desert; so it was a time of great challenge. And "challenge" may be a good word for what took place here rather than temptation: These were for Jesus opportunities to grow in grace as well as to lose it — as temptations are for all of us.

There were stones all around that looked like loaves of bread. Surely if Jesus were as holy as his reputation had it, he could command one of them to become bread (v. 3). Just one loaf! And he was famished! The temptation was to apply his power for his own use — not a sin in the usual sense, but unworthy of Jesus. Will he — alone, hungry, and tired — abide by principle and insist on divine ideals? Jesus' answer was scriptural: One doesn't live by bread alone (v. 4, citing Dt 8:3), a familiar quotation that ended with, "but on every word that comes from the mouth of the Lord." This temptation has equivalents for all of us, one of which applies to today's over-emphasis on material things for our use as individuals rather than for helping others as well: One doesn't live by them alone.

That failing, the Devil showed Jesus all the kingdoms of the world (v. 5). The fact that it happened in a single instant removes any idea of a physical taking of Jesus up higher by the Devil: It must have happened in a vision. As with all temptations in the mind, however, this temptation is no less real. To have a piece of these kingdoms' power and glory (v. 6) — the entirety of which the Devil, the father of lies, said were his own — all that Jesus need do was bend a little (v. 7). Become the kind of Messiah that the people expected. They were always looking for signs; why not give them one? Compromise. Make a deal. It's done all the time. This imperfect world is made of gray, not black and white. With that kind of power, Jesus could bring food to the poor, justice to the oppressed, and consolation to the afflicted. Wasn't that why he'd come? But Jesus showed that he submitted completely to God.

The climax of the temptations was the Devil leading Jesus to Jerusalem — Jerusalem the golden; Jerusalem the preeminent; Jerusalem whose Temple was a place of God's activity; Jerusalem to which Jesus' entire ministry was a journey; Jerusalem over which, in one of the most dramatic moments described in the New Testament, Jesus wept.

This time the Devil himself used Scripture, as he frequently does, for his own purposes: here to tempt Jesus to throw himself down (v. 9) to the Kidron valley from one of the highest points of the Temple, a drop of 450 feet. This was a temptation to fame by giving sensations. This temptation has a peculiar relevance to our times, when the image is everything and the reality nothing, the age of the public relations agent, the age when what you are is much less important than what you appear to be. If you can jump off the Empire State building and land on your feet and walk away, you must be important. Some religious leaders succumb to that temptation, and people flock to them.

But Jesus knew that religious sensationalism doesn't last. He again used Scripture (Dt 6:10) against the Devil to reject the idea of being a Messiah of the marvelous and the gaudy, even though this is the kind of Messiah many people want. Salvation comes rather by the humble way of faith; Jesus' ministry showed that the true way to real victory is the way of the cross. The Devil never, either then or now, gives up, and after he had finished with his current temptations of Jesus, he departed for a time to await other opportunities (v. 13). In Jesus' life, as in ours, the Devil's opportunities come again and again.

Because Jesus used the Book of Deuteronomy against the Devil, the Church presents a portion of it in today's First Reading to say something about how to observe Lent. In directives from God through Moses to the Israelites, Deuteronomy laid down the correct rubrics for approaching God (vv. 4, 10b) and the correct words and gestures (vv. 5-10a). The words form a creed that sums up what God had done for the Israelites throughout their history, but now especially through their harvest, just as our creed sums up all that God gave us in Christ. For all that God had done, they were to make merry (v. 11) through joyful participation in the liturgy — another lesson for Lent, when the Gospels of every day's Mass give us the opportunity to look joyfully at the life of Jesus.

St. Paul continues that notion. In his letter to the Romans, a part of which we read in today's Second Reading, he appealed that to put people in a right relationship with God they abandon the Torah's way of legalism in religion in favor of the easier way of grace that Jesus Christ gave. This involves the inner conviction of the heart as well as external words of the lips.

As Deuteronomy had presented the basic creedal formula for the Jews, Paul presented it for Christians: Jesus is Lord. That word "Lord" is all-embracing. "Lord" is the translation of the Hebrew divine name Yahweh or Jehovah; it was the title of the Greek gods; it was the title of the Roman emperors; and it applies to Jesus a title of respect like the English *sir*, the German *Herr*, the French *monsieur*, the Italian *signore*, and the Spanish *señor*. To acknowledge Jesus as Lord is central to our lives. And to believe that God raised him from the dead is an essential of Christian belief: One must believe not only that Jesus lived, but that he lives. And instead of hypocritical pious show, our personal adherence to Christ is to be in our heart as well as on our lips (vv. 9f.). And everyone shall be rescued who calls on the name of the Lord (the original of Jl 3:5, cited in v. 13).

Our life is a journey, and Lent is a small model of life. It's a special time of reflecting on life. We need that like butterflies need the morning sunshine. At that time they have to spread their wings because the scales on their wings are actually solar cells. Without that source of energy, they can't fly.

Lent tells us to treasure our basic baptismal values in the face of temptations, as Jesus did. Though tempted to acquire material possessions, he could enjoy the flowers of the field. (His life was consonant with the Chinese proverb that says: "That the birds of worry and care fly above your head, this you cannot change; but that they build nests in your hair, this you can prevent.") Though tempted to associate with the wealthy, he could weep with the broken-hearted poor. Though tempted to consort with the powerful, he could see eternal truth in the face of a child. He could accept the hospitality of despised people and handle rejection from the respected. He could love without being loved, be hated without hating. At the end, when his temptations were especially violent, he died a man of strength and peace.

How do we deal with our personal temptations? Like Mark Twain, who said, "The best way to handle temptation is to give in to it"? This Lent, we should try to find the personal weaknesses through which we might be tempted. And we should engage in the spirit of this season, penance. This means "a radical reorientation of our whole life, a return, a conversion to God with all our heart" (*Catechism of the Catholic Church*, 1431). It's a spirit that's dynamically oriented toward love on our journey through life. It's accomplished in many ways, among which are "gestures of reconciliation, concern for the poor, the exercise... of justice... , revision of life, examination of conscience, spiritual direction, [and the] acceptance of suffering" (*Catechism of the Catholic Church*, 1435).

SECOND SUNDAY OF LENT
Gn 15:5-12, 17f.   Ph 3:17-4:1   Lk 9:28-36

Faithfulness
From Death Valley to Glory Mountain; Encouragement;
Constancy; Wake Up and See God's Glory; Keep the Faith;
Life as Pilgrimage; Living Promise and Hope

Much of life is based on the consolation of promise and hope. I wasted tonight looking at television, but I promise it won't happen again. The weather seems more promising this year than last. I didn't do well financially this year, but next year somehow I'll do better for my family. Many living in tension long for the expected day of release.

The promise contained in events like Jesus' transfiguration, which the Church presents in every year's Gospel on the Second Sunday of Lent, isn't the whole of Christian faith: It has to be understood in connection with his suffering and death. There's no denying, however, that to contemplate the glorious transfiguration is an encouragement to us as we practice our Lenten mortifications.

Jesus and three of his disciples went up onto a mountain (v. 28). No specific mountain can be singled out, but the fact that they went there to pray may indicate that it was as much a theological mountain as it was a physical one, a place where God reveals Himself. And while he was praying Jesus' face changed in appearance and his clothes became dazzlingly white (v. 29).

In identical words as will be used at Jesus' resurrection (24:4) and at his ascension (Ac 1:10), St. Luke tells us that conversing with him were Moses and Elijah (v. 30) as the totality of the First Testament — Moses as the prime representative of the Law and Elijah of the Prophets — to indicate that the purpose of both the Law and the Prophets, to prepare for Christ, was now fulfilled. According to biblical and extra-biblical tradition, both men had been taken up into heaven. Among the things they spoke of was Jesus' "passage." The word was "exodus"; it meant that for Jesus it will be through death that he will pass over to heavenly glory, as the angel of death had passed over the homes of the Hebrews in Egypt, as Israel had passed over from slavery into freedom, and as we pass over from penance to salvation.

Amid all the glory, Jesus was learning the extent to which his suffering would have to go to finish his work. Moses had never quite finished his work. He had worked hard: struggling with Pharaoh, with the complaining wilderness generation, and — mostly — with God. He had been to the top of a mountain to receive the tablets of the Law. He had got through the desert, to another mountain: that from which he could see the Promised Land off in the distance. But there God took him in death. Elijah hadn't finished his work, either. He, too, had been to a mountain — just before God took him home in that low-swinging chariot. He had been on the mountain to pray, in great discouragement, thinking himself to be the last faithful person on earth. He'd worked and worked, this tireless prophet of God, and then God took him.

That could easily be a picture of the lives of many of us. We work and work, believing that soon the day will come when everything will fall into place: when I finish school, or get a job, or get married, or when the children are grown, or when loans are paid off. Often we never seem to finish, and then God takes us. But we may consider our lives as a long and difficult race, in which we can hand off the baton to another runner. Moses handed off to Joshua, and Elijah to Elisha. Today they were all making the last hand off: to Jesus.

The disciples Peter, James, and John saw his glory (v. 32). This wasn't a transformation only on the surface, as with Moses when he came down from Sinai, who didn't know that his face had become radiant (Ex 34:29). Jesus was resplendent with inner glory. He was being revealed — not only as a lawgiver or prophet, but as the Son of God. Moses had been unaware, but Jesus was very much aware. The entire scene is charged with this awareness. It's an awareness in which we can share if, unlike the Apostles, we stay alert. We miss a lot in life because our minds aren't fully awake.

What often awakens is suffering. Many an actor or writer or opera singer are technically perfect, but do their jobs without feeling. They haven't suffered enough. Paradoxically, they need a broken heart to make them whole. A teacher said of a beautiful young singer with a perfect voice, "She will be so much better when she has had to endure some of life's sufferings!"

Peter, though not fully aware, was impressed. Unable to keep his thoughts to himself any more here than on many other occasions, he blurted out that it would be a good idea to set up three tents (v. 33) for each of the glorious participants, to keep them there. He may have been thinking of the Jewish Feast of Tabernacles or Booths (Zc 14:16), the end of whose octave was now taking place. It recalled Israel's forty years of wandering through the desert, when they lived in booths, or tents. It was the idea of life as impermanent pilgrimage, a Lenten theme.

In another reference to Israel's exodus, a cloud came and cast a shadow over them (v. 34). No ordinary cloud, this was the *shekinah*, the cloud that signaled God's presence. The voice of the Father from that cloud identified Jesus as His "Son," His "chosen one" (v. 35). Equally important was the Father's command, "Listen to him." The Law and the Prophets have gone, and from now on people must listen to Jesus. His words and his example taught that life isn't all laughter, nor is it all tears, but an interweaving of both. We aren't to complain about either, as we need both for our wholeness.

When Jesus was alone (v. 36), contrasting with the thunderous awe-inspiring voice of God and the Apostles' noisy inner turmoil, there was a meaningful silence — a real, as opposed to an empty, silence. Even from Peter. In that stillness we, if not the Apostles, realize that at Jesus' tomb, two others — angels — will appear in dazzling garments and will recall that the Messiah had to suffer so as to enter into his glory (24:26). Through all the twists and turns of his life, Jesus was faithful.

We see another example of the faithful person in today's reading from the Book of Genesis. It's a story of the early life of Abraham, who with his wife Sarai left Ur of the Chaldees in what is now southern Iraq for a land that God would show them (Gn 12:1). He was still called by his original name Abram before his heroic plunge into the unknown for God's sake changed it to Abraham. Abram had become acceptable to God because he had trusted in the fulfillment of a promise by God that could not under ordinary circumstances be realized (vv. 5f.).

But when God promised Abram the Promised Land, Abram asked for a sign (v. 8). This wasn't a contradiction of his absolute faith, and in answer God sealed a covenant with Abram through symbols that Abram saw in a sacred dream. It was the first solemn covenant in all of human history, and the beginning of what we call Salvation History. It was ritualized in a ceremony. Animals were slain and divided, leaving an intervening passage. Those who were party to the covenant passed through the divided animals, thus invoking the fate of dying in the same way if they didn't live up to their obligations.

As at Jesus' transfiguration, the symbols were signs of the awesomeness of the occasion: the setting sun, Abram's deep sleep, terror, and darkness (v. 12). And, in a contrast in Genesis similar to that between noise and quiet at the transfiguration, into the darkness came God the Light, in the form of a smoking brazier and a flaming torch (v. 17): God is frequently symbolized by fiery figures. Biblical faith means that, like Abram and Sarai, we're uprooted from a merely natural way of life and are sent by God on a journey beyond that.

St. Paul, in today's part of his letter to the Philippians, tells us how to achieve that biblical faith. He doesn't hesitate to tell us to imitate him (v. 17), because he in turn is an imitator of Christ. He indicts many, however, who are so occupied with the part of Christ that includes glory that they elide over the cross (v. 18). Those whom Paul meant as the enemies of the cross in his day have their counterparts today in all those who so lack faith that they deny the need of struggle, self-denial, penance, and mortification in life — and the need for Lent.

The detachment expected of the Christian doesn't mean forbidding the love of beauty in all its manifestations. To the contrary, Christianity positively demands the enjoyment of beautiful things and a reverence for them for their own sake. But the perfection we see in them and the love we give them is relative to the infinite perfection we see in God and the absolute love we give Him. A scholar (Aldous Huxley) once remarked that when at the Reformation the puritan was substituted for the monk, the change was for the worse. The puritan practices a self-destroying asceticism, because he thinks of it not as a means to a more complete end, but as intrinsically right. The monk, on the other hand, practices self-perfecting asceticism for the attainment of a fuller completeness.

To help, Paul reminds us that our citizenship is in heaven (v. 20). Philippi, the Roman colony to which Paul was writing, was built, as were most Roman colonies, on important crossroads. For the Philippians, the privilege of being Roman citizens rather than subjects was as welcome as the thought of freedom for the imprisoned. As we suffer through our earthly pilgrimage, the thought that our citizenship is in heaven rather than here is equally welcome, and strengthens our faith.

Our citizenship in heaven, while not encouraging us to forget the cause of justice in this world, entitles us to eagerly await Jesus' Second Coming. At the Second Coming, our lowly body (v. 21) will be transformed into the glorious splendor of the transformed Christ. That's quite a promise. And, remembering all the limitations of our earthly bodies, Christ's promise is very consoling.

God has affection for everyone who struggles along the pilgrim race of this life. Along the sidelines we hear voices — some from others, the worst from inside ourselves. The worst voices say, "You're a fool." But we also hear the voice which spoke to Jesus, saying, "You're my child, the delight of my soul." Our relationship with God is more than a mere covenant (as in today's First Reading). It's even more than our being citizens of a heavenly country (as in our Second Reading). Our relationship with God through our baptism is that we be transformed into the image of Christ. Let's pray that we who have been baptized, and those Elect now approaching baptism, will continue joyfully through our penances to rely on God's promises.

THIRD SUNDAY OF LENT
Ex 3:1-8, 13-15   1 Cor 10:1-6, 10-12   Lk 13:1-9

The Need to Reform
Cooperating with Grace; Vigilance; Another Chance; Conversion

Is there a connection between how we behave toward God, on the one
hand, and our earthly fortunes, on the other? Between sin and suffering? In today's Gospel, Jesus says not in this world. He gives two examples.

When the cruel Pilate, wanting to keep the people quiet, built a
much-needed aqueduct for Jerusalem, he ruthlessly usurped Temple
money for the purpose. Many of the people were outraged at this profane use of sacred money, and they protested vigorously. In particular,
the Galileans, an excitable people, let Pilate know how they felt. So
Pilate instructed his soldiers to mingle among the gathering crowds,
with clubs hidden beneath their cloaks to beat the Galileans into submission. The soldiers went about their work so enthusiastically that they
beat some Galileans to death. The ones who were killed, says Jesus,
weren't necessarily more wicked than those who lived.

In his second example, Jesus tells the parable of the fig tree. The
fig tree was a favorite of the Jews. Genesis, the first book of the Bible,
tells that it was the leaf of the fig tree that covered the nakedness of
Adam and Eve after they committed original sin. The Book of Revelation, the last book of the Bible, compares the falling of the stars from
the sky at the end of the world with the falling of figs from this tree.
Between Genesis and the Book of Revelation there are about sixty other
references to the fig tree, including the Jews' model picture of the happy
Jew as a man sitting under his fig tree at peace with the world.

But the fig tree takes a lot of nourishment from the soil. And there
isn't much arable soil in the Holy Land. So the fig tree had to justify
its existence. In Our Lord's story, the master after three years wanted
to cut down his unproductive fig tree, but was persuaded to give it a
chance of one more year of care and fertilizing.

The fig tree in Jesus' story is a reminder of the two kinds of human beings: those who give, and those who take. What the famous
conductor Herbert Von Karajan said about orchestra conducting ap-

plies to life: "Technique you can learn. But what comes out of it is what you give as a human being." Those who only take have to justify their existence. To accept Christ's message is to be open to conversion. As the anonymous poet wrote:

> If all the sleeping folks would wake up
> And all the lukewarm would fire up
> And all the disgruntled would sweeten up
> And all the discouraged would cheer up
> And all the estranged would make up
> And all the gossipers would shut up
> then there might come a REBIRTH IN CHRIST.

Conversion means to respond to God's care for us, to devote ourselves to a life of vigilance day in and day out, and constantly to renew our cooperation with God's grace. In cooperating with God's grace, we shouldn't be under-confident of what we can do.

In today's First Reading, Moses was very conscious of his short-comings. For one thing, he was brought up by others than his parents. And he was vulnerable: When he'd seen an Egyptian persecuting a Jew, Moses had killed the Egyptian. When his crime became known, he had fled to Midian (beyond the Sinai peninsula), married the daughter of the wealthy pagan priest Jethro, and would have been content to live out the rest of his days there. He had no great gifts to talk about. He even had a speech defect.

Yet God wanted him to go back to Egypt and negotiate the freedom of his people with the great Pharaoh Rameses II. Moses mentioned many reasons not to go back: all of the above, plus that he had a good thing going in Midian and the Jews wouldn't listen to him anyhow, and so on and on. One of his major reasons for lack of confidence was the very person of the Pharaoh. We can get a picture of the power and wealth of a pharaoh from the burial treasures of King Tutankhamen, which have toured the world. Moses knew that the Pharaoh, should Moses ever get to see him, would follow other non-Jews of the time and want to know the name of his god.

They believed, you see, that knowing another's name would give them a certain power over him. In Egypt, newborn infants were given a pseudonym in order that the demons in the nether world might not know their real name and thus have a power over the infant. When

Adam named the animals in the creation story, it's a sign that he had power over them. So Moses asked God His name.

At first, God tried to give a demonstration to give Moses some idea of who He was. He appeared, as He did at other times, as a fire. Fire is a good image of God, for several reasons: Its activity is intense, giving some notion of the inner life of God; it's very much a spiritual element; and the flames of fire always go upward, toward the heavens. So this ground on which God was appearing to Moses was holy. We must all grow to see the holiness of God in our lives. As the poet (Elizabeth Barrett Browning) put it:

> Earth is crammed with heaven and every
> common bush on fire with God.
> But only he who sees takes off his shoes, the rest
> sit and pluck blackberries.

Finally God answered Moses, "I am who am" — that is to say, He who is, who was, and who shall never cease to be. This was the origin of the Hebrew word for God, "Yahweh," or "Jehovah." It means many things. It means that God is pure Being. It means that God's existence is eternal: It never had a beginning, and will never have an end. Before anything else — stars, galaxies, suns, planets — came to be, He is. Furthermore, He's the cause of everything else that is, and the one who sustains everything else in being.

Above all, "Jehovah" means the contrast between the over-arching awesomeness of God and His intimate involvement with His people's history — in technical terms, between God's transcendence and His immanence. The Israelites considered the name of God so sacred that they never pronounced it: They used a round-about word instead. The only exception to that took place once a year for one person: The high priest was allowed to use God's name on Yom Kippur in the Holy of Holies in the Temple. Even then, a blast of trumpets assured that unworthy mortal ears wouldn't hear the holy name.

Reverence for God's name has existed all over the world. A tradition going back at least to the seventeenth-century mathematician and philosopher Blaise Pascal defines God as "a circle whose center is everywhere and circumference nowhere." Muslims have 99 beautiful names for God, such as "the Merciful One," "the Compassionate," "the Almighty," "the First," and "the Last," which they often recite on a rosary. Some Muslims suggest whimsically that only the camel knows the one-hundredth name of God, which accounts for the beast's haughty air. In Africa, many traditional names have survived the influences of Jews, Christians, and Muslims in the way Africans address God. The one whom they call God includes no less than 589 names. Among these are Creator Who Spreads Things Out in the Attic of the Sky (Zambia), Father of Laughter (Nigeria), and Nursing Mother (Kenya/Tanzania). Taoist priests in Taiwan honor "That Which Cannot Be Named."

So Moses was transformed. He came to realize that, with this kind of God strengthening him, he could do anything. The rest is history: Moses' continuing to lead the Jews from their slavery in Egypt, his ongoing guidance of their trek through the desert, and their final sight of the land of promise "flowing with milk and honey."

On the other hand, our acceptance of God's grace is the story of another extreme to avoid: overconfidence. St. Paul reminds us in today's Second Reading of God's wonders that guided the Jews' journey out of Egypt. They had the presence of God as they went, symbolized by the cloud, or *shekinah*, that was over them. They were able to pass through the waters when Egypt's soldiers couldn't. They were fed by a mysterious substance that fell from the heavens every night.

But they were overconfident of themselves and forgetful of God. When Moses went up Mount Sinai to converse with God, the people at the base of the mountain fell into the idolatry of the golden calf and succumbed to fornication.

The Israelites failed God miserably also by their constant complaining. They complained that the pursuing Egyptians would overtake and kill them. They complained that Moses spent too much time on the mountain. They complained through the desert that they were going to starve, and God sent manna. They complained about the taste of the manna, and God sent them quail. They complained that their enemy nations would be too strong for them. They complained that the Promised Land wasn't worth much. And they complained that they didn't have enough water to drink.

The result? None of the generation that left Egypt, including Moses, was privileged to enter the Promised Land. They all died before they got there. It was their children who made it. Paul's message to all is to be vigilant.

Answering for our sins with suffering this side of the grave doesn't always happen. Nevertheless, we're all ultimately responsible for ourselves: our sins, shortcomings, imperfections, and "what might have been" had we cooperated with God's grace. That means the constant need to reform, and openness to conversion: assessing how we see the success of our own lives in the light of eternity. This includes such details as how we treat the person at the supermarket check-out or the irritating driver ahead of us in traffic.

Moses' people failed God. Jesus' audience failed him pitifully, too, and the Corinthians' self-serving failed Paul. We, too, can fail. As with the unproductive fig tree, Jesus is kind, loving, merciful, and patient. But he's not wishy-washy: He sets limits, and if we fail to respond he may be forced to say, as of the fig tree, "Cut it down." Times of grace, like this Lent, are times when we can satisfy the need to shore up our weakness and become more vigilant. Although we never know when our last chance will come, we know that this Lent, if we use it correctly, is a time of special grace. Am I continuing to respond to God's love this Lent?

FOURTH SUNDAY OF LENT
Jos 5:9, 10-12   2 Cor 5:17-21   Lk 15:1-3, 11-32

Reconciliation
Against Self-Righteousness; Throw Yourself on God;
Forgiveness; God's Mercy

When the history of our times is written, it will say that our popular art form is the motion picture film. Yet an aid to rapid — almost magical — learning has made its appearance. Indications are that, if it catches on, all the electronic gadgets will be just so much junk. The new device is known as Built-in Orderly Organized Knowledge. It has no wires, no electric circuitry to break down. Anyone can use it, even children. It fits comfortably in the hands or pocket and can be conveniently used. It will instantly start and stop, can promptly go forward or reverse itself, requires no batteries, and will provide full information on an entire civilization. The makers generally call this Built-in Orderly Organized Knowledge device by its initials, BOOK. The book in turn presents one of the most popular art forms of all time: the short story.

Among the most popular short stories of all time is the one in today's Gospel. Because it comes after the stories of the lost sheep and the lost coin, it gives the facetious name to this section of St. Luke's Gospel as "The Lost and Found Department." It's usually mis-called the story of "The Prodigal Son." It might better be called the story of "The Loving Father": He's the main character and real hero. He's also the same Father who listens to us as we pray. The story is realistic and reflects keen psychological insight.

The younger of two sons going to his father and asking for his inheritance was within his rights under the Law (Dt 21:15-17). But the son's coming to him like this was tantamount to saying that he wished his father dead. Nevertheless, under the law the father could choose to give his sons his property either while he was living or when he died. In either case, the division of the property would be the same. In a case like the present one, the elder son would get two-thirds and the younger son one-third.

In our story the younger son — because of immaturity, or selfishness, or irresponsibility, or a spirit of adventure, or whatever motivated the youth — chose to go his own way independent of his father. Opting for the pleasure of self-satisfaction, he came to one of the consequences of sin: isolation from community. When he was reduced to the degradation of taking care of pigs, the lowest of the low for a Jew, like an alcoholic who has hit rock-bottom he finally came to see himself as he really was. The young man resolved to return to his father's house.

All the long way home he rehearsed a manipulative speech that he hoped would persuade his father to take him back — not as a son any more, but as a hired hand. It's a tacky speech that plays on what he himself undoubtedly doesn't put much stock in — his father's reverence for God: "Father, I have sinned against God and against you." If his behavior were from someone we knew today, it would elicit our contempt. The average human father might welcome him back, but with a stiff contract: Tow the line or else! He would love him, yes: But such a son would have to prove himself before the father could really forgive or forget.

What did this father do? Even as his son was far off, he saw him; he must have been waiting and watching all that time. He threw open his arms in welcome, and never let his son finish his rehearsed speech.

The scene is well depicted in Rembrandt's painting, *Return of the Prodigal Son*. The father is embracing the young son, his left hand the large strong hand of a man, his thumb giving obvious pressure through the threadbare garment on the boy's shoulder. His embracing right hand, though, is the delicate hand of a woman, showing mercy and kindness.

The father's forgiveness was total. He ordered his workers to put on his son the finest robe as a sign of honor, a ring as a sign of authority, and shoes as a sign that he continued to be a son. His son wasn't to be reduced to the status of slave: In that culture, it was they who had no shoes. (Because slaves had no shoes even to recent times, poor African-American slaves sang the spiritual, "All God's Chillun Got Shoes." For them this meant heaven, when at last all people, even defenseless slaves, would receive their true dignity as persons.)

Again translated into modern terms, the father's behavior would receive comments something like, "The old fool! No wonder his son is such a spoiled brat! The old man will be dead of a heart attack in a year!" But if we were put in the place of having to deal with our own best beloved, it might be a different story.

During the father's celebration of his son's return, the elder son makes his entrance for the climax of the story. He's smug in having done his duty to the father all the time his brother was away. His judgments, coming from a mentality of law rather than grace, of a hireling rather than a loving son, are rash, his speech mean. Just as the father had graciously cut off the humiliating speech of his younger son to show forgiveness, the elder brother cuts off the loving speech of his father to object. He refers to his younger brother as "your son" (v. 30), and the father gently rebukes him by referring to "your brother" (v. 32).

Perhaps we should give thought to the ways — many of them self-righteous — in which we can offend. In early-nineteenth-century Vienna, a famous preacher delivered a fiery sermon to a huge congregation. He spoke of "that tiny piece of flesh, the most dangerous appurtenance of anyone's body." Gentlemen blanched and ladies blushed as he elaborated on all the horrendous consequences of its misuse. Finally, he leaned over the pulpit to scream at his listeners: "Shall I name you that tiny piece of flesh?" There was paralyzed silence. Ladies extracted smelling salts from their handbags. He leaned out farther, and his voice rose to a hoarse shout. "Shall I show you that tiny piece of flesh?" Horrified silence. Not a whisper or a rustle of a prayer book could be heard. The preacher's voice dropped, and a sly smile slid over his face. "Ladies and gentlemen," he concluded, "behold the source of our sins!" And he stuck out his tongue. That's a major way in which both the elder brother of Jesus' story and we offend.

Paul's words to the Corinthians jump out at us to let us know that we aren't God's slaves or hired help, but His children. Humankind hasn't been the same since Jesus. All people have been invited to be God's children. This means we're not creatures like the pew you're sitting on, or the clothes you're wearing, or your pet dog at home, but a creation — a new creation, the like of which no mere human could have come up with: "brand new," as a child might say. And because our heavenly Father isn't self-righteous but the best possible, we're offered reconciliation with him. And reconciliation is the essence of the Church's ministry.

Those of us who've been profligate children can take consolation not only in the Gospel story, but also in today's reading from the Book of Joshua. This book tells not scientific history in the current sense of the word, but the salvation history of God's people. The Jews on the way to the Promised Land had undergone great battles with opposing tribes, as well as other hardships, which lasted a long time. Moses had led the people out of Egypt; Joshua would lead them into the Promised Land. The Israelites had crossed the Jordan and were about to become engaged in the conquest of Jericho. Because they persevered, they made it.

Today's passage from the Book of Joshua reminds us that, no matter what our difficulties, we can make it, too. The only thing we need is persistence. Nothing in the world can take its place — not talent, nor genius, nor education. No matter what our difficulties, if we're determined enough to come to our heavenly Father during the remainder of this Lent, we can rejoice at the coming of Easter.

What lessons are in this for us? The first words of today's liturgy speak of joy, the First Reading and the Gospel of homecoming, and the Second Reading of newness. These are good themes for where we are right now on this "Rejoice" Sunday at this midpoint of Lent. We who go to church are in danger of considering ourselves to be the "saved" — the elder son in today's Gospel story. We sometimes have the elder son's smugness, coldness, and lack of compassion for those who are weak. The truth is that we're sometimes also like the younger son, profligately spending our inheritance of God's grace as though there will be no tomorrow.

Some have confused God with Santa Claus. Others believe in a pussycat God who forgives anything, even when one has neither the time nor the urge to apologize. Surely, the father of the Gospel story forgave even before the prodigal left home: There were no conditions on his love. But the forgiveness can't activate until the son comes home and asks for it. Sin isn't a debt to a banker but an insult to a friend. But if we have no adult personal relationship with God, a sense of that insult isn't likely. Some people have no sense of violating a friendship; for them God is as easy to hoax as the phone company.

No matter where we see ourselves — as the immature younger son or as the smug elder son or somewhere in between, let's accept our heavenly Father's offer of reconciliation. Our heavenly Father's pronouncement is, "You're mine, and I treasure you not for what you do but because you are." Perhaps we have to accept the hardest penance of all: to accept being loved.

Reconciliation with God — and with one another — is especially needed in our world with its many divisions. On an immediate level, the need can show itself in family rows, neighbors not communicating because of some incident that's long forgotten, words that have caused hurt. And there can be no peace without repentance and reconciliation. Sometimes it's necessary for the one offended to reach out to the offender, whose pride gets in the way of seeking forgiveness.

Overcoming those manifestations and fulfilling the proclamation of joy in the opening word of today's liturgy can be accomplished especially in the Sacrament of Reconciliation. In an address to the Second Vatican Council, Pope Paul VI defined a sacrament as "a reality imbued with the hidden presence of God."

To participate in the Sacrament of Reconciliation is especially fitting for Lent, but its frequent use at all times has many values. Every time we go to the Sacrament of Penance, or Reconciliation, or Confession — whatever we're in the habit of calling it — we acknowledge that we have culpable sins; we affirm that through the mercy of God no sin is unforgivable; we implicitly testify that God's mercy comes through the priest from Jesus, who forgives sins; we attest that the Church is a mother who loves us, even when we can't love ourselves; we implicitly confirm that God wants us to reject a part of our past life, so that the days ahead can be better than those behind; we experience God reaching out to welcome sinners home to renewed relationships with community and with ourselves; and we implicitly reaffirm that we can do things with God's grace that we mightn't succeed in doing on our own.

Thus cleansed, we can spread our reconciliation to our other brothers and sisters. Only in that way can we go down in the Book of Life as people who through Baptism have entered a new life whose story may not be short, but has significance into eternity.

FIFTH SUNDAY OF LENT
Is 43:15-21   Ph 3:8-14   Jn 8:1-11

Last Chances
Evaluating Life in the Light of God's Revelation;
Law and Justice; Come Back to Me; Right Relationship to God

One of the most picturesque names of any street in the United States in Last Chance Gulch. Now the main street of Helena, Montana, the name is a reminder of a time when you didn't criticize your neighbor until you've walked a mile in his moccasins — because, as the humorist said, by that time you're a mile away and he has no shoes. They gave the name "Last Chance Gulch" because, for the prospectors in the 1860's who had panned for gold everywhere else, it represented just about their last chance before looking for other work.

As we approach the end of Lent, we're reminded of our last chance to cooperate with God's special graces of this season. To show that our last chance with God isn't without hope, the Gospel presents an event that took place toward the end of Jesus' life, when he was accustomed to teach in the Temple by day and leave the city to spend the night on the Mount of Olives. It was daybreak (v. 2), the time of the morning sacrifice, when the people would get up early to listen to him in the Temple area (Lk 21:38). When the people started coming, the scribes and Pharisees brought a woman who had been caught in adultery and made her stand in front of everyone (v. 3). (Tantalizingly, John doesn't tell us how the Pharisees caught her: Were they spying?)

Although adultery was so widespread in New Testament times that punishment was hardly ever invoked, the scribes and Pharisees, trying again to entrap Jesus (v. 6), asked him his opinion of the Mosaic Law on the matter (v. 5). The Law said that the punishment was death, but the manner of execution wasn't precisely prescribed (Lv 20:10; Dt 22:22). The rabbis usually determined the method to be strangling rather than stoning. The Mishnah, the Jewish codified law, even laid down the method of strangulation: The executioners were to stand the convicted person in dung up to the knees, put a towel around the person's neck lest there be any marks, and pull in opposite directions until the victim was dead.

The Pharisees' question put Jesus in what we would call today a double bind. If his answer went against the death penalty, he would seem to be disregarding the Mosaic Law and would be open to the accusation of condoning adultery. If he decided for the death penalty, he might be denounced to the Romans, because the Jews didn't have the power to pass or carry out the death penalty on their own. And opting for the death penalty would lose the sympathy of the masses of the people, who knew him to be kind to sinners.

But, as someone has said, "There are no flies on the Lamb of God." Surprisingly, Jesus bent down and began to write on the ground with his finger (v. 6). It's the only occasion in which Jesus is said to have written anything, and there's much speculation about what he wrote. Some say that he was biding time to think and pray about it, others that he was stalling to bring the scribes and Pharisees to their senses, still others that he was writing the names of the Pharisees' secret sins. Seeing the leering eyes and cruel looks on their faces, the prurient interest of the crowd, and the embarrassed humiliation of the woman, Jesus wanted to hide his face from all of them in shame.

Jesus' seeming show of indifference annoyed the scribes and Pharisees, and they persisted in their questioning (v. 7). It never entered their minds that authority like theirs should be based on compassion. It was like those systems of justice that aim to be punitive and to destroy, rather than save, reclaim, or cure. There was nothing of St. Augustine's later "There but for the grace of God go I."

One of Jesus' basic principles is that no human being is to judge another. The quality needed for final, definitive judging isn't knowledge, which many people have, but goodness, which only God has in sufficient degree to make judgments. So Jesus straightened up and charged that the one among them who was without sin be the first to throw a stone at her (v. 7). In Jewish law, that would make witnesses responsible for their judgment. If a witness was later proved to have been lying, the witness was condemned to death.

When there was no action, again he bent down and wrote on the ground (v. 8), with the result that the audience went away one by one, beginning with the elders (v. 9). Perhaps the suspicious older ones, knowing their lives, thought that he was setting a trap for them in their sins. Or perhaps by now they were ashamed of having tried to use the woman's humiliation to entrap Jesus.

Whatever their reasons, this left Jesus alone with the woman standing before him (v. 9). Jesus, after allowing her an interval to reflect, asked her, "has no one condemned you?" (v. 10). To her relieved, sobbing, "No one," Jesus said, "Neither do I." He added what we hear in the Sacrament of Reconciliation: "From now on, avoid your sin" (v. 11). In Jesus' treatment, justice and mercy met.

It's important to understand what Jesus did here. He wasn't a bleeding heart, but a person of informed compassion. The lesson of the story isn't that sin is of no importance, or that God doesn't punish sin, but that God extends mercy to repentant sinners in order that they may turn from their sins. It's the lesson of the beautiful hymn, "Come Back to Me." It's last week's lesson of the Prodigal Son. With this woman, Jesus was interested, as he is with us, not only in what she was, but in what she could become. Unlike the Pharisees, who wanted to condemn, he wanted to forgive. And he wanted to challenge her — to get her to leave her sin and rebuild her life. He believed in the goodness of people, whereby one who has sinned can change. He was giving the woman another chance. Her life wasn't over yet; no life is finished until it stands before God.

And that's what today's Second Reading, from St. Paul's letter to the Philippians, is about: breaking with the past. Paul presents his mature reflections on how much God loves him, written now some twenty years after his conversion on the road to Damascus. The search of his whole life had been for a right relationship with God. In that search, when he was a Pharisee he had tried to achieve blamelessness in God's sight through perfect observance of the 613 prescriptions of the Mosaic Law. So Paul came to say that, despite his being in jail and very much alone when he wrote today's epistle, for him all that was dung. Now he realized that blamelessness comes only from a person's willingness to accept Christ.

Paul accepted the loss of all things that he might gain Christ (v.

8). To that end, he wanted to "know" Christ (v. 10). For him, to "know" didn't mean the aloof intellectual acquisition which we often mean. It meant the most intimate personal experience of another person that anyone could have. The Jewish Scriptures often used it to mean sexual intercourse. For Paul, to know Christ is the guarantee that this life is worth living, the guarantee for us of a life to come, the guarantee that the presence of the risen Lord is always with us. It also meant sharing in Jesus' sufferings. Because Christians who suffer are sharing in the sufferings of Christ, our sufferings aren't a penalty but a privilege. Thus will we achieve the resurrection from the dead (v. 11). We share the sufferings Jesus endured, the cross he carried, the death he died — and the life he now lives.

But neither Paul nor the adulterous woman nor we have yet attained perfect maturity (v. 12). The process of maturing is ongoing (v. 13). In a lively figure from sport, Paul mentions that, forgetting what lies behind but straining forward to what lies ahead, he continues his pursuit toward the goal, the prize of God's upward calling (v. 14). We seem to hear Satchel Paige's famous phrase: "Don't look back; somebody might be gaining on you." And we picture Paul struggling for breath, arms flailing, chest heaving, fists tight, sweat pouring, body bent toward the goal. That's a picture of one who takes a right relationship with God seriously.

Today's reading from Isaiah shows that a right relationship with God isn't only important, but possible, no matter how difficult the situation. Isaiah was promising redemption and restoration during, of all times, the Jews' pitiful Babylonian Captivity. When everything seemed more hopeless than even the captivity in Egypt seven centuries before, Isaiah was speaking of a new Exodus from Babylon, when God will work new wonders.

But Isaiah reminded his people of who God is. He isn't simply a God of fear and punishment, but is a loving and caring God. That God can do anything, even bring it about that powerful Babylon be snuffed out. His great deeds aren't solely wonders of the past (v. 18). God is always acting, always doing something new (v. 19).

God's story with each of us is going on right here and now. As indicated by Isaiah's prophecy and Paul's letter and today's Gospel, we must evaluate all the situations of our lives in the light of God's revelation. The newness of God's story goes on with our Elect who will encounter the dynamic Sacrament of Baptism at the Easter Vigil.

We taste the newness each time we experience the "second baptism" of the Sacrament of Reconciliation. Our passing from sin to salvation is a continuous redemptive act. And each act of God's grace with us may be our Last Chance Gulch.

PASSION (PALM) SUNDAY
Is 50:4-7   Ph 2:6-11 (both A, B, and C)   Lk 22:14-23:56

Being "Human"
What Price Commitment?; Jesus the Martyr;
The Suffering of the Innocent; Fidelity; Quality of Life

The Gospel of St. Luke is a good document from a fine human being on the human dimension of Jesus' Passion. Luke presents many unique human viewpoints of a great artist. At the Paschal Meal, for example, in Luke's Gospel Jesus begins by telling his Apostles how eagerly he desired to eat this Passover with them before he suffered (v. 15) — how wonderfully human! And after Jesus instituted the Eucharist, he asked that all humankind continue to celebrate the Eucharist in memory of him (v. 19) because, sadly, he knew how easily people forget.

Even at that table, however, there were reminders that the Eucharist is no complete guarantee against the possibility of betrayal and violation of trust. There was, for example, the presence of Judas, and the other Apostles' dispute over rank: It was poignantly tragic that the Apostles, at this of all times, hadn't shed their ideas of earthly kingdoms. Jesus reminded them — sad that he had to — that among us it shouldn't be like that. What the world needs, Jesus reminded them, is service: service not like a corporation's obsequious, "May we serve you?", or an automobile "Service Station" — all for pay — but in its true sense of helping others.

Shame overshadowed the scene even more when Jesus had to foretell St. Peter's threefold denials before the crowing of the roosters early the next morning (vv. 31-34). Peter was so overconfident that he

Note: This homily is on Luke. For Matthew 26, see Cycle A; for Philippians, Cycle B.

told Jesus he was prepared to go to prison and die with him (v. 33). Throughout history, persons, cities, and whole nations have been conquered because of complacent overconfidence like that. Peter was well-warned: Jesus had announced that he had prayed (v. 32) that Peter's loving attachment to him might never fail. In turn, Jesus asked that Peter strengthen his brothers — the lovely thought that, because of his experience, Peter would be better able to help others. He would be able to win trust by confiding, "I've been there!"

From the Upper Room, Jesus went as was his custom (v. 39) to the Garden of Gethsemane at the base of the Mount of Olives across the Kidron Valley from Jerusalem. Luke's reflective account says that Jesus went to the garden at this time not simply to escape his enemies, but to think and pray and fight his lonely battle through: No one wants to die at age thirty-three. Jesus' fight was a turning-point: He could still have refused. The salvation of the world hung in the balance. His initial prayer was that the Father take away this fearful duty, but he concluded that he really wanted the Father's will, no matter what (v. 42). So great was his fear, though, that his sweat became like drops of blood (v. 44) as his body prepared for flight or fight. Evil's darkness gathered fast. Judas' knowledge of Jesus' habit of going to Gethsemane and of a time when no crowds would be present made it easy for him to have Jesus quietly arrested.

The primal act of betrayal has always been captivating. Dante reserved the Ninth Circle of Hell, its bottom, for betrayers — Judas, the betrayer of Jesus, and Brutus and Cassius, the betrayers of Julius Caesar. They were frozen in ice, because they were betrayers of friends; through their betrayal they had ceased to have the capacity for love and so for heaven. The betrayer doesn't just commit a single treacherous act and run; his entire being — every smile, every word he exchanges — is an intimate violation of all those around him. With all modern traitors from Benedict Arnold through Kim Philby and Aldrich Ames, all their friendships and relationships become elaborate lies requiring unceasing vigilance to maintain, lies that only they can follow. Even in our jaded age, the crime of treason still has a primitive power to shock, treachery a still-compelling ability to mesmerize.

The Apostles, not fully comprehending what was going on, got excited to the point of one of them cutting off the ear of the high priest's servant (v. 50). Jesus' response was the same frustrated sad sigh as when they hadn't understood him at the table: "Stop! No more of this!" (v.

51), and he healed the wounded man's ear. As those who had come for him (v. 52) circled closer, Jesus observed that the darkness was deepening (v. 53).

The darkness closed in still more with the denials of Peter in the courtyard of the house of the high priest (vv. 54-62). Although Peter had had the courage to follow Jesus there, and certainly ran more risks doing that than the others who scampered for safety, he failed. Only Luke records that then the Lord turned and looked at Peter (v. 61). That look, that special look, the heartbreak in that loved one's eyes, stabbed Peter like a sword. Peter could have stood it more easily if Jesus had gotten angry. It was more than Peter could bear, and this strong man went out and cried intensely (v. 62).

After the guards' mockery of Jesus (vv. 63-65), he was ushered before the elders, chief priests, and scribes who, together with the presiding high priest, constituted the Sanhedrin, the High Court of the land. With an admixture of self-protective cunning, honest religious devotion, and fanaticism, the Sanhedrin's charge against him was blasphemy: Considered an insult to God's majesty, this was so serious as to be punishable by death. Jesus was asking people for simple love; the false charges insured that he wouldn't receive even simple justice.

Because by the law of the Roman army of occupation the Jews didn't have the right to put anyone to death, the entire High Court propelled Jesus to the local Roman official who had that right: Pontius Pilate. Before this outsider, the Sanhedrin's duplicity came to the fore with their deliberate change of charge from blasphemy into three crimes against the State: subversion, opposing the payment of taxes, and setting himself up as a king to rival Caesar (v. 2). When Pilate questioned Jesus about his being king, Jesus — knowing that he was certainly not the kind of king that Pilate had in mind — answered, "You say so" (v. 3). Pilate reported to the Sanhedrin that he found no legal cause of action (v. 4), thus officially declaring the case ended for want of sufficient evidence.

Because the members of the Sanhedrin weren't satisfied with this, Pilate settled for the ruse of sending Jesus to Herod (vv. 8-12). Herod, looking upon Jesus as a spectacle and considering him of no importance, was so immersed in self-centered pleasure that he was one of the few people whom Jesus found impossible to reach and to whom he had absolutely nothing to say (v. 9).

So they took him back to Pilate. The upper classes — mostly the

chief priests and the rulers (v. 13) — were afraid that through Jesus'
influence they might lose their wealth, their comfort, and their power.
So they incited the people, forming them into a mob. Pilate, a hard-
bitten Roman administrator, saw through them. Desperately trying to
give a last chance to the impartial justice that he knew to be the glory
of Rome, he proposed to appease the mob and save himself. This only
resulted in the crowd crying out, "Away with this man!" (v. 18) — the
only time in Luke's entire Gospel that the crowd ever turned from Jesus.

For the third time Pilate made a half-hearted attempt to save Jesus.
He knew that, under Roman law, any administrator of a province could
be reported to Rome for mismanagement; it would be looked into and
dealt with — because one thing the far-flung Roman Empire wouldn't
tolerate was civil disorder. And Pilate had made grave mistakes in his
past. He was vulnerable. All of us are vulnerable, and all of our pasts
can haunt us. The only way to deal with that is forthrightly and courageously. Pilate didn't. In his willingness to sacrifice Jesus to his career, he acquiesced to the leaders. The irony is that his career didn't
last much beyond this.

When the time came, the leaders deliberately put him with criminals (v. 33), to humiliate him further before the people and to have them
associate him with robbers. In the face of those insults, and the people
watching, and the leaders sneering (v. 35), and the soldiers offering
sour wine (v. 36), Jesus had things to say. He didn't say them only once:
Of his enemies, he repeated over and over again, "Father, forgive them."
In his last words to anyone on earth, Jesus kept assuring the penitent
thief that that very day they would be together in paradise (v. 43).

As Jesus' death approached, darkness came over the whole land
(v. 44): The powers of darkness were now approaching their greatest
moment of triumph. In a loud voice (v. 46) that was a shout of triumph,
Jesus' very last words were those which every Jewish mother taught
her young children to say to God as their night prayer. They were the
words of the Psalmist to God (31:5): "Into your hands I commend my
spirit." Jesus made them a more lovely prayer by adding the word "Father." He had been what God intended people to be. The crowd, seeing it, was softened (v. 48), and the women, even more touched, stood
at a distance (v. 49): powerless but for the power of prayer.

Into that scene came a final good human being: the tragic Joseph
of Arimathea, of whom each Gospel paints a brief portrait. St. Mark
identifies him as distinguished and bold. St. John tells us he was a se-

cret disciple, out of prudent fear that the Sanhedrin, of which body Joseph was a member, could turn on him for being a follower of Jesus. St. Matthew tells us that Christ's grave, carved out of the hillside near Golgotha, had been bought by Joseph for his own burial. St. Luke calls him an upright and holy man.

Though Joseph disagreed with the Sanhedrin's judgment, there's no record that he ever spoke up in court. How it would have helped the lonely Jesus if in that hate-filled assembly even one voice had been raised in his behalf! But, in the face of the usual custom to leave the body on its cross a few feet off the ground for wild dogs and vultures, at least he gave Jesus a grave. We often don't speak up until it's too late: We mention in eulogies the words of tenderness that we should have said to our dead loved ones while they were still living.

May our reflections on Jesus' suffering, death, and resurrection this week remind us that, unlike other dramas, we're not mere spectators, but participants. We're invited to ask ourselves, "Am I Pilate? Judas? Peter?" Above all, "Am I Jesus?" Do I follow him in suffering — in my attitude toward the disappointments, pains, and anguishes of my life? Do I reflect the victory over suffering and death that he showed in his total composure throughout his passion? Though suffering may have no value in itself, what does have value is the attitude toward suffering which the sufferer has — or, more precisely, the attitude toward God which the sufferer achieves in suffering. May our thoughts this day make us all-around better human beings!

EASTER SUNDAY

Ac 10:34, 37-43   Col 3:1-4 (or 1 Cor 5:6-8)   Jn 20:1-9 (All A, B, & C)

We're Winners!
Making our Baptismal Promises Meaningful;
The Power of Easter Experiences; The Risen Christ Today

No matter how we explain it, in the beginning, the earth was a formless wasteland, and darkness covered the abyss, while a mighty wind

---

Note: Today's homily is mostly on Acts. For John, see Cycle A; for Colossians, Cycle C.

swept over the waters (Gn 1:1f.). Then God created light, and the sky, the earth, vegetation, the stars, the fish, the birds, all kinds of animals, and — as the final good gift, the most noble creatures of all — people. And God looked at everything he had made, and he found it very good (Gn 1:31). The story of the human race from then on is less glorious: the fall of Adam and Eve, their son Cain murdering his brother Abel, the sometimes perverse "People of God," and the wars, pollution, destruction, murder, rape, robbery, and other evil that people have brought about ever since.

The story stimulates questions. Is it really good for the human race to have been created? Have we served any purpose? Would the universe have been just as well off had we never been? If our highest purpose is to give greater honor and glory to God, have we done so? One thing is sure: The human race made necessary a new beginning comparable to the sparkling newness of the days of creation.

That new day came with the first Easter Sunday. The resurrection of Jesus was the most momentous occasion since the week of creation. Jokes are funny because the punch lines are so unexpected and delightful; our Lord's resurrection is the punch line of the history of salvation.

New hope came with the proclamation of the Good News of Jesus the risen Lord by the Apostles, like the preaching of St. Peter in today's First Reading. On Good Friday the Church showed us a Peter who had denied even knowing Jesus, and who was reduced to tears at the realization of his failure. Here on Easter Sunday we see a different Peter; there are few more openly sincere confessions of faith than his today in all Scripture.

He typifies a boundary-breaking love for and faith in the risen Lord. Indeed, faith and love are in the history of the Church intimately connected. Faith involves an alignment of the heart, a commitment of loyalty and trust. The words for faith in the languages of the Bible don't mean only "belief" in the modern sense; to say "I believe" meant "I commit myself to, I rest my heart upon, I pledge allegiance to." The Latin *credo*, "I believe," is from *cor*, "heart," as in the English "cordial." So belief is an action word. For biblical writers and for us, the opposite of faith is not doubt, but nothingness — nothing to give our heart to, nothing to live for, nothing to judge ourselves by.

In his Gospel, St. Luke had written of Jesus' mission as traveling to Jerusalem, where his most important lessons lay. Throughout his ministry, Jesus resolutely determined to journey to Jerusalem (Lk 9:51) to work, to suffer, to die, and to rise. In the Acts of the Apostles, which Luke also wrote, he shows the Gospel message moving in accord with Christ's command from Jerusalem, on a journey that will take it to the ends of the earth (Ac 1:8).

So the book called the Acts of the Apostles represents a second journey of Jesus, working through Apostles who carry his Gospel message. The Book of Acts describes the risen life of Christ in his body, the Church. It's therefore fitting that, throughout the Easter season, the liturgy's First Reading comes from Acts. The speeches in Acts, accurately reflecting the preaching of Peter and the other Apostles, provide the basic outline of the four Gospels: the essential facts about the ministry of Jesus, the death of Jesus, his resurrection, and the witness that Jesus is truly Lord. We, living centuries later, become Christians in exactly the same way as people did then: by hearing the testimony of others. The message — called the kerygma, or proclamation of God's salvation — calls for our personal response.

Peter's speech today is, like the others, a little "creed" like the one we say at Mass and suitable to the Easter renewal of our baptismal promises that we make today after this homily. Peter says that God's revelation of His plan for the destiny of humankind through Israel culminated in Jesus of Nazareth. The ministry of Jesus is an integral part of God's revelation (v. 37). The coming of the Holy Spirit upon Jesus at his baptism showed him to be the Spirit-filled agent of God's saving will for humankind. He was a unique helper of people, doing good works and healing (v. 38).

The Apostles were witnesses (v. 39), giving testimony not only about Jesus' resurrection, but also about his ministry. They were empowered to make clear the exact meaning and interpretation of his sayings and deeds to the developing Christian community, which is the bearer of the word of salvation, in the light of his death and resurrection. Despite Jesus' goodness, the leaders performed an act of sheer horror by having him crucified — only to have God raise him up on the third day (v. 40) and to have him seen by enough witnesses to make this otherwise unbelievable event believable (v. 41).

Jesus had commissioned the Apostles to preach (v. 42) — a commission not only to the Twelve, but to every Christian. To fulfill our obligation means many things: not only words, but deeds and example. It means knowing not only the doctrines of our faith, but also the particular needs and temperaments of those we meet so as to make Jesus' message attractive to them. Peter's speeches, for example, changed to fit his audience. Today, speaking to non-Jews, he emphasized the coming divine judgment; when he spoke to Jews, he appealed to their hope of a Messiah. In both cases, the biggest result was the offer of the forgiveness of sins through Jesus' name (v. 43) — a removal of guilt that enables a new relationship with God and other people.

Because of the resurrection of Jesus, his followers have contributed to many ideas of our civilization: the principle of personal moral responsibility, for example, and the rule of tolerance, the rationale for the brotherhood of all members of the human race, the basis for the exaltation of womankind, the standard of mercy, the principle of enthusiasm, the element of optimism, and new concepts of peace. In our lives we can continue to contribute such other areas as defined by the life and example of Jesus: the guarantees of justice, esteem for human life, regard for law, the expressions of democratic ideals, reverence for the rights of minorities.

The very beginning of the First Testament says humanity failed because we tried to be like God. At the close of the New Testament humanity is promised that we can be like God. What does Jesus promise that the tempter promised but didn't deliver? In a phrase, a new life. We strive for this, or we have nothing for which to strive. Without the challenge and the promise of Jesus the rational choice is that set forth by Paul (1 Cor 15:32, quoting Is 22:13): "Let us eat and drink, for tomorrow we die."

Our Christian life should be joyful. It may be perhaps compared to the egg. The Easter egg is a symbol of the resurrection, insofar as from the egg a new life may spring. This feast of Easter, more than any other of the year, is a day filled with a new life of enthusiasm, praise, and rejoicing. Some people feel that they have little experience of the risen Christ. Perhaps the problem may be more one of recognition. Today we should pause to recognize that "heaven" is not a special place apart from our universe. "Heaven" is the universe, recognized as being in God. Let's resolve to lead a "heavenly" life on earth, witnessing God's power and love. May these joyous reflections help to give us a happy Easter!

SECOND SUNDAY OF EASTER
Ac 5:12-16   Rv 1:9-13, 17-19   Jn 20:19-31

The Meaning, Wonder, and Results of Faith
How Much Can We Learn from Experience?; Making Real the
Power of the Resurrection; The Presence of the Risen Jesus

Some teachers of creative art say that what an artist needs is experience, despite the fact that the class colors of the school of experience are black and blue. Artists are to live it up, see all of the world they can, and do everything to awaken dormant emotions. All experiences, including participation in evil, are valid and good — with the sole exception of death, which people who hold these positions greatly fear, because death is the one personal experience that no one can have twice.

Contrary to many other teachers of acting, Stella Adler didn't advise the accumulation of experiences to fall back upon — such as recalling the death of your mother when you wanted to look sad. "Don't use your conscious past," she advised her student-actors. "Use your imagination to create a past that belongs to your character. I don't want you to be stuck with your own life. It's too little."

St. Thomas in today's Gospel showed his high regard for experience when he refused to believe in the risen Jesus without probing his nail-marks and putting his hand into his side (v. 25). We may "see" mirages which don't exist; we might "hear" sounds which aren't there; likewise, all of our other senses can deceive. But when we touch something, we know it's there. That's why some call touch the sense of certitude.

Jesus accommodated himself to Thomas's makeup. The result was the most profound profession of faith in the New Testament: Thomas's, "My Lord and my God." More than an exclamation, these words are a prayer acknowledging Jesus' divinity.

The experience of the risen Jesus by the Apostles, especially doubting ones like Thomas, is the basis for the whole of Christianity. But there are dangers in too high a regard for experience. Jesus reminded Thomas of that in his beatitude, "Blessed are those who have

---

Note: This homily mostly on the Book of Revelation. For homilies on other readings, see
Cycles A and B.

not seen and have believed" (v. 29). If we believe that the verification principle of all of life is only what we can experience, the vast majority of us can't believe in God or anything supernatural.

St. John in his Book of Revelation, from which we have today's Second Reading, received images from experience and then built upon them in this, his dream. Another title of this book, Apocalypse, means an unveiling, a glimpse at hidden things, things yet to come. Apocalypses, a special type of Jewish literature, are more common in the Old Testament. They're not easy to understand. They often use the images of dreams. They were usually written to give encouragement to groups who were suffering persecution; such victims would easily have decoded the underlying message of comfort. The ultimate consolation is that Jesus will absolutely and irrevocably conquer, and we shall share in his victory if we're faithful to him. This apocalypse of John was just such a message to the young Christian churches, which at that time were beginning to feel the brunt of persecution.

The book's author, John — who may or may not be the same person who wrote St. John's Gospel — wrote this work from exile on Patmos, a small rocky island off the coast of modern Turkey. Rome had sent John there to the loneliness and pain of banishment because he was bearing witness to Jesus. John wrote essentially to console those who were suffering for their faith by reminding them that Jesus would absolutely and decisively conquer.

The hills of Patmos provide beautiful views of the glistening blue sea, and John's book is full of the broad vistas of the far-stretching water: The word sea occurs in this book no less than twenty-five times. John used other symbolism — in colors, numbers, images, and language — from his intimate knowledge of the Jewish Scriptures as well as from his own experience. Parts of it we understand, others not. It's the most difficult book of the New Testament.

John introduces himself as a brother who shares with all reborn Christians distress and endurance (v. 9). He shares our distress because people won't listen to someone who speaks of hardship from the comfort of an easy chair. He mentions endurance because he knows that the person who sits with bowed head in passive submission to whatever comes isn't real.

For nineteen centuries John's vision of the end of the world has shaken the imagination of Western humankind. John's nightmare imagery has infused our art from the medieval representations of the Last

Judgment, through the desolate horrors of Hieronymus Bosch, the poetry of William Blake, and the fiction of Herman Melville, to today's doomsday evangelists and apocalyptic movies.

John tells us he was caught up in ecstasy (v. 10) — beyond space and time. He heard God's voice, which sounded like a trumpet. Though that comparison, like every other comparison of this world to the heavenly world, is inadequate, both the Old and New Testaments often compare the voice of God to the commanding clarity of the trumpet. Examples are many. The account of God's giving the Law on Mt. Sinai says that amid peals of thunder and lightning there was a very loud trumpet blast, so that all the people in the camp trembled (Ex 19:16). When Jesus spoke of his hard-to-imagine Second Coming, he said that God would send out His angels with a trumpet blast to gather His elect from one end of the heavens to the other (Mt 24:31). And St. Paul said that at Jesus' Second Coming the Lord himself with the trumpet of God will come down from heaven (1 Th 4:16).

John goes on (vv. 12-16) to give a symbolic description of Christ in glory. He's "One like a Son of Man" — an enigmatic First Testament (Dn 7:13) title of Christ. Jewish apocalyptic literature used the title to describe a unique religious personage endowed with extraordinary spiritual power. Jesus used it frequently of himself: It was well adapted to his purpose to both veil and reveal his person and mission. On the one hand, it emphasized the lowliness of the human condition, especially in Jesus' humiliation and death; on the other hand, it expressed the triumph of Jesus' resurrection which we celebrate through this Easter season, his return to glory, and his Second Coming as judge of the world.

What John — and the Church in this Easter season — sees most is Jesus' glory. The combination of awe and fear caused in John the usual reaction of people before God or before a messenger of God: He fell down at his feet (v. 17). When there was such a great catch of fish that Peter the fisherman finally got a glimpse of who Jesus was, he had fallen at Jesus' knees. The disciples had heard Jesus' calm reassurance against fear on more than one experience-defying and imagination-challenging occasion: when he had come to them across the water, for example, and on the Mount of Transfiguration.

Then John heard Jesus give nothing less than God's description of Himself: "I am the First and the Last, the One who lives" (vv. 17f.; see Is 44:6; 48:12). These awesome titles synthesize the three stages in Jesus' career: his pre-existence, his life and death on earth, and his exaltation to eternal life. Jesus went on to give John the sublime revelation: "Once I was dead but now I am alive forever and ever" (v. 18). This is the core of the Christian creed. It's the claim of one who has risen from the dead, is alive forever, and has conquered death so that he's death's master. Because Jesus lives, we too shall live.

Faith in these truths of Jesus' resurrection bears many fruits, one of which is our common life as described in today's First Reading. It's the third summary portrait in the Acts of the Apostles, admittedly idealistic, of the Jerusalem community, creating an atmosphere of peace and fulfillment, but also of fear. God gave the early Christians the signs and wonders they needed as saving actions to spread the Good News. Among them were the Twelve's charismatic power to heal, such that the people carried their sick out into the streets so that when Peter came by at least his shadow might fall on one or another of them (v. 15), and crowds from the towns in the vicinity of Jerusalem also brought their sick, and they were all cured (v. 16). Now that Jesus has returned to the Father after curing a few people, the disciples seem to be doing even greater things than he!

But all of this provided also a note of fear: fear in those who didn't dare join the early Christian community in Jerusalem, fear in those within the community who were undergoing persecution for Jesus' sake, fear in the very first disciples huddled behind locked doors. Such fear can be, and is, overcome in the Spirit of Christ.

Fear remains a very real issue in our world: fear of illness, of poverty, of loss of relationships, of humiliation, of loss of employment, of death. If we truly believe in Jesus' Good News, though, fear is expelled. The essence of the Good News, as we recall in the Easter Season, is that Jesus has conquered death. This victory over humankind's last enemy is a conquest for everyone. What is there to fear from any of the others?

We're among those to whom Jesus says "Blessed are those who have not seen and have believed." We go beyond experience to be no less moved by this Easter season than were John the Theologian and Thomas. The encounter, far from being tame, confronts us to the core of our being. We pray for a deeper awareness of the blessings of Christ's resurrection and of our consequent new birth in God's Spirit.

THIRD SUNDAY OF EASTER
Ac 5:27-32, 40f.   Rv 5:11-14   Jn 21:1-19 (or 1-14)

Joyful Growth through Suffering
The Reality of the Resurrection; Peter the Head of the Church;
The Universality of the Church

The time after Jesus' resurrection consisted of days of anguish as well as joy, during which the Apostles had to resume their ordinary work. Life had to go on! They had families to feed and support! So, for many of them, it was back to fishing on the Lake of Galilee.

It was there that today's Gospel story of seven disciples, led by St. Peter, took place. The scene began at night, considered the best time for fishing. The boat would glide smoothly over the lake, torch blazing; the men would stare into the water until they saw a school of fish, and then, quick as lightning, skillfully throw their net or spear. Often, though, the tired fishermen would return to the dock in the morning with nothing to show for their work.

In today's story, something in the *modus operandi* of the man standing on the shore caused St. John to recognize the risen Lord. That wasn't as easy as it may sound: Jesus' body was the resurrected one, not the resuscitated one. His appearance was different from when they'd known him before; for example, he mightn't have cast a shadow. When John pointed out Jesus' identity, Peter, wanting to show Jesus his eagerness, became impatient with the slow-moving boat. He couldn't wait to tie his loose shirt so it wouldn't float when he jumped into the water. For a Jew of that time, to offer a greeting was, after all, a religious act, and for it a man must be properly clothed. Though the other disciples came quickly in the boat, it was Peter who assumed the lead. He was beginning to grow into becoming a "rock."

On shore, the fire, the fish, and the bread were another surprise. Because of the heavenly glory that was now Christ's, his presence gave a solemnity to the scene. Nevertheless, the Apostles took the time to abide by their routine of counting their fish, the usual purpose of which was to divide the catch equitably. Many Scripture scholars have used the number of fish and the unbroken net to symbolize that the Church can hold a great number of people of all kinds without the loss of her unity.

To show the universality of the Church was, in fact, one of John's purposes in writing this chapter of his Gospel. The other was to show — again — the reality of Jesus' resurrection: to insist that the Risen Christ wasn't an hallucination or a spirit, but a real person. An hallucination or a spirit wasn't likely to kindle a fire on a seashore or to cook a meal and share in eating it. The words John used for the meal — Jesus took the bread and gave it to them — allude to the Eucharist.

After the meal, the scene changed to Jesus' dialogue with Peter. He began by asking Peter three times whether Peter loved him. Not only is that a central question of every Christian's life; Jesus' followers are to be led by love and Jesus' presence is recognizable only by love. Peter was full of sadness and confusion: Was Jesus alluding to his past sin of denying him three times and asking, "Do you love me now, at last?" Or was Jesus asking, "Do you love me more than you love the nets, the boat, and a catch of fish?" Or was he asking, "Do you love me more than your fellow disciples do?"

Perhaps we recognize something of ourselves in the story of the Apostle Peter. In many ways, he's just like us. He was so simple, and yet so complex! When life got perplexing and too much for him, his strategy was direct, with his simple announcement, "I'm going fishing."

He was aware that he had often left much to be desired. When, for example, Jesus had given him permission to walk on water, and then Peter saw the first difficulty coming his way in the form of a wave, his faith began to leave and he began to sink. And there were other incidents: when he'd stupidly chided Jesus at the Lord's prediction of his passion, when he'd selfishly wanted to stay forever at Jesus' transfiguration, when he'd childishly wanted to know how many times to forgive injuries, when at the Last Supper he didn't want Jesus to wash his feet, when in the Garden of Gethsemane he'd slept and then impulsively cut off the ear of the high priest's servant, when he'd denied Jesus in his need during his last suffering. But Peter had a glorious side, too, which was the reason for his ability to grow in fidelity and loyalty. Peter's potential was the reason for Jesus' making him the leader of the Church.

Even today, though, Peter seemed insensitive. When he met Jesus — met him after having denied him — he acted as if nothing significant had happened. As if nothing required comment or apology, he quickly ate his breakfast. But next to this charcoal fire on which fish had been cooked, perhaps he was thinking of that other fire — that charcoal fire at which he warmed himself during Jesus' trial, warmed himself while he denied Jesus.

But Peter would no longer dare to say anything that would put him above the rest: no bold claims, no rash promises. He couldn't even answer with the same word for "love" that Jesus used. Jesus' word — *agapas* in the Greek of John's Gospel — involved sacrifice, and Peter remembered that, after his previous grandiose promise to lay down his life for Jesus, he had denied Jesus three times. So, unsure of whether he was capable of that highest kind of love, he answered by affirming, again in the Gospel's original Greek, *philo*, a love of feeling, of sentiment, of affection, and of attachment. Of those he was sure.

Upon Peter's reply, the consequences of true love followed: responsibility and sacrifice. Jesus indicated Peter's responsibility by directing him to "feed my lambs" and "feed my sheep." He was making Peter his great shepherd. Then there was sacrifice. In Peter's case, Jesus predicted that Peter's love would involve the greatest sacrifice of all: his life. Then Jesus said to Peter, "Follow me." Jesus' work was finished. And Peter could truly "follow" the Lord fully. Peter wasn't capable, like John, of lofty writings that soared like an eagle or, like Paul able to travel to the ends of the known world for Christ — but his determination to follow the Lord and to lead the Apostles enabled him to be the first head of the Church.

And Peter went on from greatness to greatness. His growth, like most of ours, wasn't a perceptible, continuous, eternal march upward, but a saw-toothed progress. Today's First Reading records one of his five sermons in the Acts of the Apostles. In it, Peter for the first time used the word "savior" (v. 31), that precious word referring to Jesus as the liberator of Israel and the forgiver of people's sins. To the Sanhedrin, the powerful leaders of the Jews before whom Peter spoke, this made Peter a heretic. To them, Peter and the Apostles were also a threat, because they were potential disturbers of the peace. If there were an uprising, Rome would come in to reestablish order and in the process would eliminate the Sanhedrin's prestige. The proud members of the Sanhedrin weren't about to let that happen.

The response of Peter and the Apostles showed them for what they were: men of courage, no longer aiming at "playing it safe"; men of principle, putting obedience to God's word before everything else; and men with a clear idea of their duty, which was to witness for Christ. Peter's response must always be ours: Better for us to obey God rather than people! The Sanhedrin, after giving some words of warning, dismissed the Apostles. For their part, the Apostles left the Sanhedrin "full of joy." Joy is the one unfailing sign of the Spirit's presence, and the greatest sentiment of this Easter season. Here the Apostles were full of joy because they had an opportunity to share in Christ's suffering.

This kind of love and joy provide the vision of heaven recounted in today's passage from St. John's Book of Revelation. John's heavenly vision contrasts with the anxiety of the court scene of Peter and the Apostles. John frequently took his language in this book from the Jewish Scriptures. In today's section, the hymn is to "the Lamb that was slain," that most powerful central image in the vision of John. The symbol recalled the bloody sacrifice of the Hebrews all right, but more compellingly Jesus in his death. The animal known for its meekness is now the conqueror. In John's hymns to the Lord's glory, the universal chorus of praise swells to a symphony. It reaches throughout the breadth of creation; it can't go any farther. And it goes to the very height of John's concept of Jesus: that Jesus now sits by the side of God.

For us, as for Peter, recognition of Jesus often comes slowly, sometimes in and through contact with others. We have all, like Peter and the other Apostles, responded in love. That often involves self-sacrifice, and perhaps suffering. Our modern opponents have discovered that killing people makes memorable martyrs of them, so the tactic of our day is condescending ridicule — the deception that the Church looks silly, unrealistic, decadent, and completely unworthy of the belief of a reasonable person.

We should accept that suffering — not in despair and self-pity, but "full of joy." One job of reverses like suffering is to make sure we don't get too comfortable and fall asleep and miss our life. Jesus' resurrection shows that through suffering and death one can achieve triumph. A little girl, upon finding a butterfly cocoon, brought it home. She waited with eager expectation until the day for the butterfly to come out finally arrived. A tiny head appeared, munching its way through the gray, paper-thin wall. She viewed the little creature with love, but wasn't prepared for how long it would take and how difficult a time the butterfly would have. With a small stick, ever so carefully, she decided to help the butterfly. Within moments instead of hours the butterfly was free. Then it tried to fly, but when it stretched its wings, it fell and died. "What happened?" the little girl pleaded, teary-eyed, to her father. "I even helped." "The butterfly needed that struggle," her father answered. "Without that, it was never able to strengthen its wings enough to fly."

This basic principle of the Christian life is conveyed by the Apostles' joy at suffering for Jesus' sake (today's First Reading), by John the Evangelist's comment on Jesus' words to Peter about his death (Gospel) and by the vision of the victorious Lamb that was slain (Second Reading). As in all these images, we're to be sensitive to coming to recognize his presence in family, friendships, community, and work.

FOURTH SUNDAY OF EASTER ("GOOD SHEPHERD SUNDAY")
Ac 13:14, 43-52   Rv 7:9, 14-17   Jn 10:27-30

Sheep of Christ's Flock
Our Communion with the Lord; Sheep and Shepherd;
Adapting to Change; Universal Appeal of the Good News

There was once a bird, heavier and larger than the turkey, that never adapted to change. In the course of time it became flightless. Flightless, it became silly-looking and defenseless, and then extinct. It was called the dodo bird. People who came to look silly because they were hopelessly behind the times also came to be called dodos. It's a fact of life that we have to adapt to change or become extinct.

Jesus' discourse today, from the last of his lengthy talks to the people of Jerusalem in St. John's Gospel, took place on Solomon's Porch of the Temple. This was a roofed-over walkway through columns of magnificent pillars forty feet high — something like the portico of a high court today or a university entrance. Solomon's Porch was a place where people were accustomed to go to meditate and pray and where rabbis strolled while instructing their students. The Pharisees were again asking, some in good faith, their usual questions about Jesus being the Messiah. His answers centered around himself as the Good Shepherd, an image the First Testament used for good kings.

The image of shepherd and sheep, a joy to both the Old and New Testaments but in our day seemingly meaningful only to a few rustics,

isn't an antiquated image that demands change, even in our time of
zooming airplanes, buzzing industry, efficient computers, and beckoning television screens. In the early Church, no symbol, including the
cross, was more prominent than the Good Shepherd and his sheep.
There's no better image to illustrate the intimate nature of the relationship between Jesus and us.

Whereas the image of sheep as applied to Jesus, especially as a
lamb, signifies gentleness, young innocence, meekness, and purity,
applied to us it signifies dependence — that we're weak and in need of
help. It may not occur to some of our contemporaries who have no more
contact with sheep than to eat a roast of lamb that sheep are among the
dumbest of animals. A sheepherder once said: "Sheep are born looking for a way to die." They go into gullies, become entangled in
brambles, fall into ditches, and wander into predators' territory.

No domesticated animal is as defenseless. Your pet dog likely
as not has enough intelligence to find his way home, has some acute
senses like smell and hearing to find food, and can defend himself
against other animals or make a judgment to run away from one bigger than himself. Your domesticated cat retains many of the qualities
of the wild, often owns you instead of vice versa, and is a loner with
enough cunning to take care of most situations. It's been said that with
a dog, you feed him, you give him plenty of affection, you take him
for walks, and he thinks, "Wow, this fellow must be a god." With a
cat, however, you feed him, you love him, you care for him, and he
thinks, "Wow, I must be a god!"

It's neither of those ways with sheep! For us to admit that we're
sheep is to put our trust completely in the Good Shepherd. The relationship between this kind of shepherd and his sheep is a power of
connectedness, of empathy. We need connectedness with Jesus the
Good Shepherd more than we know. If a baby is fed and warmed and
cleaned but never held, smiled at, and talked to — all of which call the
baby into life — it won't develop normally.

The relationship between the Good Shepherd and his sheep is so
intimate that it's an extension of the relationship between the heavenly
Father and the Son. Whereas Jesus speaks of his sheep, forming his
flock, being in his hand, he's also quick to put forth his heavenly
Father's auspices (v. 29). The Father's omnipotence is the guarantee
of Jesus' promises. In fact, Jesus makes one of his "hard sayings" —
that the Father and he are one (v. 30). Not "at one," but "one." He and
the Father are one in mind, will, action, and heart.

That relationship between the Father and the Son is so close that the Good Shepherd can make promises to his flock that can be fulfilled only by the Father (v. 28). He promises eternal life, a foretaste of God's own life instead of the pettiness that many people know in this present life. He promises that his sheep shall never perish — physical death won't be the end but the beginning. And he promises that no one can take us out of his hand — our life, despite the same sorrows and sufferings that others have, will be secure under his protection.

Today's portion of the Book of Revelation amplifies the picture. Its author sees God's huge flock as being from every nation, race, people, and tongue — from the press of people in the market places, in the narrow city streets, and on the quays of the seaport towns then and now. Revolutionary! For the Jews, to think of this crowd being saved needed a change of mental gears.

Christ's Good News must never be identified with any one culture, and no element of culture which isn't opposed to the Good News need be jettisoned for its sake. In some places, the image must change. In the South Pacific, for example, where the people wouldn't understand sheep or lamb, a similar message can best be conveyed (*mutatis mutandis*) only by the image of the piglet. Although Jesus was a particular human being, living at a particular time, in a particular place, and with a particular culture, the Good News about which he spoke isn't tied to any of those things.

The author of the Book of Revelation saw the Christian flock, though perhaps a bit battered and worn, victorious over the great distress (v. 14) of the fierce Roman persecutions of the early Church. In the early Church, the many who were slaves, and other workers as well, knew what it meant to be hungry all the time, thirsty a good part of the time, and have the sun mercilessly beat down on them as they worked without end in the open fields. They could easily imagine heaven as a place where they simply had enough to eat and drink and where the heat of the sun no longer tortured them.

All who suffer for Christ and persevere will share in his glory. In a few years of our time more lay Christians have died for their faith than in 250 years of on-again off-again Roman persecutions following the death of Jesus. As we said last week, though, the frequent mode of persecution of the Church nowadays is by ridicule and condescension. On TV talk shows, the unfaithful or the disgruntled get lots of time; when a carefully correct view is invited (in the name of "fairness"), it's often given by a stuffy person who uses the media badly, and sitcom priests and nuns are frequently silly.

All in all, the Shepherd promises his flock all that a person could yearn for: comfort and relief for the aches of the heart and of the soul as well as of the body. He will wipe every tear from the eyes (v. 17) of all the faithful of the flock. Whatever one most needs at any given moment, God can give.

But, as today's reading from the Acts of the Apostles shows, it's sometimes difficult for the flock to be mindful. To get to Antioch in Pisidia, which is slightly south of center in modern Turkey and almost 4,000 feet above sea-level, Sts. Paul and Barnabas had to go by one of the roughest roads in Asia Minor: Not only was it mountainous, but it was infested by brigands. The town was very mixed in population and therefore highly flammable. One thing that would easily inflame the considerable number of Jews who lived there was the expression of any idea that anybody but they were eligible for God's promises.

Despite that narrowness, Paul's sermon — his first sermon, an inaugural address, a turning point in the Church's work of evangelization — stressed important doctrines about the Good Shepherd: that Jesus' coming was the culmination of history; people didn't recognize that fact; although Jesus was crucified, he rose from the dead; his resurrection was the fulfillment of prophecy; for people who were trying to change, Jesus' message was good news; for those who wouldn't change, Jesus' message was bad news.

The reaction of the people at large to Paul's synagogue discourse was enthusiastic. The following Sabbath, a good portion of the city gathered to hear the word of the Lord from him (v. 44). But the common people's widespread enthusiasm contrasted with the jealousy of the leaders (v. 45). Nevertheless, Paul and Barnabas spoke fearlessly. Paul said that though priority of salvation was a privilege of the Jews, this didn't mean it was exclusively theirs (v. 46).

So Paul and Barnabas now went to the Gentiles — luckily for us today! In retaliation, some of the Jews stirred up a persecution against them (v. 50). The way they did it was to approach faithful women, for whom at that time the Jewish religion had a special attraction, because outside Judaism sexual morality was lax and family life breaking down. The Jewish religion preached a high level of morality. The Jewish leaders persuaded these women to have their husbands, some of whom were in influential positions, take steps against the Christian preachers. The leaders thus succeeded in having Paul and Barnabas expelled from their territory. But even as the two Apostles defiantly shook the dust of the town from their feet as they departed (v. 51), they left disciples who were filled with joy and the Holy Spirit (v. 52). With a zeal for spreading the name of Jesus that should be a model for all of us, they traveled southeast to Iconium.

Whether or not we phrase it in terms of Jesus being our shepherd and we the sheep of his flock, we're God's people and Jesus is our Lord. That's part of the essence of the ever-old and ever-new Easter message: that God offers us eternal life, the life of the risen Jesus, the life of God Himself. That's Good News — News because it's something which never happened before, and Good because it concerns what all human beings hold most dear: eternal life.

The eternal life he offers isn't simply ordinary human life without end, but the fullness of human existence. To find that fullness, we ought every day to adapt the Good Shepherd's message to the ever-changing circumstances of our lives. Today's liturgy calls us, for one thing, to renew our spirit of unity as a parish community and to revitalize our outreach to others so that we can all be one flock under the one Good Shepherd. We don't, after all, want to become spiritually as foolish or extinct as the dodo bird.

FIFTH SUNDAY OF EASTER
Ac 14:21-27   Rv 21:1-5   Jn 13:31-33a, 34f.

Extending the Hour of Glory
A New World; The Book of Glory; The Risen Christ
Present in His Church; Encouragement in Adversity

The utopian myth of humankind making infinite progress through technology has long been challenged by the specter of human ingenuity run amok: Frankenstein's monster taking revenge on his creator; Hal the computer threatening to assume control of the spaceship in the film *2001*; the machines in another film, *Modern Times*, trying to get the best of Charlie Chaplin.

There are myriad "revenge effects" resulting from our mechanical, chemical, medical, and biological meddling in the physical world. Why, for example, are the lines at cash machines longer in the evening than those at tellers' windows used to be during banking hours? Low-tar, low-nicotine cigarettes have encouraged some people to continue smoking. Widespread use of antibiotics has led to the development of drug-resistant strains of bacteria.

The growing use of computers has not increased productivity as expected; instead it has replaced one category of worker with a new category while requiring workers across the board to learn new procedures and skills. It has also led to the revenge of the body: the proliferation of back problems and carpal tunnel syndrome, caused by hours spent at a desk. New forms of transportation like trains, planes, and automobiles have enabled destructive pests to migrate to a host of new regions where they can wreak all sorts of havoc. Shipping has brought rats to more than 80 percent of the world's islands.

Whereas such developments were inadvertent, in other cases would-be scientists and entrepreneurs have deliberately introduced predatory creatures into new niches under the mistaken belief that they are improving or prettifying the environment. An amateur brought the house sparrow to North America in 1860 in the hope, apparently, that the birds would help exterminate the caterpillars near his New York home. The destructive gypsy moth was introduced to the United States by a naturalist who may have been interested in cross-breeding the creature to produce silk. Killer bees were brought here by bee dealers intent on improving their stock with imported African strains.

There are real improvements, of course. Smallpox has been eradicated, building standards and sewage systems have been improved, and seat belts and air bags have been installed in cars. But constant vigilance is required.

It's said that recent revolutionary advances in science and technology will power a new generation of cities: in enclosures, in new-generation transportation, for climate control, in communications between people, for waste-management. An equally popular theme today is the fascinating and challenging adventure of building cities in space. Writers see space cities relieving the population problem on earth, facilitating the production of chemicals that cannot as easily be made on this planet, and making possible new discoveries.

Dreams of new and adventurous beginnings are nothing new. When the Book of Revelation spoke of "a new heaven and a new earth"

(v. 1), it was revealing a dream deep in Jewish thought since long before Christ. Throughout, this book emphasizes the newness of things; that's why we read it during Eastertime, when we celebrate new life. The biblical idea of redemption always includes the earth. The earth isn't merely an indifferent theater in which a person carries out his or her daily tasks; it's the expression of the glory of God and is the divinely ordained scene of human existence. There's an inseparable unity between the human person and nature. The creation of one means the creation of the other. God's final intervention is seen as a new creation of the sin-cursed creation of old: "Behold, I create a new heaven and a new earth" (Is 65:17; 66:22).

In the Book of Revelation, the former heaven and the former earth have passed away — that is to say, the temporary nature of time will turn into the everlastingness of eternity. The author's concept is more breathtaking than models of new cities. It's based on the concept that Jesus' resurrection isn't some isolated once-and-for-all event, but a great cosmic reversal of everything that is usual into things that are surprising, wonderful, and unexpected.

Interestingly, the author saw that the sea was no more. The sea, in the thinking of the ancients, devoured ships and sailors. Sailors didn't have compasses, so they tried to sail along the shorelines. The sea's bitter storms may have given rise to the myths concerning monsters like Leviathan ruling over the primeval chaos. Anyone, even today, who has seen the power of the ocean, especially in storms, still stands in awe and finds the ancients' fear of the sea easy to understand. The author of the Book of Revelation believed that, at the time of the new creation, only God could tame the brutal power and violence of such a beast. This was the best way to describe how God could be victorious over evil — which He can be, completely, in the new heaven and the new earth, if people cooperate.

The new Jerusalem (v. 2), in which all will live, is a symbol of the Church. It's a holy city because it comes down from heaven and is consecrated to God. The Church is in God's saving plan. That plan embraces not only the entire human being and the whole of humanity, but all of creation, and the Church has all of that as her mission. In view of what human beings have already done to pollute planet earth, and in the light of what their new inventions are capable of doing even further to harm the planet and one another, it's essential that the Church's mission be not to simply look after the world but to be an agent in its renovation. The author calls the Church a bride, because marriage was a metaphor often used in the Jewish Scriptures for the covenant relationship between God and His people.

A loud voice tells the writer that God's dwelling is with the human race (v. 3). This is the fulfillment of the prophecies that foretold the intimate union of God with His people in this new era of salvation. The intimacy which the first man and woman enjoyed in Paradise and which Israel had experienced in the desert and in the Temple is now granted to all members of the People of God forever. Fellowship with God in the golden age brings happiness: He shall wipe away every tear, and there shall be no more death or mourning, crying out or pain (v. 4). The words bring us back to the Bible's beginnings, with Adam and Eve communing with God in the peaceful serenity of creation in the newness of Eden.

The words also bring us forward, to today's passage from St. John's Gospel. It's the Last Supper, and Judas has left on his vicious mission. Jesus, in anticipation of his ascension, begins to tell how best to bring about his new spiritual creation. Though he speaks at a tragic time of approaching death, it's a time of glory, a glory that is intertwined between the Father and the Son.

Thenceforward, Jesus' glory will be the cross. The cross is of the essence of life. In warfare, it's not so much the ones who come back who are memorialized, but those who gave their lives; in medicine, it's not the ones who have made money, but those who sacrificed to find cures and to ease people's pain; in statesmanship, it's not the ones who made headlines for a while, but those who have provided the best for their nation and the human race.

As Jesus continues his farewell, he calls his disciples his children (v. 33), the usual address of a master to his pupils — but now, because of his imminent death, spoken with a special tenderness. Telling them he's leaving a new commandment (v. 34), he speaks of love. But what's new about that? Two big things. For one, Jesus doesn't equate love of neighbor with love of one's fellow Israelites, as the First Testament code had done; he extends love to all people without distinction, as he had shown in his story of the Good Samaritan (Lk 10:29-37). Secondly, Jesus' commandment is new in the ideal it strives to emulate: Our love should be as he has loved us.

Those areas of newness are important. Much of what goes under the name of love is selfish, thinking of what it can get rather than what

it can give. One who loves as Jesus does acts in Jesus' way: univer-
sally, including enemies; self-sacrificingly, without limit; understand-
ingly, like people who continue to love those with whom they live and
whom they know intimately, warts and all; and forgivingly, as Jesus
loved his disciples, all of whom never really fully understood him when
they were together, and in the end left him in his need.

What will be the results of that kind of love? Today's First Reading, from the Acts of the Apostles, gives an insight into that. The
Apostles' love, now grown to a height it never achieved in the Gospels, brought about the beginning of the new City of God: The instructions the Apostles were giving, the prayers the early Christians were
offering, and the common life they were living were contributing to
the development of the Church. Today's reading reports that Paul and
Barnabas, by the end of their first missionary journey of preaching a
new power of good — the power of Easter — let loose in the world,
had strengthened the spirits of the disciples and exhorted them to persevere in the faith (v. 22). Their very successful journey established
Christianity in Cyprus, Pisidia, Lyconia, and Pamphilia to present-day
Cyprus and Turkey — a journey more difficult for them than spanning
the world by jet in a number of hours today. They learned that it was
God's will to open the Church to the Gentiles.

The people saw the necessity of Christian fellowship, and to that
end with prayer and fasting they appointed presbyters in each church
(v. 23). For all that they did, the Apostles never took the credit, but
reported what God had done with them (v. 27). Through the traveling
missionaries, God had opened the door of faith to the Gentiles, thus
offering hope for the future.

We're now living in that new place that was built by the blood
of Jesus and the love of the first Apostles. We must learn how to live
here well, so that the early Christians' love, which was to the limits of
endurance, has not been in vain. In the midst of our hardships and disappointments, which are no greater than the hardships and disappointments of Jesus and the first Apostles, we must continue to re-create
the universe and establish a new social order. This means doing everything from caring for the environment to participating in local social and political programs. It means, in short, to build and improve
our new city. That new city is not the space-age city of plastic bubbles,
climate control, living in space, and the like, but the perpetually fascinating, ever-challenging, and always needed city of the spirit.

Sixth Sunday of Easter
Ac 15:1f., 22-29   Rv 21:10-14, 22f.   Jn 14:23-29

Peace
The New Jerusalem; The Continuing Presence of God;
Peacemaking; The Dwelling Place of God

Business seminars used to deal with what they called conflict resolution. Today, realizing that — human nature being what it is — we don't really resolve many conflicts, they're more and more emphasizing the concept of conflict management. The major tactic is to try to give a full hearing to each side in a conflict and then try to mediate, seeing if each side can get what it wants without making the other side feel as though it has lost, and — most important — keeping peace.

Indeed, peace — external peace and internal peace — is vital for all of us. We continue to consider external peace in special ways at times like Memorial Day. Problems of internal peace such as undue anxiety and scrupulosity we consider all the time. Jesus made peace an important part of his last lessons the night before he died. He said that he was giving us his gift of peace "not as the world gives," and we repeat that idea in a prayer before the kiss of peace at Mass.

What the world means by "peace" is often simply the absence of war. It's a state of being left alone, like the harassed mother wants from her active young children or the worker from the public he has had to deal with for too long. Or it's not being burdened by cares or financial worries. Or it's a deep sleep, which is what the world understands when it writes "Rest in Peace" on its tombstones.

What Jesus means by peace is quite different. It's not simply a cocoon wrapping us in self-centerdness, isolating us from the pressures of daily life, and eradicating trouble. It's a positive, active thing: a virtue, a state of mind, a disposition for benevolence. St. Augustine was in the tradition of Jesus when he defined peace as "the tranquility of order." It contains certain prerequisites. It's all-involving. If you want peace, you must have a still and quiet conscience, because there's no peace for the wicked (Is 48:22). If you want peace, you must work for justice. If you want peace, you must seek God's will: As Dante put over the doors of paradise, "In His will is our peace"; T.S. Eliot added that if we do God's will we can find peace "even among these rocks" of our life.

And Jesus said that one of the essential requirements of peace is love. One problem with that is that love can turn inward and become a very private thing. By the Tiber River in Rome there is in a glass-enclosed building the *ara pacis*, a beautifully-carved marble "altar of peace." It was erected by Augustus Caesar after he and his armies had conquered practically all of Europe and the known parts of Asia. But when one bends others to one's will, that's not peace, but tyranny.

Another version of distorted love and peace is one that's syrupy sweet and sentimental. Those versions can exclude almost anybody we wish. To avoid that, Jesus calls for our obedience: "Whoever loves me will keep my word" (v. 23). That kind of discipline reaches out to the world God loves. In our often brutal world, that can call for what we today call "tough love."

To help, Jesus tried to show the Apostles that the mode of his presence was going to change. Presence — especially the presence of friends — is important to everyone, and the Apostles were dejected because Jesus' physical presence was to be no more. He assured them that his bodily presence would be replaced by something far more wonderful.

For all that, though, Jesus' presence would be no less intimate. From their having been able to physically see, hear, and touch him, they would now have God entering their lives in the deeper sense of the indwelling of the Holy Spirit. When Jesus would pass on to his heavenly Father, the Spirit would come to move people on to the next phase of union with God.

He promised the Paraclete, the third person of the godhead, to help give God's peace to us. The word "Paraclete" is also translated "Comforter," but a Paraclete does more than comfort. The word is the equivalent in Greek, the language in which St. John the Evangelist wrote, of the Latin "*advocatus*," and means a mediator, a defense attorney, one who stands by you in time of need. In time of trouble, it's a great comfort to have a lawyer take your side. What the lawyer does for pay, the Paraclete does for love. What the lawyer does with the possibility of failing, the Paraclete does with a guarantee of success for those who do their part. Although we're guilty, both Paracletes — Jesus and the Holy Spirit — plead our cause and get us a suspended sentence.

As the poet (Gerard Manley Hopkins) put it, a Paraclete is one who cheers, who encourages, who persuades, who exhorts, who stirs up, who urges forward, who calls on. What clapping hands are to a speaker, what a trumpet is to a soldier, a Paraclete is to the soul. A Paraclete is zealous that we should do the good, and full of assurance that if we try we can; calling us on, springing to meet us half way, crying to our ears as to our heart: "This way to do God's will; this way to save your soul: Come on, come on!"

Paracletes take place on a human as well as a divine level. When the heartbroken Nathaniel Hawthorne went home to tell his wife that he was a failure and had been fired from his job in a customhouse, she surprised him with an exclamation of joy.

"Now," she said triumphantly, "you can write your book!"

"Yes," replied Nathaniel, "and what shall we live on while I'm writing it?"

To his amazement, she opened a drawer and pulled out a substantial amount of money. "Where on earth did you get that?" he exclaimed.

"I've always known you were a man of genius," she told him. "I knew that someday you would write a masterpiece. So every week, out of the housekeeping money you gave me, I saved a little. So here is enough to last us for a whole year!"

From her confidence and encouragement came one of the greatest novels of United States literature, *The Scarlet Letter*.

On the divine level, deeper experiences of God do not, however, make Christians immune to problems or pain. Even as Jesus was speaking about his farewell gift of his kind of peace at the Last Supper, he was troubled. But he showed that his peace can be present even in the midst of insults, persecution, and approaching death.

The troubles of Jesus continued in his Church. The first major controversy in the Church is that recorded in the First Reading of today's Mass. It concerned whether a non-Jew becoming a Christian should be compelled to enter the Church by way of Judaism. When you consider that most of the first Christians were devout, synagogue-attending Jews, the dispute is not strange. Those Jewish Christians favoring the Gentiles having to come into Christianity by way of Judaism took the position that the Jews were God's chosen people: They pointed to God's promises to Abraham, to Moses' freeing the Jews from the slavery of Egypt, to the words of the prophets. And — very significantly — they were emotionally dedicated to their belief in their Torah, or Law.

On the other side of that dispute were those who believed that the ultimate and final word of God is not the Torah, but Jesus; he alone is our salvation. They said that if Jewish regulations like circumcision were made binding on Christians, Christianity would become nothing but a small sect of Judaism (like the Lubavitcher sect of Judaism today in places like Brooklyn). They believed that Christians die and rise in Christ through baptism, which frees us from the Torah.

In the Church's first Ecumenical Council, the Council of Jerusalem, their position won out. At that Council the early Church Fathers indicated their decision not to lay on Christians any burden which wasn't strictly necessary. And, being true peacemakers, they not only promulgated the official decision, but sent Judas and Silas out with it to help the lukewarm to accept it. With that decision, the Christian assembly officially broke ties with Judaism, arrived at a new and higher step in defining itself, and extended membership into regions of the world where it hadn't gone before.

The successors of Peter and the rest of the Church continue that authority and concern. The history of the Church has sordid pages — the Crusades, the Inquisition, the immoral lives of some Renaissance Popes, the bad politics — and is always in need of reform. But the Church is more than just a community of believers, although it is that; more than a people who study the Word of God and try to put it into their lives, although it is that; more than a people who share sacred signs called sacraments, although it is that. The Church is an assembly guided by the Holy Spirit to teach Christ's truth authentically.

That truth doesn't change. There's no new Gospel. But Christ's Gospel can be applied to new situations. The Gospel develops, but doesn't depart from its original deposit of faith. There's nothing in the oak tree which wasn't first in the acorn; yet the oak has certainly grown and developed. The Church has always confronted new problems. This shouldn't cause consternation. The Church will continue to solve life's problems as she has always done: by relying on the Holy Spirit. The Church's authority remains a sure and absolute guide in matters of faith and morals.

The vision of the end result for those who cooperate is the "New Jerusalem" described in the last chapter of the Book of Revelation, part of which constitutes today's Second Reading. Jerusalem was the Lord's choice for His dwelling. In the Holy of Holies in the Temple, He "dwelt on the wings of the Cherubim," which surrounded the Ark of the Covenant. Jerusalem represented all Israel, and was its capital. It was the embodiment of all the promises made to the Patriarchs and Prophets. Yet at the time of Christ it had become corrupt, and good Jews hated that corruption. Among the many interpretations of the Book of Revelation, what's sure is that the Book is trying to describe the kind of peace that will result, both here and hereafter, if Christ holds sway.

We face the same issues as did our forebears in today's liturgy: conflicts and their management, troubles of various kinds, and God's presence. We should know enough about conflict management to achieve peace: Jesus' unique peace, his Easter gift, wherever we go. And we need a broad enough vision to see God's presence everywhere. That's particularly true at the Kiss of Peace at Mass, when we recognize God's presence in every single person. Those realizations should have such results as deeper understanding of others and easier gestures of forgiveness, both of which in turn help further a reign of peace. That's a mode of conflict management in which everybody wins.

FEAST OF THE ASCENSION
Ac 1:1-11   Eph 1:17-23   Lk 24:46-53

Witnessing to Christ
Christ Lives and Reigns Forever; Finding Our Hope
and Our Glory; To You, Theophilus, Wherever You Are

Ascension Day is a day of mystery. Jesus leaves his disciples to go to the heavenly Father and promises to return. He concludes his ministry, and the mission of the Church begins. He commissions his disciples to establish his kingdom and pledges its fulfillment. And we're all called to this great hope.

St. Luke tries to make sense of all this for us. Today's Gospel

---

Note: This homily is on all today's readings. For mostly Matthew, see Cycle A; for
    mostly Ephesians, Cycle B.

and the reading from the Acts of the Apostles — both written by Luke — tell us some things about the mystery of Jesus' ascension. Luke's Gospel concludes with Jesus promising to send his Spirit upon us and then being taken to heaven. At that point, the Acts of the Apostles begins. That exaltation of Jesus marks the conclusion of one age and the beginning of a new one. There's a sense of urgency about it all, the emphasis being on the need for action rather than speculation.

When Jesus was lifted up in a cloud, he moved from earth where his presence was a matter of fact to a presence with us that's a matter of faith. The picture is that Jesus is taken into the cloud of God's glory: Without leaving us, he's accepted by the Father and enthroned in glory. Heaven isn't up, hell isn't down; Jesus' entry into heaven doesn't mean that he's gone away from us.

Jesus of Nazareth, a man on earth, was an objective matter of fact. As such, a few people saw him with their physical eyes, heard him with their physical ears, touched him with their physical hands. But for most people in the world Jesus hasn't been physically present. His leaving in a cloud, a biblical symbol of the presence of God who can be seen only by faith, is the story not about Jesus being taken away from us, but Jesus being given to us for all times and for all places as a matter of faith. And his presence to us right now brings him — and his warmth, his care, his love — even closer to each of us than we are to each other.

Both the Gospel and Acts record some of Jesus' last instructions before telling us of his ascension itself. Luke's Gospel says that the Apostles were to preach penance for the remission of sins "in his name" (v. 47). A frequent theme in Luke's Acts of the Apostles as well, this term expresses faith in the divinity of Jesus: What was formerly said only of Yahweh is now said of Jesus.

Also a theme of Acts is Jesus' instruction in the Gospel that all his followers are to preach his Gospel to all the nations. Our preaching and good example to those not of the faith are important works among our fellow human beings, just as undertakings among the Gentiles were important in the early Church. As the Gospel tells us, that work was to go to all the nations, beginning from Jerusalem (v. 47); as Acts puts it, the Apostles will be his witnesses in Jerusalem, throughout Judea and Samaria, and to the ends of the earth (v. 8).

It was fitting that they begin at Jerusalem, the geographic center of sacred history. Jerusalem was the capital city of the old theocracy, the site of the Temple of God, the religious center of the chosen people.

The prophets had foretold that from it would issue the glad tidings of the new dispensation in widening circles. Samaria, only semi-Jewish, was a bridge to the Gentile world. Next would be Rome, then the capital of culture. Then the whole world! Eventually it would come to embrace us, so far removed in space and time from the scene.

This universal observation is a noticeable contrast with the narrow-mindedness of the Apostles' question, "Lord, are you at this time going to restore the kingdom to Israel?" (Ac v. 6). The Apostles, reflecting their culture, thought of themselves as destined with God's help to rule the world.

Jesus then promised to send the Holy Spirit, the promise of his Father (Lk v. 49; Ac v. 8). The Gospels of both Luke and John give the impression that the resurrection, the ascension, and the giving of the Spirit on Pentecost all took place on the same day. It wasn't until more than three hundred years later that the Church began to celebrate the Feast of the Ascension forty days after Easter, perhaps in part because of the importance of each feast. In any case, the ascension didn't take place until the Apostles by many proofs (Ac v. 3) received evidence of Jesus' resurrection that was trustworthy enough to eliminate doubt.

Luke's words that Jesus raised his hands and blessed them (v. 50) deliberately took Jewish readers back to the climax of the Day of Atonement (Si 50:20). That day presented awesome majesty and aroused lofty joy at the high priest's final blessing — also pronounced only this once in the year. That was the only day of the year when the holy name of Yahweh could be pronounced, and that by the high priest in great solemnity. The occasion was a most impressive event: with the high priest fully vested entering the sanctuary, ascending the altar and, in the midst of the whole assembly of Israel, surrounded by assistant priests bearing offerings while the trumpets blasted and the people bowed down in adoration of the Most High.

Equally significant in connection with the Feast of the Atonement was its reason for being — that is, expiation for the sins of the nation. All work was forbidden on this day and the entire nation observed a strict fast. On this day the high priest, in simple white garments, sacrificed a bullock as a sin-offering for himself and the priesthood. Then he laid his hands on the head of a he-goat and pronounced upon it all the sins of Israel; thus laden, it was driven into the desert.

The idea of "scapegoat" seems deeply ingrained. The early Christians were used as scapegoats for all misfortunes — as with Nero who burned Rome and blamed them. In colonial New England, nineteen innocent women scapegoats were hanged as "witches." With the large Irish immigration to the United States for sixty years beginning around 1820, the Irish were scapegoats for unemployment. The Ku Klux Klan used Catholics, blacks, and others as scapegoats. Nazi Germany used Jews and others as scapegoats. And St. Paul tells us that the image is a picture of the atonement accomplished by our Lord for the sins of the whole world.

The Gospel tells us that then Jesus was taken up to heaven (v. 51), Acts that he was lifted up and a cloud took him from their sight (v. 9). Nowhere does it say that he rose on a cloud, as some artists have painted; the text says that a cloud took him from their sight. The cloud is the same as the cloud that engulfed the tabernacle in the desert, the cloud which surrounded the Temple when it was dedicated, and the cloud of the transfiguration. The truth is that the real nature of the ascension must of its very nature always remain a mystery. It tries to put into words what is beyond words, to relate an experience that happened only this one time and never to anyone else.

Whatever happened, the Apostles — heretofore fearful, timorous, and feeling alone — returned to Jerusalem with serenity and great joy (Lk v. 52). Whereas the ascension marked an ending — an ending of the days when Jesus was a flesh and blood person with them — it was equally a beginning. The age of the Holy Spirit, the fulfillment of the Father's promise (Ac v. 4), was dawning. The Spirit fills the cooperating individual with greater strength and with a stronger, more personal, and more appreciative union with Jesus than before.

The way Luke's Gospel put the result with the Apostles was that they were continually in the Temple (v. 53). Luke's Gospel began in the House of God with the angel announcing to Zechariah the birth of John the Baptist. Now it ends with the Apostles continually praising God in the House of God.

The final message is that Jesus will return (Ac v. 11). St. Paul, in his letter to the Ephesians of which we read an excerpt today, shows the Church to be greater than the particular churches to which he often referred in his earlier letters. This image means that the Christian community is united to Christ and, by inference, to one another. There are many other valid images of the Church, such as herald, servant, and Body of Christ, but certainly an important image for our time is the

Church as savior; no small part of that image is that we pray earnestly for that enlightenment which will bring us to know what is the hope to which God has called us.

To speculate about the exact time of Jesus' Second Coming would be futile. But we have faith that God has a plan for us. God has revealed that our history has a purpose and that it's a positive one. No matter when or how Jesus' return to planet earth will take place, his return comes to all of us when we die. We must prepare for that coming by living close to Jesus — with the joy and enthusiasm that are frequent elements of Luke's message, and which those who are filled with the Spirit can provide to a world which has so much loneliness and lack of hope. "Jesus' ascension means our salvation as well; where the glorious Head has gone before, the body is called to follow in hope" (St. Leo the Great).

Today's liturgy calls us also to be bold witnesses to the passion, death, resurrection, and exaltation of Jesus — witnesses, in other words, of Gospel joy to the world. We can't just keep looking up to heaven: We have a mission from Jesus. After the ascension, there's a bit of earth with God in heaven and a bit of heaven with us on earth. But we have work to do. We must stand on our own spiritual feet and do it. Today's emphasis on the role of the Holy Spirit assures us that in that work we don't walk alone.

SEVENTH SUNDAY OF EASTER
Ac 7:55-60   Rv 22:12-14, 16f., 20   Jn 17:20-26

Let's All Be One, for Christ's Sake!
Recognizing Christ in our Midst; The Consolation of the Church;
Results of Jesus' Having Been Here

All of us know the sadness of good-byes. We've said them to our parents, our children, our relatives, and our friends. Every farewell seems a little death. At each parting there's a wrenching and a loneliness — especially if it means separation for a considerable period of time. Those who try to be close to Jesus felt this last Thursday, the feast of his As-

cension, when we commemorated his going to heaven. Today, between
the feasts of Ascension and Pentecost, after we've marked Jesus' leave-
taking from the disciples but before celebrating the coming of the Spirit,
we speak not of Jesus' absence but of his presence, although in a different form.

The Gospel is taken from the end of Jesus' prayer at the Last
Supper. The prayer ends as it began: solemnly, intimately, in the hearing of friends, with many references to love, and filled with hope. In
the first part of this prayer (vv. 1-8), Jesus prayed for himself, in the
second part (vv. 9-19) for his disciples, and in this last part — today's
— for us and all believers.

It's called Jesus' High-Priestly Prayer, because in it he conse-
crates his body and blood for the sacrifice in which they're about to be
offered and because in it he gives his blessings to the Church that he's
about to bring forth. The end of the prayer differs from its beginning:
What went before, Jesus had spoken to the disciples; what he's saying
now is an intimate dialogue with the Father, with the disciples being
privileged to overhear. In this terrible time, Jesus didn't lose faith in
God or confidence in his people.

And his tender prayer was for his people's unity. We needn't be
reminded of its need: We often witness breakdowns of communication in families, enmity among members of the same faith community,
dissension in civil society. Jesus' unity — one of personal relationship
— is to overcome all such divisions, especially those within the fold.
Jesus wants a unity like that between himself and the Father: a unity
that preserves individuality but which is close and intimate. That union
of the Father and the Son is our model. It's a unity in which people
will love and serve each other because they love and serve him; it's
heart speaking to heart. Its key is love.

Unless the Church has the unity willed by God, it can't perform
its essential mission: that the world may believe (v. 21). That we may
be one, as Jesus and the heavenly Father are one, as Jesus prayed, Jesus
has given all of us the glory the Father gave him (v. 22). That consists,
for one, in the cross, on which Jesus wasn't so much crucified as glorified. Through suffering for God, we grow as in no other way: To carry
Jesus' cross is for the Christian an honor and a glory.

Like Jesus, we find our glory in doing not what we will, but what
God wills. When Christians preserve God's unity in love that Jesus has
given, we're the continuation of Christ as mediator and revealer of God:

We show the world that he was sent by God (v. 23). Jesus concludes his prayer with confidence that his Father (v. 25), Who alone is perfectly righteous, will deal rightly with those who have accepted the revelation of God in Christ. And even as death approaches, he sounds a note of triumph that he shall live and, through the Paraclete who is to come, will continue to make known God's name (v. 26).

One answer to Jesus' prayer began with St. Stephen. Stephen was one of the first seven spiritual and prudent men chosen to be deacons, and to do what the first deacons had as their reason for being: to distribute charity to the needy. He's celebrated as the Church's first martyr. The word "martyr" means literally "witness"; and Stephen was a lesson to all of us to stand for what's right and true — though our bearing witness is unlikely to be as hazardous as it was for Stephen. In witnessing to truth we should avoid being passive, lethargic, and indifferent; we should, to the contrary, form ourselves into a zealous people, eager to proclaim justice.

Implicitly, Stephen's prayer for the forgiveness of his infuriated audience attempts to overcome the disunity between Stephen and them as well as between them and God; forgiveness is an essential element for achieving unity. Stephen saw beyond the faces of his audience distorted with rage; and he saw even beyond time, to the Son of Man standing at God's right hand (vv. 55f.) — a position of power and authority. The Church reminds us of this today, the Sunday following the feast of the Ascension, because it's the first example in the Scriptures of a vision of the risen and ascended Jesus.

Stephen's audience was no more pleased at hearing his mentioning the significant term "Son of Man" — knowing its implication of the divine — than those who had heard Jesus use it. Considering it blasphemy, they shouted in fury, covered their ears to hear no more of it, rushed him, dragged him out of the city, and stoned him to death (vv. 57f.).

None of this was an official act of Judaism, since in Roman times not even the Sanhedrin had the power to put anyone to death: It was a lynching. The custom for such a lynch mob then was to lead the condemned to a height and throw him off. If that didn't kill him, they hurled boulders on him until he died. In Stephen's case, it was ironic that the participants in their ugly activity laid down their cloaks at the feet of a young man named Saul (v. 58), the future St. Paul, who for his part concurred in the killing.

Stephen died very much as Jesus had. Both Jesus and Stephen were accused of blasphemy. Both were tried by a mob and a kangaroo court. Both were taken outside the Holy City to be killed. Both died violent deaths. As Jesus had prayed to his heavenly Father to forgive his murderers, Stephen cried the same plea (v. 60). And both Jesus and Stephen at the last commended their spirits to God.

In the trials of our lives, which are less intense than those of Jesus and Stephen, we can be consoled by the vision of John the Theologian in today's section from the Book of Revelation. It's our seventh and last reading in the liturgy of this year from this mysterious final book of the Bible. This is the end of the book and the end of the Bible.

It has Jesus applying to himself the words used by God of Himself in the very beginning of the Bible (Gn 1:8): "I am the *Alpha* and the *Omega*" (v. 13). We call something complete when we say it goes "from a to z." To mean the same thing, the Hebrews used the first and last letters of their alphabet, "from *aleph* to *taw*," and the Greeks, as here, "from *alpha* to *omega*." It means that Jesus — and not the Torah, as the Jews had claimed — is complete in every way, timeless, and with full authority.

Those people fortunate enough to receive the right of entry into the City of God, his Church, are those who live through and in Jesus. They have the right to the tree of life (v. 14) — a very ancient metaphor indicating that anyone eating the fruit of life would become like the gods, having eternal life. In ancient pagan myths, the gods and goddesses didn't want human beings to become immortal, so they capriciously kept moving the tree of life so that no mortal could find it. Here it brings us back to the beginning of the Bible with the tree in the garden of Eden (Gn 2:9). In the New Testament, those who suffer in Christ have access to the tree of life.

John's vision next puts into Jesus' mouth two messianic prophecies that Jesus has fulfilled. He is, for one, the root and offspring of David (v. 16) — a messianic title from Isaiah (11:1). Jesus isn't only David's son, but also his Lord. In Christ, the King of kings, all hopes are realized. And John has Jesus speak of himself as "the bright morning star." The morning star is the herald of the day that chases away the night's darkness. For the Jews, it had the added meaning of symbolizing the "star" which Judaism saw as a sign of the Messiah's appearance (See Nb 24:17). That's what St. Matthew intended by his use of the star that guided the magi to Jesus' birthplace. Christ, the morn-

ing star, is the best and brightest of all hopes; before him the night, of
sin and death, flees. Jesus, who had called himself "the light of the
world" (Jn 8:12), is the conqueror of the world's darkness.

This passage, and the entire Bible, ends fittingly with Jesus proclaiming that he's coming soon (v. 20) — that is to say, in his Church.
And John's response is the warm Aramaic expression recorded also
by St. Paul: *Marana tha* (1 Cor 16:22) — the most welcoming, "Come,
Lord Jesus!": a prayer for the coming of Christ in glory.

Finished with the sadness of the good-bye to Jesus at his ascension, we pray, "Come, Lord Jesus!" We pray that he will come soon in
glory — but we pray also that he will come in our trials to make into
one all of our communities: our civic community, our local faith community, our work community, our family community. We pray that in
the unjust ridicule we receive for advocating what is true and right and
just — as, for example, condemning abortion and euthanasia — we shall
stand tall. We pray that all of us will recognize that largess makes only
networks, not community; only sacrifice makes community.

We pray to recognize that the catalyst that Jesus has given us for
fostering and developing unity is the Eucharist: To share the Eucharist
is to share the hurts and joys of the community. And we pray for the
awareness that unity goes hand in hand with Stephen's kind of forgiveness. To forgive is to reopen the lines of communication and thus foster genuine unity.

PENTECOST SUNDAY
Ac 2:1-11   1 Cor 12:3-7, 12f.   Jn 20:19-23 (All A, B, and C)

Jesus is Lord
We Can Make a Difference; Sharing our Gifts;
Openness to the Spirit; Unity in the Church; Need for Discernment

No one can have failed to observe that the Church these days contains
a great many differences. If one half of a congregation wants to go left,

---

Note: This homily is mostly on 1 Corinthians. Cycle A is on Acts, Cycle B mostly on John.

the other half will want to go right; if in a certain program there's one group that wants in, there will be another group that wants out; if some people want more music, others will want more silence. And we have our "Cafeteria Christians," who pick and choose what they will believe. We cannot, as Christians, accept these imbalances as though they must be that way; we ought to develop the view that, sharing in one Spirit, we with our individual gifts can contribute to the unity of the whole.

It's good to remember — especially on today's Feast of Pentecost when we commemorate the coming of the Holy Spirit to establish the Church (one Church) — that differences in the Church have been present from the beginning. And that Church has grown and changed.

The Church is in some ways like the squash. We're surrounded by various forms of the squash (curcubit) family: zucchini, pumpkins, gourds, cucumbers, and various melons like honeydew, cantaloupe, Persian, cassava, and watermelon. Developed in the Egyptian desert back in the mists of pre-history, squash seeds were carried by traders and travelers in their packs. By donkey and camel the seeds crossed all of Asia and across the Bering Strait in the great migrations of peoples.

Squash has a particular genius: an ability to evolve and to be transformed with each successive planting. Every time it's planted in a new soil, under new climatic conditions, at a different altitude, squash changes and develops new forms. A simple change of water can produce new forms of the vegetable.

So it is with the Church: Like squash, the Church has an uncanny ability to adapt and to take on the characteristics of the culture in which it finds itself. Planted in the fertile Holy Land countryside by Jesus of Nazareth, the original seed grew and flourished and produced a Jewish form of Church. As the Good News passed throughout the Mediterranean basin, the form of the community (Church) changed and evolved. In Greece, it became Greek; in Rome, Roman.

Which is more authentically Church? Well, is zucchini more squash than gourds? The Word of God takes root in the fertile soil of human hearts — Venezuelan among the people of Caracas, Chinese among the folks in Hong Kong, Australian among the denizens of Sydney. Watered by the Holy Spirit, it produces ever new and fascinating expressions of the divine creativity.

We celebrate that creativity in today's feast of Pentecost. Originally an agricultural feast, Pentecost among the Jews came to be identified with the giving of the Law on Sinai. With Christians, it takes on an entirely new dimension: It's the beginning of a mission to the world, a harvest of peoples instead of agricultural products. At its heart is the gift of the Spirit that established the Church and continues to move people to undertake the preaching of the Word.

St. Paul addressed the idea in today's portion of his first letter to the Corinthians. Corinth, the city to whose Christian inhabitants Paul wrote, was at that time a prosperous cosmopolitan city, very similar to most major cities in the world today: London, New York, Madrid, Lisbon, Paris, Rome, Berlin. Among the people from all over the world who lived there, the city had its hustlers, self-indulgent profligates, and sinners of all sorts. And there were factions.

Such factions have been characteristic of the human race since the pride and sinfulness of the tower of Babel. At Babel, and in today's mega-city world, human beings gather into big cities and engage in building ever higher and higher monuments to their own egos. Pentecost has the potential of being the reversal of Babel.

Corinth also had a good-sized contingent who, sick of self-seeking, had converted to Christianity. They formed an intensely lively community that burst with enthusiasm over Jesus' Good News. But the Corinthians were no simple converts: They brought to their new faith cultural and psychological problems of considerable complexity. And with Jewish Christians and Gentile Christians living side by side, there were many contrasts. The factionalism that had spilled over to the Christians in Corinth provided part of the reason why Paul wrote his letter. What was important for Paul was that in all the diversity in the Church there be unity in Christ.

One of the divisions among Christians — how like the modern Church! — involved the charismatic gifts: those extraordinary powers given by the Holy Spirit. This was in a time when, like our own, there were among pagans unabashed emotionalism, enthusiasm over prophetic trances, and orgiastic frenzies. Because this could be catching to Christians, Paul reminded them, first, that no one could get anywhere truly meaningful except by way of the Holy Spirit: The bottom-line criterion for determining the authenticity of an alleged gift of the Spirit is whether it strengthens faith and the bond of unity.

Most importantly, no one can make the unifying profession of faith, "Jesus is Lord," except in the Holy Spirit. At that time the Romans, in confronting Christian converts, tried to force them to say,

"Caesar is Lord." Most Roman citizens would have no trouble with that: For them, Caesar was indeed Lord. For others, then and since, there have been other "Lords": money, liquor, power, self, sex.

The Christian who says "Jesus is Lord!" is expressing a simplified and condensed creed and is making a statement similar to the "Credo" we say at Mass. The statement means we accept the life and teaching of the historical Jesus as being the norm of our Christian life. It also involves a sense of community, because it identifies a person as belonging not only to Christ, but also to his Church. Unity isn't uniformity, though, and those who make this profession of faith and praise, while building up one Body in Christ, retain their individual gifts.

Whatever one's gifts, they aren't purely personal; they're always the patrimony of Christ's community, the Church. To receive a gift, therefore, is to give a gift. There are various gifts, or charisms, and different works and ministries. Always, we're to use them not only for our individual wants but first and foremost for the common good (v. 7). In the verses omitted from today's reading (vv. 8-11), Paul lists many gifts: for example, the ability to express wisdom and knowledge, and to have faith; the gifts of healing, miraculous powers, and prophecy; and the discernment of spirits, the gift of glossolalia (speaking in tongues), and the gift of interpreting tongues.

None of the gifts is as earth-shaking as the gift to be able to say, "Jesus is Lord." Diverse as the gifts are, all are attributable to the same divine Spirit (vv. 4-6) and are directed to the unity of the Church. And, despite their diversity, all gifts have some features in common: that they're graces from outside ourselves, for example, that they have forms of service as their purpose, and that in all of them God is at work.

The divine choices — why God chooses to give one gift to one person and another to another — are always as mysterious as God's choice of the Israelites as His chosen people (Ex 19:3-8, 16-20, as in reading for Vigil of Pentecost). God chose the people Israel to enjoy a unique intimacy with Him, but in turn He required much of them. Through Moses, the people readily accepted that covenant. For His part, God showed His lordship of nature by a demonstration on Mount Sinai not unlike that of Pentecost: peals of thunder and lightning, a heavy cloud, a loud trumpet blast, a rushing wind, smoke, and fire, so that all the people trembled (Ex 19).

Many people, if given their choice of gifts for themselves, would pick the most spectacular of them: gifts which would show up like what the Apostles did on this first Christian Pentecost. But most of us have gifts which are much more quiet: the gift of being practical enough to manage a household, for example, or the gift of getting along with people, or the gift of loving patience to raise children, or the gift of being able to handle the details of a business. In their use, instead of attracting attention to ourselves, we're to help bring others to Jesus and to one another. Diversity and unity are both important to the Christian community, but only when they go together.

Let's all ask ourselves, "What are my gifts? What am I uniquely able to do that is of most help to others and to Christ's work?" Mother Teresa put it this way:

> I slept and I dreamed
> that life is all joy.
> I woke and I saw
> that life is all service.
> I served and I saw
> that service is joy.

Let's pray with Eucharistic Prayer #3, "Grant that we may be filled with the Holy Spirit and become one body, one spirit in Christ." Then let's accept our gifts from the Holy Spirit and continue to use them to unite people and make us one in the Body of Christ that is his Church. Next to the gift of faith that enables us to confess that "Jesus is Lord!" are other gifts as diverse as those of the humble squash. Our diversity can, if we use it wisely, contribute happiness to the human family.

TRINITY SUNDAY
Pr 8:22-31   Rm 5:1-5   Jn 16:12-15

Becoming and Remaining in the Image of God through Largeness and Unity
The Experience of God in Our Lives;
The Intrinsic Unifying Element in our Spiritual Life

Every year in the United States pollsters survey public opinion on a variety of topics. One of the questions they ask is, "Do you believe in

God?" About 30%, or 60 million Americans, have stated that they don't believe.

But everyone has a god. What answers all the ultimate questions of life for you is your god. Scripture speaks of those whose god is their belly. Included in that are gods of pleasure, comfort, and the "almighty dollar." Other people believe in a kind of spider god, who lurks in wait for the unwary. Still others believe in humanity as their god, and state that, in the entire realm of being, there's nothing higher than people, nothing finer or nobler, nothing more worthwhile.

Maybe pollsters should also ask, "In what *kind* of god do you believe?" For those in our Christian tradition, no god of the belly or gold or pleasure or humanity suffices. In fact, no god that would be fully understandable by the finite human intellect would suffice. Such a one would be too small to be God.

When we assert our belief in God, we refer to those wonderful attributes presented so poetically by the Book of Proverbs in the First Reading of today's Mass, and by today's Responsorial Psalm. The Book of Proverbs reminds us of many facets of God. There's the creative action of God the Father, forming the world and all that it contains. It brings us to realize that we have a wonderful idea of God because we live in such a gorgeous world; if we lived on the moon, our sense of God would reflect that more barren landscape. St. Catherine's best-known image for God is the ocean. And Proverbs portrays God not as an authoritarian remote figure, but someone intimately accessible to the created world.

One of the aspects of God that neither Proverbs nor anywhere else in the First Testament fully revealed is that, as God Himself later told us, ours is a triune God. Now that our long celebration of the drama of Easter, which concentrated on the Second Person of the Blessed Trinity, is over and we've commemorated the Holy Spirit at Pentecost, today we have an opportunity to stand back a bit and see some of the fuller context of God being three Persons in one nature.

The full, clear, and explicit realization of the doctrine of the Trinity took time to come to us. Amid the many ancient gods — the forces of nature, and emperors, and statues, in addition to the gods we already mentioned — the ancient Jews hung on to God's revelation of Himself as one and absolute, infinite, and alone the Creator. Their knowledge of God's oneness prevented them from falling into idolatry, and was so important to them that they put out of their minds any notion that would compromise it, including foreshadowings of God's triune nature.

So when ideas such as the Trinity threatened their belief in one God, the early Christians, as well as the Jews from whom they sprang, had problems. God the Creator they understood. They had greater difficulty with the fact that, unless their eyes and ears were deceiving them, Jesus — even though their experience showed him to be a human being like themselves — was also Absolute God. And he had taught them about their having the Holy Spirit of God so as to be able to speak with authority and even to forgive sins in God's name.

Even today, much that we know about God is according to our way of thinking and talking. For example, feminists find difficult the masculine terminology about the Trinity: especially "Father" and "Son." They prefer such terms as God the Creator, God the Redeemer, and God the Sanctifier. Whether we refer to God as Father, Mother, Yahweh, Great Spirit, or whatever else a particular culture at a specific time dictates, God is so filled with the energy of Being-at-its-fullest that the Father eternally generates the "Living One," a beautiful title for the Risen Jesus.

The Life which leaps and sparks between these two is in turn so dynamic, so joyous, and so fertile, that another Living Person, the Holy Spirit, powerful and life-giving, comes forth eternally. The essential meaning of the Trinity has to do with life generating life. The life energy that is thus generated overflows into the entire universe, creating and renewing the face of the earth.

In our limited way of thinking and talking, we appropriate to the three persons of God various works. We say that the Father creates us and keeps us in being; the Son redeems us and strengthens us throughout our earthly lives by his word and sacraments; and the Holy Spirit fills us with love and helps us find our way through this life and into the next. But the truth is that in each of those works that are outside of God — creation, redemption, and making people holy — all three Persons of God are present. Whatever may be said of one Person of the Trinity, as far as attributes go, may also be said of each of the other Persons: the Father is almighty, the Son is almighty, the Holy Spirit is almighty; the Father is eternal, the Son is eternal, the Holy Spirit is eternal; and so on.

It's within the Godhead that the divine Persons' relationship is distinct. Furthermore, the Persons are intensely active, more active than the energy exploded from nuclear fission. But the three Persons are also one. And their unity is an intensity of love and communication between one another, infinitely more than what may exist within the most lively and loving community we know of on earth. The Father is eternally begetting the Son, the Holy Spirit is eternally proceeding from the Father through the Son.

In the First Testament, the Father revealed Himself as love. Because of His transcendence, though, He seemed to be awesome and far away (reflected in the Psalmist's wonderment expressed to God, "What are people that you are mindful of them?"); the Son became a human being in order to show the love of the Father and to show us what God intended for us from the beginning. The Holy Spirit manifests to us and in us the life of the Son and of the Father.

Today's portion of St. John's Gospel shows Jesus at his Last Supper praying to the Father, speaking of himself as the Son, and promising the Holy Spirit. Here, he emphasizes the Spirit. The Spirit represents the continued presence of Jesus among humankind, sustaining the disciples, clarifying Jesus' message, and bringing a fuller understanding of God's revelation in Jesus. Although the Spirit is the Paraclete, the advocate, intercessor, consoler, and comforter, here Jesus emphasizes the Spirit's role of abiding guidance. The very word for "spirit" in Hebrew, Greek, and Latin is the same as the word for "breath" and "life." The last two verses of today's Gospel come nearest to providing an insight into the actual "life of love" at the heart of the Trinity.

St. Paul mirrors the beginning of the Christian tradition in today's part of his letter to the Romans. He reflects on God's love that establishes the new covenant relationship and identifies the various actions of God in its descriptions of new life. Salvation is through God's gracious action in Christ.

Our whole Christian life is caught up in the life of the Trinity. Liturgically, we pray to the Father through Jesus and in unity with the Holy Spirit. And we're taught to imitate the Trinity, which means entering more and more fully into the life of God, a life which is never static or selfish. Many in our tradition have followed this injunction and become saints.

Our reflections show that our imitation of God is important especially in two ways. First, though God is so great that He can never be fully comprehended by the human mind, we should be in that tradition of greatness. *Allahu Akhbar*, say the Muslims: "God is great!" For the ancient Greeks, greatness was one of the ideals for the development of the human person: that one become a *megalopsychos* — from *megalos*, meaning large, from which we have such words in English as "megalomania" and "megalopolis," and *psychos*, meaning the soul or the spiritual aspect of persons, from which we derive such English words as "psychology" and "psychosomatic." The Romans copied the idea in their word *magnanimitas* — magnanimity — which means essentially the same thing.

Our second conclusion as a result of our contemplation of the Trinity is unity. Just as the three Persons in God are intensely active and separate but at the same time one, so should we be with other persons. God calls us to be united in a community of active love, even as the three Persons in Himself.

We should make our faith in God a matter of reality that will through our largeness of spirit and oneness in love bring others to a meaningful faith in our triune God.

SOLEMNITY OF THE BODY AND BLOOD OF CHRIST (CORPUS CHRISTI)
Gn 14:18-20   1 Cor 11:23-26   Lk 9:11-17

The Meal that Fully Satisfies Hunger
Response to and Reverence for the Eucharist;
Communion and Community; the Abundance of God's Love

People in many parts of the world hunger for food. But hunger is much larger than that. In a world that is in many ways unfair, we hunger for justice. In a world that seems on the brink of war every day, we hunger for peace. All of us hunger for understanding, love, and friendship. We hunger for growth into proper maturity.

And we hunger for spiritual nourishment. Sometimes people aren't even aware that that exists. There was to be a baptismal party for the new baby of a soldier and his wife at their home on an Army base. Before the ceremony the post chaplain took the new father aside.

"Are you prepared for this solemn event?" he asked. "I guess so," replied the soldier. "I've got two hams, pickles, bread, cake, cookies...." "No, no!" interrupted the chaplain. "I mean spiritually prepared!" "Well, I don't know," said the soldier thoughtfully. "Do you think two cases of whiskey are enough?"

Nevertheless, our spiritual hunger is the greatest of all hungers. Today's liturgy of the Solemnity of the Body and Blood of Christ is about that. Whereas on Holy Thursday we celebrate the origin of the Eucharist, today's feast is a celebration of, and an act of faith in, the Real Presence of the risen Jesus with us in this sacrament. All of today's readings are about meals: Abram's victory meal, the Last Supper, and the feeding of the crowd. All refer to the "meal" we call the Eucharist: to what goes beyond people's hunger for food, or for intellectual stimulation, or for psychological growth.

So important to spiritual nourishment is Jesus' multiplication of the food that it's the only one of Jesus' miracles told by all four evangelists. Sharing food with people isn't as simple as it sounds. Ask any political candidate who has followed the campaign ritual, eating his way caterpillar-like through ethnic neighborhoods: the kosher hot dog, the Irish soda bread, the Italian cannoli, the Polish kielbasa. Food is tribal bonding: I eat what you eat; vote for me. And food can become a sounding board for politics. It can become a slogan: "A chicken in every pot." An impulse to revolution: "Let them eat cake." Or a derogatory nickname for an entire tribe: the "limeys" of England, "krauts" of Germany or "frogs" of France.

Social divisions were more pronounced in Jesus' time than in ours — and yet, it would seem that he made sharing food on an equal footing with everyone one of the key points of his way of relating to the world of his time. Just think of the alien groupings who might have been present in the people Luke has sit down together. Men and women of the time would normally not have eaten together, nor would those who were ritually pure with those who were unclean. Then there were Jews and Gentiles, not to mention peasants and those of a higher social order.

St. Luke's version shows many facets of Jesus in his attempt to satisfy hunger: Jesus' compassion, for example, and the abundance of God's generosity. Although he had taken the Apostles away from the crowd for a well-deserved rest, when over 5,000 people came to see him he not only tolerated their disturbing his plans but, in contrast to the abhorrence of the Twelve, actively welcomed them. You can get some idea of his kind of heroism if you imagine your hard-earned vacation being disturbed by a crowd of acquaintances, hangers-on, or unknowns coming to your vacation retreat to freeload.

Some say that the people wouldn't have come to such an out-of-the-way place without having brought their own food with them; basically selfish, they wouldn't break their rations out into the open, because they didn't see anybody else's provisions and so were afraid that they might have to share their own. Jesus' miracle, according to this version, consisted in overcoming this selfishness by making the people share what they had.

But most believers interpret the miracle in the literal sense: Jesus took five loaves and two fish and multiplied them into enough food for over five thousand people to eat. That we haven't a clue as to how he did it we can easily find were we to try to cater a meal, even for ten, with a loaf of bread and a can of sardines. But that isn't as important as knowing that he did it. And the overtones all refer to the Eucharist. The same God who could perform this miracle could do anything, including changing bread and wine into his body and blood.

The miracle shows also the abundance of God's love for individuals: each person ate, everybody had more than enough, and there was a lot left over. Scripture associated this abundance with the Messiah. God had given this same abundance in the manna which He had freely provided the hungry Hebrews as they wandered through the vast and trackless desert in their exodus from Egypt. God offers the same abundance of results today to all who use the Eucharist properly.

All the evangelists deliberately wrote in the same terms as the oldest written account of the institution of the Eucharist — today's portion of St. Paul's first letter to the Corinthians, which antedates the Gospels. The brevity of this passage shouldn't blind us to its tremendous importance. Paul was dealing here with a situation of disunity and selfish behavior when the Corinthian community gathered at the Lord's Supper. As an antidote to the Corinthians' divisions, selfishness, and mindlessness — even as they celebrated their most sacred liturgical act — Paul presents the idea of self-sacrifice as being of central importance in the Lord's Supper.

Paul presents a profound theology. He uses the Greek word *anamnesis*, which we translate as "remembrance," or "memory." This in turn translates the Hebrew *ziccaron*, a First Testament word which means "memorial sacrifice." Among the Hebrews, these words came to be used of one memorial sacrifice *par excellence* — their Passover. Paul is trying to convey the concept that the celebration of the Eucharist is a memorial sacrifice by which God remembers to show mercy upon us because of the death of His Son. Through the Eucharist, Christians of all times have found themselves again with their Savior in making present Jesus' great redeeming sacrifice. We've so often heard the words of the Eucharist at every Mass that we could easily take them for granted; imagine the amazement, if not the incredulity, of the Apostles when they heard them for the first time.

In the last sentence of this reading, Paul uses the word "proclaim" — that, every time we eat this bread and drink this cup, we proclaim the death of the Lord until he comes. Well, Paul's word (*katangellete*) means "to celebrate in a living way, to bring to the present and make effective here and now." In other words, when we proclaim the death of the Lord until he comes, we're bringing Christ's death to the present and making it effective in ourselves.

So the Eucharist is not only to be a memory, but a living contact with Jesus. As Paul wrote to the Corinthians, one can't at the same time be self-centered and truly celebrate the Eucharist. Paul's understanding was that this sacrifice was functional: It's for you. This understands the egalitarian aspect of Jesus' activity, and addresses the question of social divisions in the group with regard to eating together: The rich Christians who had plenty of leisure came early and ate the best food, not waiting for their fellow Christians who were slaves to arrive. And this is a new covenant: It's the fulfillment of God's promises to Jeremiah (31:31) to replace God's Mosaic covenant.

The Church points out that Jesus was in a unique position to do this. The line of Jesus' priesthood wasn't from Moses' brother Aaron, from whom the First Testament priesthood derived, but — as we heard in today's reading from Genesis and in the Responsorial Psalm — from the mysterious First Testament priest Melchizedek, who in his sacrifices to God used, instead of the customary bulls and heifers, bread and wine. Today's First Reading commemorates Melchizedek's sharing a meal of blessed bread and wine with Abram to memorialize Abram's victory as God's instrument over four powerful kings.

The Eucharist, the most exalted of all the Sacraments, is essentially a meal, like the one that Jesus shared with the people in the meadow. It intends to bring together not only us with God, but us with

E. not an end in itself!

one another. St. Thomas Aquinas said that the ultimate change that God sought in the Eucharist isn't the transubstantiation of the bread and wine into Jesus' body and blood, but the transformation of ourselves into Jesus' presence. Our communion means that we receive the body of Christ in the Eucharist and perceive the body of Christ in our neighbor. We can't share fruitfully in the first if we're unmindful of the second.

When as a family we have a meal at home together, we're drawn closer by that sharing more than by anything else. When we provide hospitality to friends by way of a meal — or they for us — we have the opportunity for closeness with them that nothing else has. In the Eucharist, God is providing the same opportunity, with the addition that the closeness, intimacy, union, and other rewards are provided by God and with His unique abundance.

If we want the Eucharist to contribute to our spiritual nourishment, intimacy, and love — as Jesus intended — we must approach it with reverence and awe. Jesus' request at the Last Supper, that we do this in memory of him, is among the most poignant of his statements in the entire New Testament. What he meant by this is what he himself did: to bless and thank God for his life, death, and resurrection. This is to last forever.

And this is a simple thing that's gone on throughout Christian history. Christians have found nothing better than this to do for condemned Christians as the lions roared in the nearby amphitheater; for kings at their crowning and for criminals going to the scaffold; for armies in triumph and for wedding couples in little country churches; for a sick old woman about to die and for Columbus setting sail; for an exiled bishop who had hewn timber all day in a prison camp and for an old monk on the fiftieth anniversary of his vows. The Eucharist has been celebrated in every conceivable human circumstance and for every conceivable human need, in every century since Jesus, on every continent, and among every race on earth.

It's as though Jesus said, "Remember me, and all that I've said and done in your presence. Remember my love. If at first some people don't understand, have them remember the yearnings of all people's hearts and the need of sacrifice to express their love. And I hope all of you will remember that I in turn love you so much that I'm giving all I have, my very blood, for you."

Without the Eucharist, there can be no sufficient satisfaction for our hunger for peace, or justice, or love.

TENTH SUNDAY IN ORDINARY TIME
1 K 17:17-24   Gal 1:11-19   Lk 7:11-17

Our Duty To Be at the Same Time Prophetic and Compassionate
Our Tradition and Conduct toward the Unfortunate; Transformation, Resuscitation, and Resurrection; Helping the Bereaved

A movie star, visiting a refugee camp for the publicity of it, was repelled by the sight. On his first morning, he washed his hands about a
dozen times. He didn't want to touch anything, least of all the people,
all covered with sores and scabs. Then, just as he was bending down
to one little tyke, mainly for the photographer's benefit, someone ac-
cidentally stood on the child's fingers. The child screamed, and in a
reflex, the movie star, forgetting the child's dirt and sores, grabbed him.
He always remembered that warm little body clinging to him and the
crying instantly stopping. At that moment he knew he had much to learn
about loving, but he knew, too, that at least he'd started.

Today's Gospel is about compassion. It presents all the charm,
color, suspense, and pathos of a good short story. As Jesus entered the
town of Nain in Galilee, two crowds met, approaching from different
directions. One was the large crowd (v. 11) that accompanied Jesus.
The other was the large crowd from the city (v. 12) in a funeral procession. Few processions, even today, evoke as much awe as that which
wends its way to the cemetery. Today, the headlights of the hearse,
followed by an automotive train of mourners, declare, "This is the
march of death; stand back!" Cars stop at intersections; other drivers
avert their eyes; children on their way to or from school, as well as some
adults, gape wide-eyed at crosswalks.

The crowd in today's Gospel funeral procession contained not
only relatives and friends engaged in the merciful work of burying the
dead, but also hired musicians and mourners whose flutes and cymbals and shrill cries created a kind of frenzy. St. Luke's description of
the dead man as the only son of a widowed mother contains the age-
less sorrow of the world, and the tears: the world of broken hearts.
Whereas others held back, the widow can hardly get near enough to
her son's body. This is the burial of her last hope. She's present now

as she was the day she gave him birth, mother now as she was mother then. She grieves as one who would be willing to change places with the deceased, to enter death in order to restore life. Surrounded by friends, she is yet alone.

To all that pathos, Luke adds the compassion that underlaid Jesus' being the best of what we mean by being human. Jesus, far from being, as some people picture him, apathetic and aloof, was again and again overwhelmed with pity, moved to his depths at tragedy. Luke adds to Jesus' compassion his power: For the first of many times, Luke calls Jesus "Lord" — the only evangelist to use that expression before the resurrection. Jesus stepped forward and touched the coffin (v. 14). The coffin of the time meant the long open wicker basket in which mourners placed the linen-wrapped body. Then Luke the physician records that, to the surprise of everyone, the dead man sat up (v. 15).

Now, there are those who see here only a miracle of diagnosis: that is, that Jesus, with a prescience beyond the times, saw that the man wasn't really dead, but in a cataleptic trance. Jesus would thus have prevented the man from being buried alive, as then happened to some because of poor medical skills and quick burials. But we must remember that the one writing is Luke the physician, who we may presume was more observant than the ordinary person about things like this. Even more, the person performing the miracle is Jesus, who showed that he's Lord not only of life but of death.

It would have been lacking in compassion at such a time to speak to the lonely widow the lines that the unknown poet put into the mouth of God to parents upon the death of a child:

> "I'll lend you, for a little while, a child of mine," He said,
> "For you to love while he lives, and mourn when he is dead.
> It may be six or seven years, or twenty-two, or three.
> But will you, 'til I call him back, take care of him for me?
> He'll bring his charms to gladden you, and shall his stay be brief,
> You'll have his lovely memories as solace for your grief.
> "I cannot promise he will stay, as all from earth return,
> But there are lessons taught down there I want this child to learn.
> I've looked the wide world over in my search for teachers true,
> And from the throngs that crowd life's lanes, I have selected you.
> Now will you give him all your love — not think the labor vain,
> Nor hate me when I come to call to take him back again."

I fancied that I heard them say, "Dear Lord, thy will be done.
For all the joy this child shall bring, the risk of grief we'll run.
We'll shower him with tenderness and love him while we may,
And for the happiness we've known, forever grateful stay.
And should the angels call for him much sooner than we planned,
We'll brave the bitter grief that comes, and try to understand."

Rather, Jesus gave him to his mother. Jesus must have taken him, and well-nigh carried him, and placed him in the arms of his mother. When the mother's arms had closed round the body of her son, only then did Jesus step aside and go his way, possibly to hide his tears.

Luke consciously relates his story of Jesus to similar stories about the prophets Elijah and Elisha. The story of Elijah in today's First Reading is part of the "Elijah Cycle" of stories which, like so many other stories about the prophets, is told to enhance the reputation of the prophet and thus help give authority to his word.

The climax of the Elijah story isn't so much the physical restoration of the life of the young man whose death made his widowed mother destitute as it is the widow's profession of faith. The widow, who was a non-Jew from the region of Sidon, received the spiritual gift of salvation through looking after Elijah and hearing from him the word of God. Whereas Elijah had raised the son of the widow at Zarephath and Elisha the son of the widow at Shunem with dramatic symbolic rites, Jesus did it just by the power of his word.

St. Paul, too, like Jesus and Elijah, was a prophet and, like them, had to face calumnies, envies, and mistrust. In today's portion of his letter to the Galatians, Paul defends his Gospel; his thesis is that his Gospel is not of human origin (v. 11), but comes from God, and is the common possession of all the Apostles. This Gospel Paul received through a revelation of Jesus Christ (v. 12) while he was on the road to Damascus to kill Christians. This doesn't mean that the facts about Jesus were communicated miraculously to Paul: He did have to depend in addition on traditional teaching.

Paul's life proved what trust in God can do. His former way of life in Judaism (v. 13), humanly considered, hardly provided the psychological background from which his Christian Gospel would have developed. As a Pharisee, he had persecuted the Church of God beyond measure and tried to destroy it. As a Pharisee, he had strongly rejected everything that departed from the Mosaic Law and its interpretations by the rabbis. Toward the Church of God, which he would eventually come to see as reflecting the First Testament assembly of the People of God in the desert (*qehal Yahweh*, Nb 16:20; 20:4), he had a scorched-earth policy.

But the time came (v. 15) when all that changed. When that profound conversion happens — when a person completely changes values and does a thorough turn-about in life — there has to be an explanation. Paul's explanation was the intervention of God. And God's action wasn't haphazard, but planned: God chose to reveal His Son through Paul (v. 16). Paul didn't see himself chosen for honor, however, but for service — the same as the housewife who prepares her children for school or the engineer who builds a bridge.

To think through what had happened to him and to speak with God before he in turn spoke to people, Paul first went on a retreat. His next stop took courage: It was Damascus, to which Paul had been traveling to persecute the Church when he was knocked off his horse. All Damascus knew that. And the Christians knew what kind of man Paul had been. They wanted no part of him.

Paul's next step took an equal amount of courage: He went up to Jerusalem (v. 18). The Christians in Jerusalem, as his former victims, unable to believe that he had changed, might well ostracize him. His former Jewish associates there, too, might well have nothing to do with one whom they considered a deserter and a traitor. But we have to have the courage to face our past. There are, after all, at least a hundred ways of falling and only one way of standing up. Paul wanted to confer with Kephas — Peter, the head of the Church — and to do that he had to pay the price of facing whatever in Jerusalem might await him. His fifteen-day meeting with Peter was successful, and he also met James, a relative of the Lord. Both Apostles broadened and deepened Paul's faith and trust in the Lord.

All the people in today's readings — Elijah, Paul, and Jesus — are prophets: that is, people who speak on God's behalf to others. And they're all compassionate: that is, they feel for the needs of others. Paul didn't get either prophecy or compassion correct at first, but he learned. Jesus, unlike Elijah, wasn't asked to intervene; what moved him was his extraordinary degree of compassion. We're all, like them, expected to be both prophetic and compassionate — persons who by word and example show people how to be God-like but who at the same time understand people's weaknesses. Some good people try to speak for

God, while being oblivious of the needs of people. Other good people feel deeply for others but, because they aren't in touch with God, their feelings are only on the surface.

No matter where we find ourselves, like Paul we can learn. We can learn today to cooperate with God's grace to raise us beyond the limits this world imposes, so that we may be free to love as Christ teaches. That love is life-giving, supporting, transforming, healing, and compassionate. Like Jesus, our compassion must take us, even when not asked, wherever there's the misery of crushed hearts and tears of the bereaved, so that we may promote the unending praise of our heavenly Father and the honor of His Son.

Eleventh Sunday in Ordinary Time
2 S 12:7-10, 13   Gal 2:16, 19-21   Lk 7:36-8:3

Mercy and Love over Correctness and Smugness
Women in the Life of Christ; Faith vs. Legal Observance;
Mercy vs. Smugness; Putting Yourself Right with God

Today's portion of St. Luke's Gospel contains a story that is one of the world's most touching and infinitely tender: It's the story of Jesus' forgiveness of a "bad" woman. A Pharisee named Simon had invited Jesus to dinner (v. 36). Why, we don't know. Likely as not, it was simply because Simon had heard of Jesus, thought it might be interesting to have a celebrity in his house, and asked him to come; this would explain Simon's combination of respect and discourtesy. Jesus accepted the invitation.

A sinful woman in the city (v. 37) heard of the dinner and invited herself. Her crashing the party was easy, in view of the custom that when a rabbi was at a meal as a guest, anyone was free to come and listen to him. What could she have looked like? Well, they say that an artist can look at a pretty girl and see the old woman she'll become. A better artist can look at an old woman and see the pretty girl she used to be. A great artist can look at an old woman, portray her exactly as she is and force the viewer to see the pretty girl she used to be. More

than that, he can make anyone with only the sensitivity of an arma-
dillo see that that lovely young girl is still alive, imprisoned inside the
old woman's ruined body. Jesus was, at the least, a great artist.

The woman was attracted to come either because she had had
some contact with Jesus in his wanderings, or simply because she liked
what she had heard of him. In writing of her, Luke is very delicate: He
mentions neither her name nor what her sins were. She was probably
either a prostitute or married to an outcast like a tax-collector. It's obvious that most people don't like tax collectors even today.

What may be less obvious is that most people still don't like prostitutes. In the United States, the highest arrest figures aren't for murder, robbery, or rape, but for prostitution. A third of all female prisoners are incarcerated for prostitution. In many cases, prostitutes were
seriously abused as children sexually and in other ways by their fathers.
Rape of prostitutes is rarely reported, investigated, prosecuted, or taken
seriously. In one study, female prostitutes reported being raped an average of 16 times annually by their pimps and 33 times a year by their
clients. Many times street prostitutes are robbed, harassed, beaten, and
murdered — in ancient times as now, living at all times on dangerous
ground. The system largely ignores the role of men who hire prostitutes.

Most people suspect that this woman's sins were of the sort that
we're embarrassed to admit in confession, but love to read in the "tell
all" autobiographies of media stars. She had going against her not only
the prohibition against close female contact with men outside the home;
she had the added handicap of being known as a sinner. So, although
she had been brave enough to come, she stood behind Jesus at his feet
as he reclined at table (v. 38), where he couldn't see her right away.

Like other Jewish women, she wore around her neck an expensive vial of perfume. She intended to anoint his feet with it. As she
stooped to do so, she was so overcome with emotion that she unex-
pectedly burst into tears. She hadn't foreseen this outburst, and she
spontaneously loosened her hair and wiped and kissed his feet repeat-
edly before anointing them.

Through it all, the host Simon was silently condemning Jesus for
not being prophet enough to perceive the known character of the woman
(v. 39). Jesus proved himself to be a prophet by reading Simon's secret thoughts. In answer to Simon's thoughts (v. 40), Jesus presented a
rabbi-like case study about two men who owed money, one a great deal

and the other less (v. 41). The creditor wrote off both debts (v. 42). When Jesus asked Simon which of them will love the creditor more, one can almost feel the insolent coldness in Simon's answer: "The one, I suppose, whose larger debt was forgiven" (v. 43).

Then Jesus showed Simon for what he was. Jesus' phrases about expected courtesy (vv. 44-46) beautifully portrayed the Oriental etiquette of the time. When a guest entered a house, he could expect the host to show certain marks of respect. The host was to place his hands on his guest's shoulder and wish him *shalom*, the most-prized gift of peace. Another duty of hospitality was to cleanse and comfort the guest's feet with cool water after the dust of the dirt roads had penetrated his sandals. And the host could be expected to place a few drops of attar of roses on the guest's head. Simon, probably thinking Jesus a country bumpkin, and being unmindful that courtesy, like bravery, is saved through being spent, had fulfilled none of these duties.

The woman made up for it. And, as in Jesus' case study, her many sins were forgiven, whereupon she showed great love (v. 47). The tables had turned: It was now Jesus who was inviting Simon. We aren't told Simon's response. The friend of sinners then said to the woman, "Your faith has saved you; go in peace" (v. 50).

Through the contrasts between the woman and Simon, Jesus enabled us to see her superiority over the Pharisee. She expressed the love that stems from repentance, whereas Simon's pride prevented him from even acknowledging his sinfulness. Her self-giving attitude was in stark contrast to the devout Simon's calculated reserve. But the major contrast between them was that Simon wasn't conscious of any personal need, therefore felt no love, and so couldn't receive forgiveness; the woman was conscious of nothing but her need, therefore was overwhelmed with love, especially for one who understood, and so was forgiven. The one thing that shuts us off from God is self-sufficiency; a sense of need will open us to God, Who is love.

After this incident, the synagogues were no longer as open to Jesus as they had once been, so he preached as he wandered. And, as he journeyed from one town and village to another, preaching and proclaiming the good news (8:1), he accepted the help not only of the Twelve Apostles, but of many women. And, as with the Apostles, the women were startlingly different from one another (vv. 2f.). Luke's Gospel is noted for his attention to the underprivileged, outcasts, sinners, and women. Jewish society of the time had little regard for any of them, non-Jewish society even less. When we consider that women couldn't be disciples of a rabbi, and were thought incapable of understanding the Mosaic Law, the dignity that Jesus assigned them is amazing.

From the lowly sinful woman today's liturgy takes us to a sinful king: David who, though mighty in earthly power, received no special treatment from God. The First Testament painted this great figure with his warts as well as his glories, his fall from grace as well as his faithfulness to God. David, softened by success and affluence, was captivated by the beauty of Bathsheba and committed adultery with her. Learning that he had gotten her pregnant, David sent for her husband Uriah, hoping Uriah would sleep with her and thus eliminate suspicion from David. David's plan failed: David, from whom violence was never far, had Uriah killed, and he married Bathsheba, who bore him a son. David's intoxication by prosperity had led him to forget the God Who gave him prosperity, and to adultery and murder.

It's only natural that one who's wronged should ask, "How could you do this to me, after all I've done for you?" And that's what God said, through His prophet Nathan, to David (vv. 7f.). God had chosen and anointed David as king, rescued him from being killed by Saul, given him Saul's house and wives in accord with custom, presented him with a united kingdom, and done still more (v. 8). Counterbalancing God's goodness to David was David's terrible sin (v. 10). Nathan, like Jesus, told a story to illustrate how important taking responsibility for sin is as a first step on the road to repentance. David wound up sincerely sorry (v. 13). And so he was forgiven.

St. Paul, to put himself right with God in the same way that David and the sinful woman had, had been trying with all the intensity of his dynamic personality to be correct in his observance of the Mosaic Law. His attempt failed, which left an ever deeper sense of frustration and helplessness. It isn't through mere correct legal observance (v. 16) that a person is put right with God, "but through faith in Jesus Christ" — that attitude by which a person accepts the divine revelation made known through Jesus and responds to it with complete dedication (v. 19).

Therefore, Paul valued only the new condition received from Jesus, who is the source of holiness (v. 20). Faith in Jesus reshapes one internally, supplying not just a new psychological make-up, but a new principle of life in the very core of one's being. So in Paul Jesus proved to be more powerful than the Mosaic Law. The Law is an external set of rules; Jesus is a living presence, doing what the Law could never do: changing a person from within. Jesus' indwelling reshapes one's life, and must eventually penetrate one's psychological awareness as well. Our being right with God, therefore, doesn't come from any law, but from the sacrifice of Christ. To say otherwise is to nullify the grace of God (v. 21).

What's the key to forgiveness? Like King David and the woman in the Gospel, it's taking responsibility for our evil and being sorry for it. We need to see and understand our situation before we can change. If we've observed the law to an extent that we've become smug like Simon the Pharisee, we need to recognize that when the pharisee inside us suppresses the sinner who also lurks there, we need to throw ourselves at the feet of Jesus, wash them with the tears of our responsibility, and beg forgiveness.

TWELFTH SUNDAY IN ORDINARY TIME
Zc 12:10f.   Gal 3:26-29   Lk 9:18-24

Life through Death
Quality of Life through Christianity's Paradoxes

A paradox is a statement that is inherently contradictory or seems opposed to common sense and yet is true in fact — for example, "mobilizing for peace," or "all of us have a perennial longing to be what we're not." There is paradox all around us. For example, common sense tells us that the earth is flat, but in fact it's round; that the sun goes round the earth, whereas in fact it is the opposite; that if you fire a bullet from a revolver at the same time as you let another bullet fall, the latter will hit the ground before the former, whereas in fact both will reach it at the same time.

Jesus used paradoxes often. Today's Gospel is full of paradox. Let's consider the scene. Jesus and his Apostles were in the north, outside their own territory, near the town of Caesarea Philippi, named "Caesarea" in honor of the Emperor, and "Philippi" in honor of the sycophant tetrarch Philip who built it, to distinguish it from the many other towns and cities dedicated to Caesar. In this pagan area there were no crowds around Jesus. And Jesus was feeling very deeply the rejection of his own people. He prayed, as he had done before when he had faced important events such as the selection of the twelve.

Needing a feel for his identity, he first asked his followers, "Who do the crowds say that I am?" If the crowd's answers were wrong, then despite his popularity at such times as the multiplication of the loaves and fish, this opinion poll would show that he was a failure. If their answers were correct, he would have at least a glimmer of hope and could go further in his teachings. All of their answers — that he was John the Baptist, or Elijah, or some other prophet — had overtones of the "Conquering King" concept of the Messiah. So he would have to turn their ideas upside down. Somehow, he would have to get across the paradoxical connection between the Messiah and the cross.

Timorously now, he approached an even more important question: "But who do you say that I am?" These men were his closest trainees — more, his closest friends. More was hanging on their answer than on the crowd's. For Peter, Jesus was the realization and concretization of all Israel's hopes. So, in the impulsive way that was his custom, he answered that Jesus was the Messiah of God. Jesus was relieved. Now he could tell them what God expected of them and of him, what sort of death was reserved for him, what glory would be his, and what demands would be made of his followers. He could refer to such First Testament prophecies of his suffering as the third-century B.C. collection known as "Zechariah" in today's First Reading and, if they all believed what Peter had said, they wouldn't be scandalized.

Again the paradoxes: Jesus' life and their lives, judged perhaps failures by other standards, by God's standards were a success; and, because of the false current notions of Messiahship and the danger of further unnecessary misunderstandings, he still had to forbid their telling anyone of his being the Messiah.

Referring to himself in the words "Son of Man" from the Book of Daniel — an assertion of divine authority — Jesus spoke of the sufferings which he must endure. It's interesting to see in St. Luke's Gospel the times when Jesus used this word *must*: when, as a child, his parents were looking for him in Jerusalem, he said, "I must be in my Father's house"; when his ministry in Galilee was so successful that the people tried to keep him from leaving them, he said, " I must proclaim the good news of the kingdom of God to the other towns"; when threatened by Herod and the Pharisees in Jerusalem, he answered, "I must continue on my way"; and over and over he mentioned that he must go to his cross. And now, he must suffer greatly, be rejected, and be killed (v. 22).

Jesus' next words have no "must" about them: "If anyone wishes to come after me... whoever wishes to save his life." They're an invitation — an invitation to the three elements that constitute the essence of being Christian: denying oneself, carrying one's cross, and following. To be baptized into Christ, in the words of St. Paul in today's excerpt from his letter to the Galatians, means adopting Jesus' attitude. To be Christian has as many implications as the titles we use in other areas of everyday life. When we use "Mr. and Mrs.," for example, or "boss," or "brother/sister," each of these titles conjures up relationships and obligations. So does the title "Christian."

But we're free. Only a few people contemplate the observation of the philosopher (Kierkegaard) that "life can only be understood backwards, but it must be lived forwards." For many, life is mindless; "saving" life comes from no deeper a level than trying to acquire all the comforts possible, and they prefer the manipulative logic of the TV commercial to Christ's honest laying out the cost as well as the invitation. But, in truth, the consequence of accepting Jesus' invitation is to pay the price in daily installments, to wholeheartedly take up one's cross each day — remembering, though, that it's God Who leads, and He asks us but to follow.

The greatest paradox of all is the last line of today's Gospel, that whoever clings to life will lose it, and whoever lets go of his life for Jesus' sake will save it. Yet people in a society that's trying to be smokeless, low-fat, and caffeine-free seem to be attempting to save their lives all the time.

But — again paradoxically — the saying is also good psychology. If we examine the varieties of meanings for the word "life" — from ordinary bodily life to eternal life in the kingdom of God — we see that, unless we live this life without seeking personal advantage, we never find true happiness. People who are always letting go of their life are like the Lake of Galilee, which is constantly giving forth the waters it receives — so its waters are fresh, wholesome, useful, and needed. People who are always clinging to their life are like the Dead Sea which, with no outlet, keeps all the water it receives and gives nothing — so its waters become stale, useless, and unattractive: a salty waste. It's through today's paradoxes of Christianity that we find our freedom, joy, and fulfillment.

Now, Jesus asks the important question, "Who do you say that I am?" of every one of us. Our answer has to be a deeply-felt personal one. It can't come solely from the Pope, or the Church, or anyone else: To be meaningful, it must come also from ourselves. And there's something wrong if our answer is the equivalent of saying that Jesus is something remote and strange, like an android; or only powerful, like Rambo; or, worse, a wimp.

Even though every age, every culture, and every person has been presented with the same question about Jesus' identity, the answers have been as diverse as the cultures from which they arose. For the early Greek Christians, Christ could best be understood in terms of the *logos*, the divine Word, the principle of wisdom, perfection, and harmony in the cosmos. For the first Jewish Christians, Jesus was the sacrificial paschal lamb, the reconciler, and the fulfillment of the Law.

For a feudal society, the notion of Christ was based on the idea of ransoming: Christ was the one who paid the price for salvation and ransomed us from the evil one. For the reformers during the beginning of commerce, Christ was tied in with justification: He was the one who satisfied the "debt" owed to the Father. For the new-Scholastic philosophers, Christ was the king who ruled the universe and in whose total spiritual sovereignty the Church shared. For some in the early twentieth century, influenced by discoveries in new sciences, especially psychology, sociology, and anthropology, Christ became the purpose and goal of the evolutionary process, the Omega Point.

Today, different scholars sketch the historical Jesus variously as a political rebel, an ancient magician, a maverick Pharisee, a thoroughly Jewish prophet announcing that God was about to restore Israel, or a Hellenistic gadfly with no mission beyond questioning the world's conventions. For many of the well-fed and well-off, Christ has taken the form of a palliative, satisfying the hungry spirits of a sated consumer society; in this perspective, Christ satisfies people's search for meaning and provides a remedy for the nothingness and despair of existence.

For those beset by fears of nuclear holocaust or a polluted earth, Christ becomes a principle of hope. In Latin America, where Christ had been traditionally the guarantor of law and order, liberation theology now sees him as the liberator for the masses — like his Father, setting the captive free, feeding the hungry, and sending the rich away empty.

Still others seem to find justification in the New Testament for their own personal views of Jesus' identity. Aware of this, the Church, as a guardian of the deposit of faith, has over the centuries sought to define a minimal core that all Catholics must accept. Most often these ecclesiastical pronouncements have sought to declare what was "out of bounds," rather than to settle arguments between opposing schools or individuals when both sides maintain these "core" beliefs.

The upshot of it all is that we must stress the primacy of the Christ of faith over the historical Jesus. It's only the Christ of faith whom we encounter in prayer, preaching, and the sacraments, who reveals the Father to us and enables us to journey to the heavenly Father through the process of continual conversion.

May we realize Jesus' full identity, use our freedom to follow him on his terms and, like him — paradoxically — grow to find life through death!

THIRTEENTH SUNDAY IN ORDINARY TIME
1 K 19:16, 19-21   Gal 5:1, 13-18   Lk 9:51-62

Resoluteness
Becoming Free; We Don't Walk Alone; Single-Mindedness;
Courage; Renunciation; Sacrifice; Purification

Soon after a Texas oil well caught fire, the company called in expert fire fighters. The heat was so great, however, that they could get only within 2,000 feet of the rig. In desperation, the manager asked the local volunteer fire department for assistance. Several minutes later, a little old fire truck rattled down the road and came to a stop 50 feet from the fire. The men jumped off the truck, quickly sprayed each other with water, and then proceeded to put out the flames. The elated company president was so grateful that he presented the fire chief with a $10,000 check. When asked what he planned to do with the money, the chief muttered, "Well, first we're going to fix the brakes on that lousy truck."

The firemen's resoluteness and courage are not, of course, the kind that Christianity recommends. Yet, we don't see many artistic representations of resoluteness and courage in the life of Jesus. In the art museums of the world, there are many paintings of him. The paintings follow certain patterns which are appealing either because they're people themes like mother and child, or because they represent important aspects of his life: his birth, the compassion of some of his miracles, his teaching the people, his passion, crucifixion, resurrection, and ascension. One, El Greco's painting of Jesus driving the moneychangers from the Temple, shows a manly, angry Jesus.

Only one painting, to my knowledge, has been attempted on one of the greatest scenes in all Scripture: the opening line of today's Gospel — that, even though Jesus knew he was to die in Jerusalem, he resolutely determined to journey there (v. 51). That painting is a popular one by Hoffman. This Jesus, firm of jaw and resolved, takes us away from the sweetly sentimental Jesuses of much of art. Although Jesus had been in Jerusalem for many reasons before, this time it was to be a solemn visit. Hereafter in St. Luke's Gospel, we see the crowds grow, and we see Jesus providing more and more credentials. With each episode the opposition grows and the tension mounts.

On this occasion, for unknown reasons Jesus decided to travel south to Jerusalem by way of Samaria. This was the more direct route, but not the customary one. The ordinary Jew would have gone roundabout through Perea, in order to avoid fights with their age-old enemies, the Samaritans, as you would avoid a bad neighborhood after dark. This would have been especially true if a Jew's destination was Jerusalem, because one of the sources of the fights was that the Samaritans thought that the true worship of God should take place on their Mount Gerizim instead of in the Jerusalem of the Jews.

When the Samaritans didn't welcome Jesus, the "sons of thunder" — James and John — increased the mounting tension by wanting to imitate Elijah, who had called down fire from heaven to consume the king's soldiers sent to capture him (2 K 1:10-12). Jesus reminded them that his is not the way of destruction, but of mercy and salvation. In his view, peace comes through respecting the freedom and ways of the other. His way of facing the foul-ups and rejection we all experience is to understand the viewpoint of the other. His way suggests that we at times question to what extent we ourselves are responsible for others rejecting Christianity, and how the witness of our lives may give margin for misunderstanding. His way takes every bit as much strong courage as the display of weaponry that the "sons of thunder" and their successors recommend.

Many of us may be tempted to follow James and John with fire and brimstone against the inhospitable, but unlike them Jesus was meek in the face of rejection. The strong Abraham Lincoln was in this same tradition when, in response to his counselors after the Civil War who were recommending that he destroy his enemies, replied, "Don't I destroy my enemies when I make them my friends?" It's the tradition also of the wise man who said that the shortest distance between two people is laughter. Life is often serious, but some serious matters may be taken care of by laughter.

Other episodes also showed the mounting tension. The ever-gentle Jesus' teachings — of peace, light, love, and life — were before crowds with a sprinkling of spies from the establishment. By this time, he had offended all establishments — religious, political, and business — and the die was cast for him in this city called "holy." This entailed a profound sacrifice that in turn involved many other qualities, among them purification, service, and personal fulfillment. Jesus wants sacrifice also from his followers. We see that through the three men who came to him in today's Gospel.

To the first man, who said he would follow Jesus wherever he went (v. 57), Jesus' honest advice, in modern terms, was, "Before you follow me, count the cost." His reply was in the context of poverty. He himself, he said, had nowhere to rest his head (v. 58), and that was true: He'd been driven out of Nazareth, disregarded in Galilee, rejected in Samaria, and threatened with death at Jerusalem, and the house in Capernaum which he now used as a base in Galilee probably belonged to either Peter or Matthew. That didn't mean, however, that Jesus walked alone: He had companions who actively participated in his mission, some who — like James and John — weren't afraid even to make suggestions, and people who helped him.

In dealing with the first man, Jesus knew the tendency of people to be calculating and cautious. Before acting, they study popular trends and graphs, listen to polls, see which way the wind is blowing, and in their hearts treasure security. Jesus had sacrificed security, and we're called upon to do the same to follow him.

The second man illustrates the fact that to follow Jesus one must even sacrifice one's own idea of duty. This man responded to Jesus' invitation by saying that he wanted to go first and bury his father (v. 59). His father wasn't yet dead, or the man wouldn't have been here: It was their custom to bury their dead the same day they died. Jesus made the point that, in everything, there's a crucial moment when one is expected to act. This was this man's crucial moment, and he missed it.

We do the same when we don't realize the benefits of self-discipline. A self-enlarging process, the pain of giving up is the pain of death, but death of the old is birth of the new. The pain of death is the pain of birth, and the pain of birth is the pain of death. The farther one travels on the journey of life, the more births one will experience, and therefore the more deaths.

The third man wanted first to say good-bye to the folks at home. Jesus' answer showed that we must be prepared to sacrifice, if necessary, even affection in our resolve to follow Christ — as he had sacrificed even the affection of a family. "No one who sets a hand to the plow and looks to what was left behind is fit for the kingdom of God" (v. 62). Everyone in that rural audience knew that, if one wants to plow a straight furrow, he has to pay attention to what he's doing and not look elsewhere.

Everyone there also knew the story of Elijah and Elisha as recounted in today's First Reading. In order to follow the prophet Elijah for God's sake, Elisha dramatically used his wooden plowing equipment as fuel to barbecue his oxen for his workmen. (And, having twelve yoke of oxen, he had been rich!) Thus he gave up all his assets, said good-bye to his parents, and broke all ties with his comfortable life; his deeds declared that there was no going back. As Elisha would be considered irresponsible in things that pertain to the world, the worldling is as irresponsible as a streak of lightning in the things that pertain to God.

People who want to sort out life have to remind themselves that Jesus is the way to do it. It's not all hardship, and it's at times a great sense of liberation — an emancipation from all other burdens, which St. Paul mentions in today's Second Reading. We, like Paul, have to make courageous choices for Christ's values over other tensions from outside, and between the flesh and the spirit within.

Today we have many more distractions from resolve and single-mindedness than the rural people of Jesus' audience: easier ways to "go places," television, beckoning amusements. There's a constant search for "where the action is," and fewer opportunities for meditation and quiet. Although we aren't necessarily called to sacrifice security, or our personal idea of duty, or the affection of a family, as Jesus was, today's liturgy challenges us to re-examine the attachments that may be holding us back from a liberated and joyful following of Jesus. Attachment literally means "staked to." That may be a plow or a family or a corpse, by way of a strong chain or a golden thread.

Let's choose God with the same responsible abandon of Elisha following Elijah, the same true freedom mentioned by Paul, and the same firm resolve of Jesus going to Jerusalem. Let's each of us discern the Jerusalem we must face in our lives: whether it be someone we dislike, or a relative with whom we're on the outs, or a duty we've been avoiding. That kind of commitment and effort frees us from the games people play, from the rat race, from peer pressure. It makes us free to be different without being afraid. It's exhilarating, and filled with joy.

FOURTEENTH SUNDAY IN ORDINARY TIME
Is 66:10-14   Gal 6:14-18   Lk 10:1-12, 17-20 (or 10:1-9)

Peace and Rejoicing
Missionary Christianity; Faith; Universality of the Gospel Message

One of the most beautiful words in the English language is "peace." Peace isn't merely the absence of war, and isn't limited to maintaining a balance of powers between adversaries. It's "the tranquility of order"; it's the work of justice and the effect of charity (*Catechism of the Catholic Church*, #2304). And it makes demands.

In fact, the history of humankind seems to be the story of its wars. Of the 3,400 years of recorded human history, 3,166 were years of war and the remaining 234 were years of preparation for war. Our own country was created by war, has a constitution that calls for the funding of its military to fight wars, has averaged a major war every thirty years, regularly boasts of being the world's greatest military power, is the world's largest arms dealer, and has four military academies to train professional soldiers.

A poet has said, not without great truth: "Give me the money that's been spent in war and I will clothe every man, woman, and child in the attire of which kings and queens would be proud. I will build a schoolhouse in every valley over the earth. I will crown every hillside with a place of worship consecrated to the Gospel of peace."

Less poetically, think of the real-life advantages of a country not having to support a military establishment: a better standard of living; a high percent of its national budget for health; a high literacy rate; choice education free at all levels; well-stocked public libraries; theaters and symphony orchestras that are state-subsidized but not state-controlled; a public transport system that's cheap, clean, and punctual; paved roads that are a dream, with scarcely a pothole to be seen; many national parks; and a well-funded ecology program that could convert the republic into a mecca for bird-watchers, and provide clean air and safe water.

Yet not everybody's for peace. The ancient Greeks looked upon war between their own city-states and between themselves and the "barbarians" as part of the order of nature. To Machiavelli, war is necessary to survive. The German philosopher Hegel taught that people must accept war or stagnate. Another German philosopher, Nietzsche, was a representative of the romantic cult of war. He invented the word "superman" (*Übermensch*) and, for the supermen he wanted to create, war is the supreme witness to their superior quality; supermen should never descend to the "slave morality" of Christianity, with its accent on humility and turning the other cheek.

Not all Christians have been complete pacifists. Theologians like St. Augustine approved of what they called a "just war." In the Middle Ages, when the papacy had temporal as well as spiritual power, it also had military strength, and used it. With the advent of nationalism, people like St. Thomas More in his *Utopia* advocated a pragmatic idea of war to defend one's land or allies. And Dante maintained that peace must be attained by the imposition of a world law — paradoxically, by war if necessary.

The seventeenth century, because of growing international commerce, saw the desirability of permanent peace. The eighteenth-century "Enlightenment" had as one of its tenets the law of the "eternal progress" of the human race, in which humanity would eventually secure peace. In the nineteenth century, movements toward peace became more prolific, even if as ineffective as ever.

In our own century, World War I convinced the human race that war is an absolute evil. The League of Nations was established, and after World War II the United Nations, in the belief that wars are permissible on behalf of the maintenance of world peace. World War II also introduced nuclear weaponry, giving the world a preview of possibilities to come. As for nuclear war, multiply by ten the combined atrocities of Attila the Hun, Tamburlaine, Genghis Khan, the barbarians of the Dark Ages, Stalin, and Hitler — and you won't begin to match this crime against the human race. Reflection upon this has resulted in a greater obsession with peace.

In the face of these varying views and problems about peace, today's liturgy is a breath of fresh air. In the Gospel Jesus sends seventy-two disciples "like lambs among wolves" (v. 3) to spread his message of peace — a reminder that, when Moses was worn down with work, the Lord had him designate seventy-two elders to help him. We can't identify Jesus' group as laity, bishops, or presbyters. Whoever they were, their mission was to proclaim the Good News about Jesus.

That Good News, though, was tough and realistic. It included the truth that Jesus didn't come to bring perfection to this world, and that we must not only be grateful for his salvation but must actually share it by carrying our responsibilities. Although we can't offer instant solutions to all problems or suffering, Jesus' Good News can alone provide true peace.

Realistically, the disciple must be able to live in accord with St. Paul in today's closing words of his letter to the Galatians. This is his only letter which lacks a "thanksgiving" section — the reason being that Paul was very angry when he wrote: He felt that he had absolutely nothing to thank the Galatians for. There remained the tension between him and the Jewish-Christian trouble-makers who, even though they believed that Jesus was the Messiah, were insisting that all Galatian Christians abide by Jewish religious law. To Paul this was blasphemy. As Paul discovered, peace isn't easy. Yet he wished the Galatians peace.

Jesus recognizes that his message of peace is subversive. His idea is that, if the world wants peace, the wolves must swap power for trust, manipulation for solidarity, greed for sharing. That isn't a world that the wolves of war and violence can survive in. It makes them very angry, and vicious in their attack.

Jesus tells us through his emissaries that the kingdom of God "is at hand for you" (v. 9). The kingdom of God is "at hand" and "for you": It's not up in the sky or across the sea, but right here with us whenever and wherever we want to call upon it. With our cooperation, God's power can transform this world, with all its problems, into a place of peace and justice.

The characteristic quality of this kingdom, as pictured in today's section of Isaiah, is the Hebrew *shalom*; *salaam* in other Semitic languages. This beautiful word is untranslatable, but peace is its dominant characteristic — and also harmony, joy, well-being in every sense, and prosperity (as it's translated today in Isaiah). Metaphorically, the "city of peace" — "Jerusalem" — can be wherever we are if we're a child of peace.

God's kingdom already looks to a heavenly city on earth and, interestingly, Isaiah's dominant images for this relationship between God and us are feminine: the child at the large, consoling breast of its mother and the mother comforting her children. The image suggests a privileged intimacy, a wondrous dependency, even a child's first ecstasy — a nursing babe, arms outstretched and lost in speechless delight. Isaiah also proclaims that, if people cooperate, God will send peace flowing like a river through any landscape that's dry of it.

Jesus' advice that one isn't to greet anyone along the way isn't to mean a cold unfriendliness, but a reminder that there's a seriousness and an urgency about seeking and spreading peace; we mustn't indulge in distractions, but get on with the work. Jesus further advises that his missionaries for peace take no walking staff, traveling bag, or sandals — this to dramatize one's willingness to trust in God's providence. The person then becomes vulnerable, making it possible for God to work through our vulnerability. Jesus' true disciples must have no bag of tricks, no dog-and-pony show (thus different from the hucksters of religion we see in the streets of that time and on TV today).

How we can find peace is contained in the words Dante put over the door to heaven: "In His will is our peace." Peace, in the final analysis, means oneness with God's will. The search for peace must begin with individuals like you and me, then radiate out — to family, community, nation, and world. In that process, we recognize the truth of the Chinese saying that "the first step is the longest." Peace isn't a given; it has to be continually worked for, and worked at. If you haven't found Jesus' deep peace, take the first step — the long one — of praying for a heart to welcome it. When that's achieved, we have peace of soul, even in the world's imperfection.

May all of us be free of discouragement, impatience, and anger in failure in our efforts for peace, and be sincere, humble, and wise in seeking it; peace-seeking and peace-making are the highest callings within civilization; in our daily lives we must reflect nonviolence as a positive force. Let's repeat constantly the beautiful words Jesus advised: "Peace be to this household" (v. 5). Peace is our greeting, and peace is our mark. Peace is one of the signs of the presence of the kingdom. May God's peace be in our hearts and in our homes.

FIFTEENTH SUNDAY IN ORDINARY TIME
Dt 30:10-14   Col 1:15-20   Lk 10:25-37

Christ's Teachings:
Stimulus to Human Growth and Potential
Christ's Teachings: Best in All the World; Christ's Laws: Too High for People?

If you help a person on the street whose life is in danger and if you're in any way considered negligent, you may be legally liable. For this reason, many physicians won't stop at the scene of an accident. So some jurisdictions have enacted what are called "Good Samaritan" laws — that one who attempts the rescue of a person in peril, provided the attempt wasn't made with complete recklessness, can't be charged with contributory negligence if the victim's condition worsens. To know the law about daily activities is important.

In matters of eternal life, it's even more important; thus the scholar of the law in today's Gospel who posed the question to Jesus about what he must do to inherit eternal life (v. 25). It's a lawyer's question. Jesus, knowing the complexities of the matter, sent the lawyer back to the law: "What is written in the law? How do *you* read it?" (v. 26). And the lawyer's answer, to love God wholeheartedly and one's neighbor as oneself, is the heartpiece of the Jewish Scriptures. The first part of the answer, to love God from the heart, with generosity and love, is from the Book of Deuteronomy.

Today's portion of that book is one of the most consoling and joyful ever written. It says simply that God is our life, and that our lives can reveal God. It recounts an important moment in our understanding of humanity and God. The words of Moses reveal a stage in the revelation that God's love, which created the universe, is always with us. The all-powerful Creator will in time become the child of Bethlehem.

As for Deuteronomy's heartpiece, religious Jews still put it in the little boxes (phylacteries) which they wear on their forehead and on their arm when they pray, place it at their door posts, pray it daily during life, and want it on their lips as they die. When Deuteronomy speaks of this command enjoining you *today* (v. 11), the "today" means whenever the passage is read. We're not to think of God's commands as remote and far from our minds, but as something very near (v. 14).

The second part of the lawyer's answer, to love "your neighbor as yourself," is from the Book of Leviticus (19:18), and is more problematic. It was that part that the lawyer grasped at to show that he had had sufficient reason for asking the question in the first place and that he wasn't to be dismissed as a mere schoolboy. He asked, "And who is my neighbor?" (v. 29). The Jews' regular answer embraced only their fellow-Jews. Jesus' answer was part of his moral revolution. It was the story of the Good Samaritan.

The story was about a man as he went down from Jerusalem to Jericho (v. 30). The road connecting Jerusalem, which was about 2,500 feet above sea level, and Jericho, about 800 feet below, dropped about 3,300 feet in a little more than twenty miles. The road was narrow, at times consisting of no more than boulder-bordered paths. It had many sudden turns — all of which made it a hunting ground for brigands. The traveler of the story may have been foolish for traveling alone along this road, and may have had no one but himself to blame for his falling victim to robbers. Anyone could have used that as an excuse for not helping him.

The first to pass by, a Jewish priest (v. 31), a symbol of religious power, could have the excuse that, for ritual purity, he would have to avoid coming near a corpse, which the wounded man appeared to be: The robbers had left him half-dead (v. 30). The next to pass by was a Levite (v. 32), an assistant at the Temple, a symbol of secular power. He, too, could say that he had to take every precaution to remain "pure," or he wouldn't be able to perform his duties.

The one who possessed the secret of eternal life was the last to arrive: a Samaritan (v. 33). He reached the secret without the lawyer's learning, without priestly or levitical concern for purity, and without their status. He was moved with compassion — spontaneously, kindly, on a person-to-person level. In his act of mercy the known world of religion and power were turned upside-down.

Jesus' choice of the Samaritan as the hero of his story made his audience wince. The Jews and the Samaritans didn't get along at all, for the same reasons some modern peoples don't get along: race, politics, religion. In this case, it was a combination of all three. Racially, the Samaritans were Semites the same as the Jews, but they had for a long time intermarried, which the Jews strongly opposed. Politically, although the Samaritans shared part of the same land as the Jews, they had often collaborated with the enemies of Judah. And religiously, the Samaritans didn't accept all the Jewish Scriptures, ignored Jerusalem, and looked to their own Temple on Mount Gerizim as their center. Jewish law considered Samaritan testimony worthless in court. In retaliation, the Samaritans refused hospitality to any Jew passing through Samaria.

This Samaritan — who would himself be excluded from being a neighbor in the then-current Jewish meaning of the word — didn't stop to consider that bandits then as now at times used decoys in the road to fake injury. He wasn't afraid of losing time. He didn't grudge the trouble. He generously paid the innkeeper two days' wages — even though, because of the danger of robbers, it's not likely that he had much money with him. He poured oil and wine over the victim's wounds and bandaged them. Oil and wine were the common remedies for bruises and cuts: the wine for its cleansing, astringent properties, the oil for its soothing and healing. And his credit was good: He promised to pay any further expense on his way back, and his promise was accepted.

When Jesus asked which of these three was neighbor to the robbers' victim (v. 36), the lawyer couldn't even bring himself to say the despised word "Samaritan": He answered that it was the one who treated him with mercy (v. 37). This was a new definition of neighbor. In the Book of Leviticus, the neighbor was one who was to be loved, such as a countryman. The new definition of neighbor is one who loves. Jesus was at the same time answering the important question that should have been asked: "Who is capable of becoming a neighbor?"

Jesus' admonition to go and do likewise was a date to be remembered in the history of humanity! He was saying what no other reli-

gion in history ever said: that everyone in the world, without exception, is our neighbor. Every place we go is from Jerusalem to Jericho.
If we love like the Samaritan loved we will be compassionate, attentive, and affectionate to all. The human race grows in sensitivity. Just
as we look back in history at some practices of people and call them
barbarous, we, too, may be looked upon by future generations as insensitive in many ways — to gays, for example, and lesbians, and victims of AIDS. The human race has had God's invitation for almost
2,000 years now to grow into Jesus.

That's what today's portion of the letter to the Colossians is about.
To a non-Jewish church at Colossae, confused about the identity of
Jesus, this section of the letter — written by St. Paul or in his name by
one versed in his way of thinking — is one of the most highly developed theologies of Jesus. It beautifully tells us, in brief, that Jesus —
and not the Torah, as the Jews believed — is everything. In himself,
Jesus is the image of the invisible God (v. 15). Jesus is also everything
to creation: All things in heaven and on earth were created through him
and for him (v. 16).

Jesus is everything to the Church, of which he's the head (v. 18).
Head signifies the principles of authority and vitality. He's the Church's
beginning, not only in the sense of time, as 1776 was the beginning of
the United States, but in the sense of being the source, like the bub-
bling brook is the beginning of the stream and remains with it. Jesus
is, in fact, everything to all things: For in him all God's fullness was
pleased to dwell (v. 19).

Today's liturgy teaches us to ask not only, "Who is my neighbor?", but also, "Am I a neighbor?" Have I become so used to seeing,
either in real life or in vivid color on TV, the suffering of the victims
of violence, of famine, or of injustice, that my heart has become so
hardened that I find it difficult to love? Do I consider my religion a
vertical one, containing only my going up to God and God coming down
to me, or also a horizontal one, embracing broken humanity as well,
through whom we might find God?

Do I, like the priest or Levite in Jesus' story, make rational-sound-
ing excuses to relegate caring for the sick only to doctors, nurses, chap-
lains, and others who work in pastoral or health care? Do I, like the
scholar in today's Gospel, have faultless book-knowledge of the law,
but am careless about living it? Or do I, like the Samaritan, listen to
my heart and put my religion into practice? Am I repelled by those who

aren't beautiful, or who reek with the stench of alcohol or urine, or who are weak or foolish or unintelligent?

Or does my love, like the good Samaritan's, prompt me to end up not only in feeling sorry for the misfortunes of others, but in doing something about them? Every day God counts on our human hands to help raise the unfortunate from dung-heaps. Jesus seeks people committed to the love and care of one another and the earth under the guidance of God's peace and justice. That should be us! But we often miss the victims on the side of the road. Real love seeks not legal limits, but opportunities to help.

SIXTEENTH SUNDAY IN ORDINARY TIME
Gn 18:1-10   Col 1:24-28   Lk 10:38-42

One Thing Only Is Required in Life
Thinkers and Doers: Divided?; The Duties of Hospitality;
What to Remember in Times of Worry

The ancient Greeks said that all human temperaments depended on which of the four elements — fire, earth, air, or water — of which they thought the universe was made was dominant in a person. Modern psychological theories are more detailed and sophisticated. They look to whether you're, for example, creative, inspirational, an achiever, an objective thinker, emotional, a perfectionist, or going in many other directions.

Today's Gospel shows two temperaments that were completely different from each other: Martha and Mary. They were both close to Jesus. Bethany, the village where they lived, was just a few miles from Jerusalem. Jesus was on his way through to Jerusalem, where he was going in order to die. Jesus' visit to Martha and Mary was characterized by graciousness, gentleness, and mutual respect. That a woman could be mistress of a house and invite a man into her home would be almost inconceivable in the patriarchal society of first-century Palestine. Nevertheless, Jesus treated the sisters as two responsible persons who could run their own lives.

Mary sat at the Lord's feet listening to him (v. 39). That meant real listening, which is love in action and is hard work. Most people don't listen well: Even though we may feel in our social relationships that we're listening very hard, what we're often doing is listening selectively, with a preset agenda in mind, wondering how we can end the conversation as quickly as possible or redirect it in ways satisfactory to us. Even in marriage, where listening as love in action is most appropriate, couples often don't truly listen to each other.

Jesus didn't think it unbecoming to converse with a woman like this, although all other rabbis of that time would. Jesus, rejecting the Talmudic view that it was "better to burn the Torah than to teach it to women," welcomed her. And, challenging the then-current notion that a woman was unable to learn, he taught her.

Martha welcomed Jesus, possibly because her temperament was dominant over her sister Mary's, and she was probably also the elder of the two. It was therefore she who undertook the duties of hospitality. Showing a familiarity which suggests that she had known Jesus for a long time, she complained to him about being left alone in the kitchen (v. 40). Why, then, didn't Jesus simply go into the kitchen, where he could be with both Martha and Mary, and thus settle the difficulty? Because, for one thing, the idea of a house as a home as we know it didn't take shape until much closer to our own time. The interior design of a house at the time of Jesus would allow for only a very small kitchen. Such attributes in the home as ease, comfort, and leisure as we know them hadn't yet developed.

Martha's eagerness to abide by the laws of generous Middle Eastern hospitality was turning into criticism. She was giving the wrong kind of hospitality; Jesus didn't want what she was offering. Jesus, with the press of the crowds from which he'd come and to which he was going to have to return, with the tensions of his confrontations, and with the suffering that was before him, wanted most of all an oasis of peace and quiet. When we're trying to be hospitable, we shouldn't try to do it in our way: We should try to think of what the recipients of our hospitality need and want. Mary understood this, and Martha didn't. Jesus' gentle, loving, and inoffensive correction of Martha (v. 41) was directed at her being preoccupied to the point of distraction about many things. The problem was not that Martha was working, but that she was obsessed with working.

One's home has been called the setting in which both the most ardent ties of love are formed and at the same time the deepest hatred simmers. The Scripture stories of Cain and Abel and of Esau and Jacob, as well as of Martha and Mary, show that since ancient times family rifts are common. As siblings grow, feelings are often hidden, but old patterns don't always stay buried and can surface during tense moments.

Jesus then spoke to Martha those often-misunderstood words that apply to all of us: There's need of only one thing (v. 42). What is that one thing? Many have thought that Jesus was contrasting Martha with Mary, that Martha had missed out completely, that there's a conflict between listening and doing, that there are two opposing states of life — contemplation and work — and somehow the contemplative life is better.

Work isn't separable from contemplation. Work is whatever we expend our energy on for the sake of accomplishing or achieving something. Work in this sense isn't what we do for a living, but what we do with our living. Parents and teachers both work at the upbringing of children, but only teachers receive paychecks for it. The housework of parents is real work, though it brings in no revenue. The schoolwork, homework, and teamwork of children are all real work, though the payoff isn't in dollars. The opposite of work isn't leisure or play or having fun, but idleness — not investing ourselves in anything.

So we have to look at Martha and Mary together. It just happened that at this particular moment Mary attended to God by sitting still; at another time, perhaps even in the next moment, Mary could have attended to God's interests while helping with the work. All Christians must balance both action and contemplation. Thinking without doing produces unrealistic types who have their feet firmly planted in midair. Doing without thinking produces people who efficiently speed through life without enough regard to the right direction.

The true follower of Jesus is one who, like Mary — and like Jesus himself — can go aside at times from the clutter of the less important details of life to be alone with the Father, and who, like Martha — and again like Jesus — can go about doing good for others. Work and prayer together have remained a good Christian tradition. The Benedictines encapsulate it in their inscription, *Ora et labora*: "Pray and work." This requires us to face many difficulties in prayer, some unique to our day: erroneous notions of prayer, the mentality of our world, seeming failure in prayer, distraction, dryness, lukewarm faith, and selfish laxity, among others (*Catechism of the Catholic Church*, 2726-2733).

The story of Martha and Mary also preeminently entails hospitality. In Judeo-Christian belief, there's no finer work. One of the great adages in the Christian tradition is, *Venit hospes, venit Christus*: "When a guest comes, Christ comes." This notion characterized early America: It was a rare day then when some stranger didn't sit at the family table. George Washington recorded that his family didn't once sit down to dinner alone for twenty years.

Many folktales tell of gods and of kings who travel in disguise and who reward people who show them hospitality. Today's reading from Genesis shows hospitality as it was perceived by Abraham, our father in faith. God dropped in on Abraham unannounced and anonymously through His messengers, and Abraham fussed as much as Martha about the details of entertaining. In fact, the whole scene prepares us for the visit of Jesus to the home of Martha and Mary.

So strongly did Abraham conceive the duty of hospitality that, even though he didn't know the identity of the three visiting strangers, he actually ran from the entrance of his tent to greet them (v. 2), bowed to the ground before them, and addressed as "Sir" the leader of the group (v. 3). This was in a tradition of hospitality which demanded that one take strangers into one's home, furnish them with a meal and a bed for a night, and provide them protection. Abraham's three messengers from God are a frequent subject of Eastern holy pictures, where the messengers are often depicted with halos.

Abraham had water brought to wash their feet and suggested that they rest in the shade of his tree (v. 4). Then he spoke of bringing them a little food (v. 5). He told his wife Sarah — who as a woman was out of sight, as was then the custom in contradistinction to Martha and Mary with Jesus — to prepare a half bushel of fine flour (v. 6): the very best. They were also to be fed from a steer (v. 7) and provided with yogurt and milk (v. 8). The food proved to be quite a meal, even by modern standards. Abraham and Sarah would be eating leftovers for a long time!

It was only when Abraham heard the leading visitor promise a miraculous birth of a son to his aged wife Sarah (v. 10) that he realized that somehow this was the Lord. But Abraham had already received that promise several times. The assurance is that hospitality is rewarded.

Today's portion of the glorious letter to the Colossians reveals the special and unique insight that the kind of generosity given in hospitality finds its heroic fulfillment in suffering for others. But how can the letter's author claim that he was completing what's lacking in

Christ's suffering (v. 24)? Was Jesus' sacrifice somehow insufficient? No, but by God's own will the Redeemer's work of salvation is not yet complete: Jesus wants his followers to continue his work by sharing in his afflictions, thus building up his body in every age. We need to realize that we can do something for the salvation of the entire world. That's at the root of the communion of saints.

It's Jesus who teaches today's lessons: that the one thing necessary in our lives is love, that we show it in both action and contemplation, that it expresses itself preeminently in outgoing hospitality. Throughout, little things mean a lot: Whereas a religious spectacle in a huge cathedral may be an empty show, a private cup of water to a needy person may mean salvation. But let's not get so bogged down in unimportant details that we forget to treat each other as brothers and sisters, and let's use our insights into our particular psychological temperaments to grow into Jesus.

SEVENTEENTH SUNDAY IN ORDINARY TIME
Gn 1:20-32   Col 2:12-14   Lk 11:1-13

Can Prayer Change Sin City?
Bargaining our Petitions with God; How to Pray; Perseverance in Prayer; Prayer: to Change God, or Ourselves?

All of Jesus' thoughts, words, and actions were directed to God. That's what prayer is. His was a life of prayer.

In today's Gospel, the disciples saw how Jesus' prayer illumined his countenance. And they were aware that religious groups were marked by their own prayer customs and forms. The Pharisees, the Essenes, the disciples of John all had their own prayers which distinguished them from other groups. The disciples, too, wanted an "Identification Prayer," a distinctive badge that would bind them together and be an expression of their chief beliefs (Lk 11:1). So they timidly asked Jesus to teach them to pray in the same way as he did.

Jesus answered by giving them a prayer which, in its simplicity, contrasts sharply with many of the very fulsome formulations used in

Jewish and Greco-Roman prayers of his day, not to mention some of today's equivalents. Despite its brevity, Tertullian called the Lord's Prayer "truly a summary of the whole Gospel." In it we ask, not only for all the things we can rightly desire, but also in the sequence that they should be desired (*Catechism of the Catholic Church*, 2763, citing St. Thomas Aquinas).

Jesus didn't intend what he gave to be the only prayer, but the model of prayer. Because a vital part of our prayer — but not the only part — is supplication, that's what the Lord's Prayer demonstrates most. The Lord's Prayer also deals with prayer's other major elements: adoration, contrition, and thanksgiving ("ACTS").

The Lord's Prayer in the early Church was spoken with great reverence and awe. Clement of Alexandria said that our prayers often move in a circle around our own small "I," our own needs and troubles and desires. Jesus teaches us to ask also for the great things — for God's almighty glory and kingdom, and that God's great gifts and the endless mercy of God may be granted us. That doesn't mean that we may not bring our small personal needs before God, but they mustn't govern our prayer.

St. Luke's version and St. Matthew's, though slightly different from each other, both put God, His glory, and the reverence due Him first, then — and only then — ourselves and our needs. The very first word in Luke, "Father," transports us at once into a new era. Though we may take the privilege of calling God "Father" for granted, the early Christians were thrilled that they were allowed to use the word.

He with Whom Jesus wants us to speak in prayer is less the Creator of the universe, the Lord of heaven and earth, than *Abba*, a diminutive of endearment that was used by adults as well as children for their own fathers: the word that could express most adequately the most intimate, most personal relationship anyone could think of.

Some people find difficulty with the word "Father" as the name for God. Some say to address God as "Father" seems no longer to have any experiential basis in their lives. Pity! For others, it's too male-chauvinist. But the Fatherhood of God in the Jewish Scriptures contains also something of what the word "Mother" signifies to us: tenderness, mercy, care, and love. In the Gospels we find the word "Father" for God on the lips of Jesus 170 times.

The first "you" petition — "Hallowed be Your name" — isn't to be understood primarily in its causative sense (only God hallows, makes holy), but above all in an evaluative sense: to recognize as holy (*Catechism of the Catholic Church*, 2807). The second "you" petition — "Your kingdom come" — is intimately connected with the first. To do God's will means in practice to let His kingdom, that is already present, rule our life. The petition means, "Lord, let nothing except the presence of Your kingdom rule and determine all my actions." This is difficult: Jesus literally sweat blood over it.

Taken together, the words mean that whatever we believe the kingdom of heaven to be like, we work to achieve here and now. Is heaven a place of unity for God's people? Then we should strive for unity here. Is heaven a place of peace? Then we should attempt to make peace here. Is heaven a place where justice reigns? Then here and now we should seek to right all injustices. Is heaven a place where all are welcome? Then we strive that none are strangers to us now.

In the first of the "we" petitions, we ask that God give us each day our daily bread (v. 3). Food and meals aren't just a means for staying alive — at least not for Orientals. For them every table fellowship is a demonstration of brotherhood. Jesus' eating and sitting at table with sinners and outcasts was correctly understood by his opponents: Because Jesus ate with sinners, he was also receiving them.

Because we're asking here for material needs, this petition is circumscribed with caution. The request is to give us — thus mindful of the needs of others as well as ourselves. We're to come daily, as children to their parents, like the Israelites with the manna in the wilderness, and like the birds in the sky. And it's our bread we ask for: bread we've earned. Finally, there are nuances of the eucharistic bread as well: That's one reason why we place the Lord's Prayer in the Mass.

Jesus advises us to pray next that God forgive us our sins (v. 4). The great gift of the age of Jesus is forgiveness — a time when human beings live in the presence of God with the knowledge that God has forgiven them and created new communion with them. The magnitude of God's forgiveness makes it ridiculous for us not to forgive one another our petty offenses. If we don't forgive one another we're demonstrating, in effect, that we've not really accepted the great forgiveness of God's love offered to us. Our forgiveness of one another, therefore, becomes the sign of how far we've accepted God's great gift of forgiveness that's offered to us.

But the phrase "as we forgive" shouldn't be taken as a comparison that God would forgive us in the measure that we forgive. It's daunt-

ing to realize that God's outpouring of mercy can't penetrate our hearts
as long as we've not forgiven those who have trespassed against us.
Love, like the Body of Christ, is indivisible; we can't love the God we
can't see if we don't love the brother or sister we do see. This petition
is so important that it's the only one to which the Lord returns and which
he develops explicitly in the Sermon on the Mount (*Catechism of the
Catholic Church*, 2840-41).

The prayer concludes with a petition that God prevent our being
subjected to a final onslaught of the Devil. Whereas God tempts no one,
no one can obtain the kingdom of God who hasn't passed through testing. We must also discern between being tempted and consenting to
temptation.

Then Jesus told a parable to signify that our petitions are always
heard. In the Holy Land, travelers often moved by night to avoid the
daytime heat of the sun. The friend to whom one such traveler came
(v. 5) was indeed hard-pressed. On the one hand, he was out of food;
bread was baked at home and was made only for a day's needs lest it
go stale. On the other hand, the duty of hospitality was serious and
sacred (v. 6).

No one would knock on a shut door (v. 7) unless the need was
really urgent. Doors were wide open during the day, to offer hospitality. To remove the large bar to open the closed door at night was noisy,
and would disturb the whole house. Understandably, the householder
initially refused. But his visitor was shamelessly persistent, and that
persistence got him what he needed (v. 8). Because our relationship
with God is between parent and child, we have a claim to keep on asking, seeking, and knocking in prayer (vv. 9f.), and to expect that we
shall receive, find, and have the door opened.

Jesus isn't guaranteeing that the exact object of every prayer will
be granted as asked — but only that God will hear our prayer and give
us what's best for us. That, after all, is the way it was with him: His
condemnation as a sinner, his unjust trial, and his cruel death show that
not every prayer is answered as asked. But instead of rescue he received
resurrection, which is better. As parents give their children good things
(vv. 11f.), how much more do we have the right to expect that our heavenly Father will give us all good things (v. 13)?

Today's First Reading is a lovely (and humorous) account that
shows that even Abraham, about eighteen centuries before Christ, had
the perseverance in prayer about which Jesus spoke. In the picturesque

language of this part of Genesis, the Lord God said, "I must go down" (v. 21) to earth and be involved in human history.

The discussion between the Lord and Abraham concerned God's threatened destruction of Sodom and Gomorrah. Whereas Israelite tradition was unanimous in ascribing wickedness to these two towns, the tradition about the exact nature of the corruption has varied. According to Isaiah (1:9f; 3:9), it was a lack of social justice. Ezekiel (16:46-51) described it as a disregard for the poor. Jeremiah (23:14) saw it as thorough-going immorality. According to Genesis (19:4ff.), the sin was homosexuality.

Like people in an Eastern bazaar, Abraham haggled with God, and the Lord was open to one who approached Him thus. Underlying Abraham's huckstering were many presuppositions, including the idea that there's more injustice in the destruction of a few innocent people than in the sparing of many guilty ones. Abraham pushed the limit, and God heard his prayer. Abraham couldn't find ten good people, though, and the destruction of Sodom and Gomorrah under fire and brimstone was complete.

Also giving hope is today's reading from the letter to the Colossians. It tells us that the Just One, God's Son Jesus, sufficed for God to pardon the sins of the whole human race. That's because, when we consider the degree of the evil of an offense, we look to the dignity of the one offended; but when we judge the extent of retribution, we look to the worth of the one acting. So we can approach the heavenly Father with confidence because we've been redeemed by His Son. The sign of that redemption is baptism. The life of the baptized is called new (v. 13) because it's vital, liberated, emancipated. Jesus has removed our bill of indebtedness to God because of the merits of the cross (v. 14). The true Christians are those who live out their baptism by their ongoing relationship with Jesus.

Such an ongoing relationship must have prayer as a major ingredient. Beginning with this Mass, let's always recite the Lord's Prayer slowly, knowingly, and lovingly. God, in turn, will be even more responsive than we've experienced good persons to be: our parents who gave us daily care and love, friends to whom we can go at midnight if necessary, and loving people who have been good to us. God is like all of these — only more so, as Jesus shows us.

EIGHTEENTH SUNDAY IN ORDINARY TIME
Ec 1:2; 2:21-23   Col 3:1-5, 9-11   Lk 12:13-21

Having Our Priorities Straight
What Is the Good Life?; Wealth as a Sign of God's Favor;
Against Vanity; Money and the Good Life

Some of the most famous tourist sights in the world are tombs. Among them are the Great Pyramid of King Cheops in Egypt, which was built of five million tons of stone and took as many as 400,000 men two decades to build; the elaborate sarcophagi of ancient Rome; the Taj Mahal in India, containing the body of a beloved princess; Père Lachaise cemetery in Paris, with the graves of Marcel Proust and Oscar Wilde, and the Jewish Cemetery in Prague, where Franz Kafka is buried. At temples throughout the Far East, despots made sure during this life that provisions for the next life would be left at their grave: food, clothing, jewels, their favorite chair. In China, at Xian, an "enlightened" emperor, rather than having his servants buried with him as had been the custom, had thousands of beautifully made life-like terra cotta figures of his army buried with him instead.

The United States has Bellefontaine Cemetery in St. Louis, which contains the striking mausoleum of Adolphus Busch, patriarch of the Anheuser-Busch beer empire, which bears the words *"Veni, Vidi, Vici,"* and the grave of Gen. William Clark, of the Lewis and Clark expedition, topped by an obelisk. Buried on the shaded grounds of Calvary, a Roman Catholic cemetery next door to Bellefontaine, is playwright Tennessee Williams, whose large, upright, pink-marble slab is inscribed with a quotation from his play, *Camino Real*: "The violets in the mountains have broken the rocks." In the palm- and pine-studded cemeteries of Hollywood, many of the interred seem to have thought that when they died they would be able to "take it with them."

In local graveyards some gravestones and mausoleums appear to suggest that death is just a little stumble in the scramble for eternal status, and that a good death, like the good life, is identifiable with a sizable bank account. John (Bet-a-Million) Gates, who made a fortune by introducing barbed wire to Texas, remembered himself at Woodlawn Cemetery in the Bronx with bronze doors on his mausoleum, which were made by the same artist who designed the friezes on the United States Supreme Court building. Nearby Frank W. Woolworth, who opened 2,000 dime stores, has two sphinxes guarding his mausoleum. H.D. Armour, the meat-packing tycoon, lies in a huge tomb the color of liverwurst. The structure of the Vanderbilt family mausoleum at the Moravian Cemetery on Staten Island, the largest mausoleum in America, is an exact copy of a twelfth-century chapel in Arles, France; it looms high over New York harbor, giving the Commodore and 25 of his relatives a perpetually great view.

Modern alternatives are no less grandiose. On the Internet, there are web sites where you can post, for perpetuity, a picture of the deceased, accompanied by a favorite song, a spoken greeting, and even a bunch of electronic flowers to leave in the virtual memory garden. For the ashes of those who are cremated, funeral directors often try to sell the bereaved a full-size coffin or a fancy jewelry box. And for those who want to stop or even reverse the aging process, there is cryonics, the freezing of a just-deceased person for later reviving.

A sign on a hospital maternity ward bulletin board read: "Research Shows That the First Five Minutes of Life Can Be Most Risky." Penciled underneath was this anonymous postscript: "The Last Five Minutes Ain't So Hot Either."

The Book of Ecclesiastes, which is a series of glimpses into life written in the third century before Christ, gave thought to these phenomena. Herman Melville in *Moby Dick* (ch. 97) states that "the truest of all books is Ecclesiastes." Its influence is strong even today. One day in the summer a vacationing man trekking through the Maine woods met an old hermit who hadn't lived in so-called civilization for forty years, but who seemed uncannily wise. When asked how he got his wisdom, the hermit pulled from his pocket the only book he'd read in all that time: a tattered, yellow copy of Ecclesiastes.

As Qoheleth, Ecclesiastes's author, looked about the world, he came up with one main word to describe it: vanity, which in Qoheleth's Hebrew appropriately connotes "vapor" or "a chase after wind." Aside from the title and the epilogue which were added later by someone else, "vanity" is this book's first and last word. The author uses the term "vanity of vanities" to indicate the superlative.

Vanity is well illustrated by Aesop's fable of the fox and the crow. The coal-black crow flew to a tree with a stolen piece of meat in her beak. A fox, who saw her, wanted the meat, so he looked up into the tree and said, "How beautiful you are, my friend! Your feathers are fairer than the dove's. Is your voice as beautiful? If so, you must be the queen of birds." The crow was so happy in his praise that she opened her mouth to show how she could sing. Down fell the piece of meat. The fox seized upon it and ran away.

In our time, vanity would be applicable to the young lady of sixteen conceitedly preening before a mirror whose father reminded her: "You can take no credit for beauty at sixteen. But if you're beautiful at 60, it will be your own soul's doing. Then and then alone you may be proud of it and be loved for it." Even worse was the case of a woman who, aiming to prove her contention that men are more vain than women, said in a speech: "It's a pity that the most intelligent and learned men attach least importance to the way they dress. Why, right in this room the most cultivated man is wearing the most clumsily knotted tie!" As if on a signal, every man in the room immediately put his hand to his tie to straighten it.

The pursuit of life as a sole end is vain. Qoheleth heightens the futility of that by his concrete description of the trials inherent in the world of work: the toil under the sun, the anxiety of heart, the sorrow and grief, and the restlessness at night.

Jesus, who knew more about life than Qoheleth, in today's Gospel seems to confirm his observations. The rabbis of his time were often consulted about civil affairs, especially inheritances. But despite the fact that Jesus was a new Moses and was the subject about whom Moses had taught, he refused to hear the case about inheritance put before him. There were courts of law to settle secular matters; Jesus refused to get involved in them. Had the man before him seemed capable of perfection, Jesus would probably have said to him, "Give your share joyfully to your brother and follow me."

Surely all of us have met people like the man in Jesus' story — sometimes, sadly, he's ourselves. An anonymous author wrote:

> First I was dying to finish high school and start college.
> And then I was dying to finish college and start working.
> And then I was dying for my children to grow old enough for
>   school, so I could return to work.
> And then I was dying to retire.
> And now I am dying... and suddenly I realize
> I forgot to live.

The man in Jesus' story had the wrong priorities. The first was that he never saw beyond himself. His plan of life was a constant repetition of "I" and "my." Contrary to his thinking, it's been said that life's five most important words are "I admit I was mistaken"; the four most important words are "What is your opinion?"; the three most important words are "If you please"; the two most important words are "Thank you"; and the one most important word is "you." From many points of view, life's least important word is "I."

The man's second wrong priority was that he never saw beyond this world. His whole basis of security was wealth. He believed in the modern axiom, "Money talks; learn its language." The driving force today is, no less than in Jesus' time, to build bigger and bigger barns. Upper management receive obscenely high salaries, while workers are laid off by the thousands. Big companies use bankruptcy laws to default on debts, which little persons have to pay. Corporations seem ruled by a dog-eat-dog philosophy which encourages people to climb over the bodies of others to reach the top.

The man in the Gospel was a rich man (v. 16) — one who people might say owned property, but in reality the property owned him. He never thought in terms of the later proverb, "There are no pockets in a shroud." God called him a fool (v. 20). In the Sacred Scriptures, a fool is one who is "mindless" — even to the point of denying God's existence. Thus, the psalmist said, "The fool says in his heart, 'There is no God'" (Ps 14:1).

The author of today's section of the letter to the Colossians tries to identify what's essential in life and to separate it from what's not. Some Jews had been trying to get the Christians of Colossae to go back to "the good old days" of Judaism by practicing Jewish feast-day observances and kosher rules. But the author says that the old rules were merely human precepts dealing with things that perish, a principal effect of which was to indulge pride. He challenges them to the new way, life in Christ.

The correct priorities (vv. 1-4) — which are on things above and not on things of earth — change our whole idea of the good life. We're to join ourselves to Christ. This doesn't mean a withdrawal from care for the world and its problems. On the contrary, it means a truer love for the world. But that love is with a difference: We're to see everything in the light of eternity.

For the writer of this letter, it meant a great deal to say "Christ your life" (v. 4). Sometimes we say of a person, "sports are his life," meaning that such a person finds the meaning of life in sports. Many such people forget the experience of a famous basketball coach who, at the age of 47, was suffering from terminal spinal cancer. Looking back on his life, he told a story about himself as a 23-year-old coach of a small college team. "Why is winning so important to you?" the players asked him.

"Because the final score defines you," he said. "You lose, so you're a loser. You win, so you're a winner."

"No," the players urged. "Participation is what matters. Trying your best, regardless of whether you win or lose — that's what defines you."

It took 24 more years of living for the coach to say, "Those kids were right. It's effort, not result. What a great human being I could have been if I'd had this awareness back then."

The author of Colossians, though, refers to something more far-reaching: We must find our present resurrection as well as our future resurrection in Christ. This richer and higher life is to begin now, not after we die. This means putting to death all the evils in our nature that are earthly (v. 5), taking off our old self (v. 9), and putting on a new self (v. 10) who grows gradually into what Jesus wants.

We who are trying to live out our baptism have a new set of values. We think of giving instead of getting, serving rather than ruling, forgiving and not avenging. We're grateful for life given by God without cost, friends provided without price, eternity promised without merit. We have the insight that our worth isn't measured by what we own but by what we share and that we have the opportunity to grow in the lasting wealth of love. We see that wealth isn't necessarily a sign of God's favor, and that poverty can be.

We're not to define ourselves by our salary, by our material possessions, or by our accomplishments on earth. We're to realize that it's possible to "spend less and enjoy more," "to live simply so that others may simply live," to reject greed and grow rich in God. We're to prepare to move into the dwelling place prepared for us in heaven rather than building bigger barns. Do we have our priorities straight?

NINETEENTH SUNDAY IN ORDINARY TIME
Ws 18:6-9   Heb 11:1-2, 8-19 (or 11:1-2,8-12)   Lk 12:32-48 (or 12:35-40)

Integrating our Faith into Our Lives
Preparedness; Readiness for the Lord's Coming; Let Go and Let God!;
Urgency and Watchfulness; Trust in God

Imagine that a catastrophe has occurred that's so great that our knowledge of the natural sciences is all completely lost: Physicists have been killed, books destroyed, laboratories sacked. All that's left are fragments, bits and pieces of theories, experimental equipment whose use has been forgotten, half-chapters of books, single pages from articles. Some of the scientific terminology survives, but its meaning is largely lost. Heated debates develop over scientific concepts that are only dimly understood.

That's what has in fact happened — not to science, but to our understanding of the language of religion. People continue to use many of its key expressions, but have — largely, if not entirely — lost their comprehension of many aspects of religion. Charity now typically means patronage of the poor by the well-off. Love means what goes on between movie stars, off and on screen. Service equals unpleasant menial duties or one sector of the economy. Grace is a girl's name or a period of time before one pays a bill. Redemption is the process by which you get value for your stamps. The supernatural is that which has to do with hobgoblins and spooks. Faith is believing what's not so.

How different the Church's definitions! The term "faith," for example, is so important to the Church that there isn't one definition, but many! The one in today's letter to the Hebrews, written for Jewish converts to Christianity, is a good one: Faith is the assurance of things hoped for and the evidence of things not seen (v. 1). If the object of faith is seen or known by experience, it isn't faith; but faith is more than mere opinion, because God's own assurances are behind it. So even when we don't understand the events of our lives, we have faith that God will fulfill His promises to us.

Faith entails leaving behind all things that are less than God in order to be able to accept the God Who contains all things. Even all science rests on a basis of faith, for it assumes the permanence and uniformity of natural laws — a thing that can't be demonstrated. So the person of faith goes beyond the humdrum world of the everyday into a new vision and adventure. Faith gives a new outlook, a new set of values, a new world of meaning. It has an excitement analogous to the world of sports, from which the letter to the Hebrews derives so much of its imagery. (Its sports imagery is perhaps one of the reasons why this letter is wrongly attributed to St. Paul, who often used such imagery.) Faith is backed by the best evidence in the world: God's word.

Most of the rest of the reading from the letter to the Hebrews is an illustration of its definition of faith. Faith puts us into the world of such First Testament models as Abraham and his wife Sarah. God promised Abraham that he would father a son through whom his descendants would be as numerous as the stars. Because it was God speaking, the couple believed. But they were in the dark as to how and when God would fulfill His promise.

As time wore on, they thought of several cultural solutions offered to childless couples of their time: adopting the first most trusted slave of the household, for example, or having offspring by Sarah's maidservant. But God made it clear that none of these, though acceptable to their culture, was to be their route, and as they waited they relied on their confident assurance concerning what they hoped for. Only when their confident assurance was stretched to the limit — when Sarah was long past the age for childbearing and Abraham as good as dead — did God fulfill His promise of so many years earlier.

Abraham's faith wasn't according to the principle of most people, who, cautious and comfort-loving, put safety first; his faith went into the unknown, where it couldn't see the end of the path. Abraham did everything God wanted of him — and, sure enough, ultimately his wife conceived and his son Isaac was born. Then, when God asked him to leave the comforts of his home-town Ur in the Chaldean mountains for what came to be known as the Promised Land and endure all the problems of a stranger in a strange land, he did it — even though he wasn't sure where God was leading him. God, to test him even further, some years later asked him to give his young son Isaac as a living sacrifice. Despite his hope that through Isaac he would have descendants, he prepared to do as God asked. It was only at the last moment that God prevented him from going through with his sacrifice.

We, like Abraham, should let go and let God! Some researchers in India wanted to keep a monkey out of the trees and on the ground for various tests they wanted to perform. Knowing that the monkey loved coconuts and peanuts, they hollowed out a coconut, filled it with peanuts, and put it in a place where the monkey would be sure to come upon it. When the monkey did, he put his hand inside and grabbed hold of the peanuts. This kept the monkey out of the trees, but they couldn't get the monkey to let go of the peanuts so he could get his hand out of the coconut. It took the researchers several hours and many subterfuges to get him to let go. We're often like that! With regard to what holds us back, St. John of the Cross said that it doesn't matter if a bird is shackled by a chain or a thread: So long as its movement's thwarted, the bird isn't free.

God tests the faith of all. Today's First Reading is an example from the last book of the First Testament to be written: the Book of Wisdom, written less than a hundred years before Christ. As with the letter to the Hebrews, it was written for people who were tempted to abandon their faith. Its author wrote to the Jews in Alexandria in Egypt that, rather than the skeptical and secular attitudes of the pagans around them with whom they were having frequent contact, the Israelites should be characterized by courage and joy (v. 6).

The Book of Wisdom reminded the Jews of a sign of faith and hope for all time. The "you" of the passage refers to God, to Whom this excerpt is an ancient prayer of thanks for deliverance. The "night" to which the reading refers was the night of the Passover: the night on which the angel of death destroyed the first-born of the Egyptians but passed over the homes of the Hebrews, the night on which those who were unprepared were destroyed and those who were prepared were saved.

Today's Gospel urges a similar attitude for Christians. Its two stories tell us to be ready for the Lord's coming into our lives. They begin with the servants awaiting their master's return during a wedding. In Our Lord's time, on the day of the wedding the bridesmaids assembled at the house of the bride. After sunset the bridegroom, accompanied by his male friends, went into the bride's house, where they were greeted by the bride and her bridesmaids, and then both parties returned together in a joyous procession that was illumined by lamps or torches, to the wedding feast in the house of the bridegroom. No one knew the exact time when the bridegroom would arrive. Our Lord then tells us — not without humor — that he will come into our lives like the unexpected arrival of a thief. How would we like him to find us? Certainly at peace with everyone and with ourselves.

Finally comes Our Lord's story of the steward. This man's first mistake was doing what he liked while his master was away. We make the same mistake all the time. We do it every time we faithlessly divide our lives into compartments, like the sacred and the secular. We deceive ourselves if we think that we can give one part of our lives to God and another part to worldly pursuit: The secular penetrates the sacred, and the sacred the secular. The steward's second mistake was in thinking he had plenty of time to put things right before the master would return. Those who have thought about it even a little realize that life is short, and the time is now.

To retain a vibrant faith, Jesus makes three demands of his followers. First, we're to share with the needy (v. 33f.); the only worthwhile treasure is that which awaits us in heaven. Secondly, we're to be vigilant, prepared, and living lives that are integrated by our faith. And thirdly, whatever our task in life, we're to carry it out faithfully and responsibly in a spirit of service.

The faith of Abraham caused him to leave familiar territory and later to consider sacrificing his only son. The faith of Moses and the Israelites caused them to pull up stakes in the middle of the night and leave Egypt. Jesus was the faith-filled person *par excellence*. To become like all of them, our faith must be renewed and deepened daily. We battle constantly in the face of non-belief and apathy.

At the heart of Christian faith is the notion that God, Who called me by name from eternity, made me unique, and loves me with a love that is infinite. But, as we said in the beginning, we aren't living in an "Age of Faith." That time did exist in the Western world many hundreds of years ago, when everything was at one with Christian faith: one's peer group, one's family, the marketplace, and the world of entertainment. Today, we must be constantly on our guard to preserve our faith and to find the strength and courage to share its light with those who don't understand it.

Solemnity of the Assumption of Mary
Rv 11:19; 12:1-6,10   1 Cor 15:20-25   Lk 1:39-56

Mary as Model, First Disciple
Involvement; Concern; Christianity as Revolutionary;
The New Ark of the Covenant; The Locus of the Holy; The Human
as Home for the Divine; Woman as God-Bearer

On the Nevsky Prospekt in Leningrad (now St. Petersburg) under the
Communist regime was a museum in a former church, Our Lady of
Kazan, dedicated to "The History of Religions and of Atheism." It
pointed out, among other things, Karl Marx's theory that religion is
the opiate of the people. Marxism claims that history attests that those
in power have used religion to keep under their thumb the miserable,
the oppressed, and those who aspire to better their lot. By concentrat-
ing these people's attention on the next world, Marxist theory goes,
religion makes people forget their unhappiness in this world. If, however, we look at Jesus Christ, his religion, and his first disciple, his
mother Mary, we see that, far from being an opiate that puts people to
sleep, our religion, if properly understood, wakes people up in a revolutionary way.

Today's portion of the Book of Revelation was written to demonstrate a different idea: that all-pervasive superstition takes over when
true religion is absent. Even some Christians succumb. Some, for example, find the number 13 unlucky. At the Last Supper, it was the 13th
guest who betrayed Jesus. Thus, the fear of dining at a table of 13
plagued Napoleon, J. Paul Getty, and Franklin Delano Roosevelt; in
France a *quatorzieme*, or professional 14th guest, can be hired at a
moment's notice to make a dinner party safe. Fear of the number 13
(*Triskaidekaphobia*) costs the United States roughly a billion dollars a
year in canceled travel plans and missed work. The number nine,
though, is considered to be a relatively lucky number. Real estate is
often leased for 99 years, and nine appears in several sayings: A stitch
in time saves nine; a cat has nine lives; a blissful person is said to be
on cloud nine; a well-tailored person is described as "dressed to the
nines."

Note: For other approaches to the Assumption, see Cycles A and B.

The superstitions at the time of the Book of Revelation were worse: a world of gods and goddesses, mythological stories, signs and portents, dragons and monsters. It was a world of Babylon and Persia, and especially of the apparently invincible and persecuting Roman Empire. It was also a time of a worldwide movement toward one who might be a savior from all this, of persecutions suffered by Christians, and of knowledgeable women who embraced Jesus and converted their menfolk to him.

The Book of Revelation, a book most difficult for us to understand, is in the realm of apocalypse, that strange and often enigmatic Mideastern literature which speaks in the language of dreams and visions, of a world of symbols and of wonder. It's likely that the imagery in today's passage was intended to refer in an involved way to the very popular Greco-Egyptian goddess Isis, who was said to have emerged from the sea clothed with the stars and the moon. But because women from the beginning of the human race were part of the mystery of birth and a woman was now to take an essential role in the birthing of the messianic new age, Christians apply the imagery to Mary, the mother of God and the prototype of redeemed humanity. The mythical dragon was seen as the epitome of all the forces of evil opposed to God.

Today's excerpt from St. Paul places before the eyes of all humankind the image and the consoling proof of the fulfillment of our final hope — namely, that Mary's glorification is the destiny of all of us. He's opposed to those cultured Greeks of his time who considered all matter, including the human body, to be evil, and the person's soul to be one's only good side.

The Gospel on this feast of Mary's being taken into heaven presents Mary pronounced by Elizabeth to be blessed because she is the mother of the Lord, the first time that word is used of Jesus in the Gospel. And we see her as not only helping someone in need — her aged cousin Elizabeth in the sixth month of her pregnancy with John the Baptist — but also saying a beautiful prayer. The *Magnificat*, as it has come to be known from its first word in Latin, not only shows important roots in the canticle of Hannah (1 S 2:1-10) and other allusions from the past, but also the revolutionary newness of Christianity. Three verses of this prayer especially demonstrate this.

Mary says that God has dispersed the arrogant of mind and heart (v. 51). This is the beginning of the moral revolution which Christianity has begun and which even today is nowhere near completion. In all the Western world, those who achieved the very highest level of wisdom and intellectual greatness without God's revelation were the ancient Greeks, who had reached their peak about 500 years before Mary. Their achievement has never been exceeded for any people or culture without God's revelation. That includes today's secular humanists, who try hard to go through life without God. Christ's religion surpasses them all.

So high is the moral standard God asks of us that we need models to help us achieve it. Mary's the moral model we need. She's passionately holy and, as such, the symbol of redemption at work, the reminder that salvation is possible. It's interesting that the doctrines about Mary that we consider today initially arose in an evolving context of mistrust for the body, fear of sexuality, and denial of death. A seventeenth-century preacher (Paul Beurrier) revealingly remarked, "Our bodies resemble glasses that break when they touch one another." And the body was considered nasty and disgusting. In the 13th century an influential treatise commented: "Man is nought but fetid sperm, a bag of excrement, and food for worms… In life, he produces dung and vomit. In death, he will produce stench and decay." In Mary, all is holy, and the salvation even of woman's sexuality and bodiliness has begun.

Mary then asserts that God has thrown down the rulers from their thrones but lifted up the lowly (v. 52). This is the beginning of a social revolution — again, barely begun and certainly not yet over. We hear the mouthings of politicians and others about respect for women and helping the poor, but not much seems to get done outside the Christmas and voting seasons. To a great measure this is the fault of Christians who don't make those in power act. Christians often forget Mary's example of concern, of putting herself out, and Jesus' radically new conduct with women and his identification of himself with the lowest of the low.

A story's told of a wandering university student in the Middle Ages. As with many university students in those times when universities were being founded, he traveled to wherever he heard the good teachers were. Also as with many of his fellow-students, he was dirty, ill-fed, and ill-clothed. He fell seriously ill, and was taken to the hospital almost dead. The doctors consulted around his bed. They said that his life appeared worthless, and the best use they could put his body to would be medical experimentation. They spoke in Latin, not realizing that he was a university student whose classes were in that language.

Hearing them, he opened his eyes and said to them in Latin, "Call no man worthless for whom Jesus has died." That lesson is indispensable to the social revolution that our religion tried to start.

In this social revolution, Mary is again a model. The symbolism of the feast of her Assumption shows woman rising, soaring, affirmed. Woman whole and free. Woman ascending to new heights. Woman liberated from (sometimes superstitious) oppressions that have kept her down and humiliated her. Woman sharing in the resurrection of Jesus, the symbol of redeemed humanity. Woman showing what God intended for all of us.

Lastly for our consideration, Mary said that God has filled the hungry with good things and sent the rich away empty (v. 53). This was indicative of the economic revolution started by Christianity — a revolution hardly begun even today. In the economic world, it's pretty much all people for themselves, getting and spending. Christians, though, should always have regard for the Church's teachings about social justice and an openness to new ways to help put high economic standards into existence. For example, it was only little more than 100 years ago (in 1886) that a tiny band of firebrands came up with a dangerous idea: an idea so far out, so impractical, and so dangerous, that it was roundly attacked as anarchistic, communistic, and just plain crazy. The idea was simple. We call it the eight-hour day.

All Christians should be uneasy while anybody else is in dire need and they have an abundance. Among today's more than five billion people on this planet, one out of four goes to bed every night hungry. This is certainly against the way that Jesus and his first disciple, Mary, want it. And it's that way because Christians haven't been Christian enough.

Jesus has given the power — and the duty — to his brothers and sisters in this world to participate in the moral, social, and economic revolutions he intended by his coming. And in his first disciple, Mary, he has given an example of what we ought to be. In Mary's assumption, we have an affirmation of that: In this celebration Mary, the symbol of redeemed humanity, has opened a window for us on the radical transformation possible through the power of Jesus. Mary is the woman for our times. She embodies our rebirth, our new life, our new experience of time and space. With her, woman, the God-bearer, births the divine in herself and then into human history.

It's hard to understand that there could have been a time when anyone like Karl Marx could write that religion is the opiate of the people. Marx undoubtedly met Christians who gave the impression that religion is just an otherworldly affair, and there are clearly some Christians who give the same impression today. But we're proud of those Christians in Latin America, Africa, Asia, and other places in our world — including our own — who give their lives for Christianity's revolutionary teachings. God wants to give no one the impression that our religion puts anyone to sleep.

TWENTIETH SUNDAY IN ORDINARY TIME
Jr 38:4-6, 8-10   Heb 12:14   Lk 12:49-53

The Christian Life Is Not a Spectator Sport
Life Is a Race; Keep Your Eyes on Jesus; The Personality of Jesus;
Commitment; Jesus' Strength; Doing What You Have to Do;
Telling the Real from the Fake

Each of us has two aspects about us that are important: personhood and personality. Personhood embraces our reasoning powers, which enable us to transcend immediate needs and understand what life is all about, and our will, which enables us to love. Personhood is where good and evil reside. Personality, on the other hand, consists of those surface characteristics which appear to other people and attract or repel them: A nice way of laughing, a good way of talking, and gracious manners attract, while their opposites repel. A bad person can have an attractive personality, and a good person can have a repelling personality. We like to believe that it's one's personhood that matters, but when all is said and done it's often personality that wins out.

With Jesus, it's helpful to know not only that his personhood consisted of the two natures of God and of man, but what his personality was like. Those who overemphasize the gentleness of Jesus' personality traits are scandalized by a Gospel passage like today's, which emphasizes Jesus' strength. Many pictures and statues of Jesus overemphasize Jesus' humility, gentleness, and kindness, depicting him as almost a long-haired sissy.

Today, Jesus speaks with a mixture of anguish and fear about having to light a fire on the earth and undergo a baptism. Both fire and water are ambivalent symbols. Fire from the earliest history of human-kind has fascinated people. It's both awesome and wondrous on the one hand, and terrifying on the other. Fire is so wondrous that early civilization created the story of an ancestor, Prometheus, stealing it from the gods. It was around the fire that the household gathered, that hu-mankind perfected speech, made up songs, and explored the mysteries of life. It was around the fire that our ancestors sacrificed to their gods, and smoke that carried prayers heavenward linked religion and domes-ticity.

Although many of those benefits have been broken by stoves and furnaces that provide nothing to gaze into for that reverie and compan-ionship which is important to every human being, we still approach fire with near religious devotion. To some primitives, the fact that fire always burns upward and never in any other direction symbolizes the direction of God. To the early Hebrews, in fact, fire symbolized both the presence and the activity of God. ("The Lord, your God, is a con-suming fire" [Dt 4:24].) When the Jews were going from Egypt to the Holy Land, they were preceded at night by a pillar of fire, the symbol of God leading them.

Fire has also been terrifying. When God came to Moses with the ten commandments on Mt. Sinai, the mountain was surrounded by fire. When on another occasion Moses conversed with God, God was sym-bolized by a burning bush. God used fire on Sodom and Gomorrah to show His judgment. The Jews were instructed to consume their offer-ings to God in fire, to show sacrifice. And many passages in the Jew-ish Scriptures show the use of fire to symbolize testing, dividing, puri-fying, and judging. In our time, burning buildings and blazing forests also witness to the terrifying nature of fire.

The encounter with the living God refines, purifies, and trans-forms those who are open to conversion, but destroys those who per-sist in asserting the self as independent of God and God's reign. The symbolism suggests an interpretation that hell can be, whatever else it is, painful self-damnation and self-destruction in such many-faceted ways as a human life offers.

Jesus also said that he had a baptism to receive. This brings to mind another ambivalent symbol of God's activity: water. This scorched planet, after it cooled enough to have a crust, seemed impossible for life. The atmosphere was poisonous — chiefly methane, ammonia fumes, and hydrogen sulfide. (If there had been any human beings about, the stench would have been awful!) Two of its most common elements were hydrogen and oxygen. Together, then and now they create the only liquid that forms naturally on the earth's surface — a supple, sparkling substance which rises and falls in ocean tides, spirals and crashes in surf, forms fluffy clouds, and reflects the splendor of sunsets.

For about one and a half billion years, water performed its wonders on a rocky, dead, volcano-tortured globe. In time, steam erupted from volcanoes, formed dark clouds, then fell as rain in century-long cloudbursts that drenched the rocks. Many elements were dissolved out of the rocks and poured into the great mixing bowl of the seas: iron, calcium, sodium, phosphorus, potassium. Finally tiny living cells appeared with those elements in them, sensitive to their surroundings, endowed with energy systems dependent upon water and its nutrients for their existence.

When animals emigrated from the sea, elaborate arrangements like threads of bloodstreams had to be made to keep every cell in their bodies in a watery environment. Human beings, when God created them, were 70 percent water, and this level must still be constantly maintained: You can die of dehydration in six days. In addition to providing nutrition, water purifies. Like fire, it separates and renders judgment, as with the exodus from Egypt when the waters saved the Jews and killed the Egyptians.

In today's Gospel, fire and water mean that Jesus was going to have to be purified by being submerged in his suffering and death. Hence his mixed feelings in looking ahead to it. Nevertheless he would do what he had to do. His "fire on the earth," with its lack of exterior peace, was originally meant for Jewish Christians ostracized by their families, and Gentile Christians cut off from the mainstream of Greco-Roman culture; it also applies to all who must go against received opinions and disturb the status quo.

So today's Gospel puts a hard face on Jesus' personality. He was realist enough to know that his message would bring a sword, even to people who were closely related to each other.

But we must take the message of the Bible as a whole, and not just one passage here or there. As he says elsewhere, Jesus really came to bring peace. The peace he came to bring isn't peace as some people may define it, but the peace of God. The difference is that human peace is basically extrinsic, a matter of temporary trade-offs and compromises, but the peace of God is basically a matter of truth, integrity, and love that always provides inner harmony. God's peace is that loving communion with Him, with one's neighbor, and with oneself which comes from living the beatitudes. It's the kind of peace that Maximilian Kolbe had when in the Nazi concentration camp he gave his life to save another inmate and was starved to death; the kind of peace that the Japanese martyrs in Nagasaki had when they sang hymns of praise to God as they were being crucified; the kind of peace that the Ugandan martyrs had when they were being burned alive.

Jesus had God's peace as he fulfilled his mission. So did Jeremiah in today's First Reading. Jeremiah's ministry took place in those fateful twelve years between the first fall of Jerusalem and its final destruction in 587 B.C. As the armies of Babylon were preparing for an assault on Jerusalem, Jeremiah spoke the truth as he heard it from God about the inner rot of his nation. He told the weak King Zedekiah and his people that, unless they repented and returned to God, they would be destroyed. The leaders said that Jeremiah's message was demoralizing the people, and accused him of treason.

Jeremiah's punishment was to be put in a cistern to die of exposure, hunger, and thirst. Every town had such cisterns, its walls built out of rock and plastered with limestone to collect and hold precious and scarce rainwater. The cistern's opening was narrow, to prevent the loss of water by evaporation. By the time of Jeremiah's punishment, which was at the end of the dry summer season, most of the water had been drawn, leaving the bottom mud in which Jeremiah was trapped.

Even at the orders of the inept king, no Judean would soil his hands on Jeremiah, and he had to be rescued by a foreigner, the Ethiopian Ebed-melech. Faith-filled and patriotic, Jeremiah really loved the city and its holy Temple. More, he loved his people. Despite his pain, Jeremiah, like Jesus in the future, did what he had to do. And in that awful summer his words were fulfilled: Jerusalem fell to the Babylonians. By an irony, just before that Jeremiah was kidnapped and taken to Egypt with refugees; there he died in exile.

What do we do in response to today's disregard of God's messages? The letter to the Hebrews has the perfect answer. First, remember that life for us Christians is a participatory race, not a spectator sport. Secondly, we must keep our eyes on Jesus, who's our goal, our model, and our companion.

The Christian life means we must be willing to pay the price for being in the race, just as athletes do by their training to win. But just as some athletes are handicapped, we're handicapped by the encumbrances of sin. Our sins may result from the habits we've formed, the companions we've made, the weaknesses we've tolerated, the passions we carry with us, the personality we've developed. But we're also surrounded by what the letter to the Hebrews wonderfully calls a "cloud of witnesses." These are the countless people who have gone before us in the faith and won their race of life — at that time the heroic First Testament figures, in our time adding the heroes and saints who've lived ever since. They knew all the struggles of running and the joy of winning. In running our life's race, it helps to picture this cloud of witnesses cheering us on. Through it all, we must imitate the personality of Jesus in both his gentleness and his strength.

TWENTY-FIRST SUNDAY IN ORDINARY TIME
Is 66:18-21   Heb 12:5-7, 11-13   Lk 13:22-30

Who in the World Will Be Saved?
To Whom Does Salvation Come?; Education in Christ; Salvation: What Does It Mean?; Is Salvation Easy?; Are We Smug?; Discipline and Correction

Anthropologists have never encountered a culture where people do not laugh to express merriment and sociability; even deaf people sometimes laugh out loud. Babies begin laughing at the age of two or three months. The rate of laughter picks up steadily for the next several years, until around the age of six, when the average child laughs 300 times a day. After that, social training and the desire to blend in with one's peers conspire to dampen liberal laughter. Estimates of how much adults laugh vary widely, from a high of 100 chuckles daily to a dour low of 15, but clearly adults lose their laughter edge along with the talent for finger-painting.

Some authorities view that decline as a blow to the health of body and spirit. When you laugh robustly, you increase blood circulation, work your abdominal muscles, raise your heart rate, and get the stale air out of your lungs; after a bout of laughter, your blood pressure drops to a lower, healthier level than before the buoyancy began. And there are subtler effects of laughter on the immune and neuro-endocrine systems. Big business is beginning to be persuaded of the financial value of laughter on the job.

Our Judeo-Christian tradition includes both comedy and tragedy; we often forget the comedy. Some artists — Botticelli, for example — never painted saints smiling. A Renaissance genius with great poetic imagination, fantasy, and elegance, he became famous for the softness of his light and his skillful use of perspective. Among his renowned paintings on religious themes are many Madonnas, his exquisite "Adoration of the Magi," and a solemn "Nativity." But, deeply affected by Savonarola's preaching, he never painted smiling saints.

Although the Gospels don't record any instance of Jesus laughing outright, there are instances of his humor; it would be most surprising if he didn't enjoy, for instance, the wedding ceremony and reception at Cana. All the expressions in the Jewish Scriptures about joy and laughter were, after all, his tradition.

And laughter is an essential part of our Western heritage. That heritage has pointed out that to laugh is proper to human beings. We instinctively know that at times we must quickly laugh for fear of having to cry, that it's fitting for us to laugh because hope has a happy place with us, and that our destiny, heaven, must contain an inextinguishable laugh. Even though the world be mad, we're born with the gift of laughter. Children jingle with laughter as though they had swallowed sleigh bells, and their laughter is natural until life takes — or we take — it away from them.

And of all the people who have ever lived on this planet not one is known to have ever died of laughter. To the contrary: When you laugh, your diaphragm vibrates as though dancing, and you have dancing cells. All your cells are happy, and when you're happy you have a longer life.

But it's also important to be serious, and today's liturgy deals with that. In St. Luke's Gospel, as Jesus was going through towns and villages, teaching as he went and making his way toward Jerusalem (v. 22), someone asked him a serious question that has always intrigued people: How many people will be saved? (v. 23). Isaiah's answer had been general: "a remnant" (Is 10:19-22). The prophet Amos had been more specific: one-tenth of the population (5:3). The questioner here probably expected an equally precise number.

But the person had asked the wrong question. The right question is, "How do you get to be saved?" So Jesus made the three points that are the message of today's liturgy — salvation requires effort (v. 24); you should seize the present moment (vv. 25-28); and no one should be smug about salvation: Some "outsiders" will be accepted and some "insiders" will be turned away (vv. 29f.).

With regard to salvation requiring effort, two erroneous religious traditions have grown up. One is the conviction that baptism or religious heritage alone — being Catholic, for example — will be a ticket of admission. The other is the delusion that we can earn salvation by some kind of spiritual athletic exercises alone. Jesus' narrow door is somewhere between these two. Jesus is saying that we're not to travel with the mob, but to struggle with all our might in our own particular circumstances. One thing's certain: No one just saunters in.

As for seizing the present moment, Jesus' parable isn't only told; like a gun, it's aimed — at the Jewish leaders. The time will come when it will be too late; the door to salvation is going to be locked (v. 25). At that time, the leaders will come to the master of the house — Jesus himself — and try to remind him that they ate and drank in his company and he taught in their streets (v. 26). Their efforts will be in vain. There comes a time when, in the words of St. Augustine, the lackadaisical must come to realize: "Too late have I loved you, O Beauty so ancient yet ever new! Too late have I loved you!"

As for smugness, the labels we hang on "outsiders," like some of the Jewish leaders hung the label "evildoers" on non-Jews, may be reversed (v. 27). The leaders, and sometimes we, are like little children who form secret clubs with secret passwords for the membership of those whom they like and the exclusion of the unpopular. When the door to salvation is opened the smug, arrogant, and self-satisfied leaders will be surprised to find inside the very ones they would have excluded: non-Jews from every corner of the earth (v. 29). The sole key to inclusion is transformation, made possible by loving, grace-filled commitment.

Jesus' words reflect today's First Testament imagery from Isaiah which speaks of bringing people from all the nations to the holy mountain of Jerusalem. Today's portion of Isaiah — the finale of the whole book — opens a vision of a glorious future in which humankind's covenant with God is opened to the whole human family. Returnees from every part of the globe known to people of that time (v. 19) in which God's people had been scattered from around the entire Mediterranean, from Spain to Turkey, will come back to Jerusalem. (Their strange names in the reading come from Gn 10, the "Table of Nations.")

Their procession is almost liturgical. Nations of diverse cultures and races will lead the Israelites home (v. 20), using horses, chariots, carts, mules, camels, and every other form of transportation imaginable. A joyful concept, and a joyful procession indeed! Both Isaiah and today's Responsorial Psalm highlight the teaching of Jesus that salvation extends beyond the borders of Israel.

Yet, why do people suffer so much for salvation? Why does God seem to treat His children so poorly? Today's portion of the letter to the Hebrews addresses that question and continues the lessons of the Gospel. The unknown scholarly author gives practical advice in handling the consequences of being a true follower of Christ — both those who have been on trial for their faith and those who must suffer the minor tribulations of trying to lead a Christian life in a non-Christian ambience.

 God begins by encouraging them. All of us who travel the road to salvation, both the strong and the weak, need encouragement. The word "encourage" comes from Latin and French words meaning "one who fills the heart." You can encourage by a personal note, a greeting card, a phone call, a small gift, a favorite food, a funny story, or even just a smile, a wink, a hug, or a handshake. Encouragement is oxygen to the soul. No one ever climbed spiritual heights without it; no one ever fully lived without it. All of us must bask in the warmth of approval now and then or lose our self-confidence.

As artists find joy in giving beauty to others, so anyone who masters the art of encouraging will find that it blesses the giver as much as the receiver. There's much truth in the saying, "Flowers leave part of their fragrance in the hand that bestows them." A near miracle happens to people whose self-esteem has been raised: They suddenly like other people better; they're kinder and more cooperative with those around them; they want to like you and cooperate with you. (Nowhere are these realities truer than in marriage!)

In the style of the rabbis, the author of this letter chose one word as God's encouragement of us and as the answer to the problem of following God: *paideia* (v. 5). Literally the word is from *pais*, child, and means everything that adults want to pass on to their children: formation, culture, civilization, education. Someone once observed, "There are only two lasting bequests we can give our children — one is roots, the other wings." Giving both to our children and to others means empowering them with the freedom to rise above negative scripting. Instead of transferring negative scripts to the next generation, we must change them.

Often, as here, *paideia* is translated into English as "discipline." When we teach our children discipline, we're teaching them how to suffer, yes, but also how to grow. What are the tools, the means of experiencing the pain of problems constructively that is discipline? There are four: delaying of gratification, acceptance of responsibility, dedication to truth, and balancing.

The letter gives as its first key image that the Lord disciplines as a father does his child, but with even more love and even greater wisdom. God's children can, for their part, have many attitudes toward discipline. We can simply be resigned and accept it, with the defeated recognition not of a father's love, but of his power. Or we can accept it with the grim determination of getting it over with as soon as possible. Or we can take it with self-pity. Or we can take it as a resented punishment from a God Who's vindictive, which is the way many see Him. But the attitude advised here remains the best: to accept it as coming from a loving father, asking, "What is God trying to teach me through the discipline of this suffering?"

If God didn't discipline, that kind of non-caring lack of love would be a worse punishment. All discipline from God has its source in love and is aimed at good. In the face of the fact that life's way to salvation is often tough, there are always members with drooping hands and weak knees (v. 12). Sometimes that includes us. So the letter returns to another key image: We're in a race, and we must persevere despite occasional pain that goes right down to our very bones.

As we go, and perhaps wonder about our salvation, let's remember that there will be surprises, and there's hope. Amid our contemporary promotion of selfishness as the way to freedom, we find in the life of Jesus in today's liturgy at least two elements that are clearly worth imitation. First, Jesus was committed — disciplined, as the letter to the Hebrews might say — to face up to all the consequences of his life-choices before God, right up to death itself. Secondly, his penetrating vision cuts through human pretense to the core where the true person lies under whatever we may have acquired of complacency, narcissism, self-inflation, or other detritus. May God help us on our way, through both laughter and tears, to salvation — no matter what the number of those who accompany us.

TWENTY-SECOND SUNDAY IN ORDINARY TIME
Si 3:17f., 20, 28f.   Heb 12:18f., 22-24   Lk 14:1, 7-14

Part of Correct Etiquette at the Banquet of Life: Humility
Humility in the Scheme of Things; Compassion Made Real in Gentleness;
The Paradoxical Nature of Christianity

Fagin, in Charles Dickens's *Oliver Twist*, offered this personal tip to Oliver: "Some conjurers say that number three is the magic number, and some say number seven. It's neither, my friend, neither. It's number one." He was, of course, referring to himself. Egomania knows no bounds. For example, on his deathbed, the French philosopher Auguste Comte was heard uttering this mournful cry as he expired, "What an irreparable loss!" Almost a century later, the equally chesty American novelist Theodore Dreiser had the gall to prepare his last words: "Shakespeare, I come!" At a dinner, the painter James McNeill Whistler, was overheard muttering, "If other people are going to talk, conversation becomes impossible." Winston Churchill once admitted, "We are all worms, but I do believe I am a glow-worm."

Perhaps one reason we find these sayings tolerable is that so many are willing to kid their own egotism. George Bernard Shaw, for example, once confessed, "I often quote myself. It adds spice to my conversation." And W.S. Gilbert once revealed that "You've no idea what a poor opinion I have of myself — and how little I deserve it." Yet all of these are topped by Mark Twain's tongue-in-cheek statement that recognized human pride: "Twenty-four years ago... I was so handsome that human activities ceased as if spellbound when I came into view, and even inanimate things stopped to look — like locomotives and district messenger boys and so on. In San Francisco in the rainy season I was often taken for fair weather."

By way of refreshing contrast, in the later years of John Millais, the painter, an art gallery in London had a show of his collected works. A visitor saw the painter coming from the collection with tears in his eyes. To the visitor's questioning gaze, Millais looked up and said, "In looking at my earliest pictures I'm overcome with chagrin that I have so far failed in my maturity to fulfill the full potential of my youth." That's humility.

There seem to be two acceptable types of humility. The first is self-effacement: the habit of doing good deeds, or indeed just daily work, secretly or anonymously, without expecting thanks. A good example of that is a teacher who in preparation for Thanksgiving Day asked her class of first graders to draw a picture of something they were thankful for. She thought of how little these children from their poor neighborhood had. She imagined that most of them would draw pictures of turkeys or tables with food.

But the teacher was taken aback with the picture little Douglas handed in: a childishly-drawn hand. The teacher showed it to the class to decide whose hand it was. "I think it must be the hand of God that brings us food," said one child. "A farmer," said another, "because he grows the turkeys." When the others were at work, the teacher bent over Douglas' desk and asked whose hand it was. "It's your hand, teacher," he mumbled.

It was only then that she recalled that frequently at recess she had taken Douglas, a scrubby forlorn child, by the hand. She often did that with the children; it had obviously meant a lot to Douglas. For herself, she was grateful for the chance, in whatever small way, to give self-effacedly to others.

The second acceptable type of humility is linked to the first: the habit of being under authority. This doesn't necessarily have anything do with parental strictures or school rules or the necessary procedures of the office; it means simply the acknowledgment, all the time, of a power much higher than these, in whose hands we are and to whom we owe allegiance.

A fitting model for all aspects of humility is the early flowers of Spring — the primrose, violet, wood anemone. They bloom in hidden places: in woods, on broken ground, under hedges. We often smell these flowers before we see them; they spread their sweetness without asserting themselves, and wither as soon as they're picked and brought indoors to be admired. Their beauty lies in their self-effacement.

One of Our Lord's cherished characteristics is his special love for humble people. In today's Gospel passage St. Luke, following the classical Greek style of his day, organized different material into a unity. Because Jesus speaks in connection with sharing a meal on a Sabbath with some Pharisees (v. 1), the section is described as "Jesus' table talk." Jesus didn't refuse invitations, even an enemy's: You can't make enemies into friends if you refuse to meet with them and talk.

Yet Jesus was under the Pharisees' surveillance (v. 1). Few things are more trying than their kind of scrutiny of Jesus: It ordinarily makes you edgy, aloof, impersonal, careful. But Jesus remained serene, concerned, and fervent. There's some humor and irony in the situation: They're watching Jesus closely for some social gaffe, but Jesus' observations lead him to criticize the values they betrayed by their table-manners. He addressed his first lesson to the guests. Using their conduct at dinner as his jumping-off point, he lifted them to the more important eternal feast of heaven. The Pharisees took for granted that at that heavenly banquet they would have the places of honor; they never thought it possible that God might have a different seating arrangement.

The first part of Jesus' straightforward lesson was that everyone who exalts himself will be humbled (v. 11). Jesus used this proverb frequently, in all kinds of different settings. His use on this occasion shows that he wasn't teaching only social etiquette at table, even though etiquette comes before law in getting along with other people; you can't get away without etiquette any more than you can decide not to use language. But what Jesus was doing here was drawing theological conclusions about the kingdom. God invites into membership those who are humble enough to recognize their need of salvation.

The warning here was pointed, but more kindly than Jesus' former rebukes to Pharisees. As Jesus showed here, Gospel humility isn't a religious sado-masochism instigated by self-hatred, or an obsequiousness motivated by a desire to be noticed. And it doesn't preclude assertiveness, as Jesus showed when he used a whip in the Temple. But both humility and assertiveness require that we be true to our dignity as images of God.

The latter part of Jesus' lesson to the guests was that the one who humbles himself will be exalted. A nervous lector once read this verse mistakenly to an amused congregation: "The one who humbles himself shall be exhausted." Despite the mistake, it's true that humility requires effort and is difficult to achieve.

After thus addressing all of that to the guests, Jesus applied the lesson of humility to his host. To invite your friends or your relatives or your neighbors (v. 12) to a dinner is good, Jesus said, but can be calculated to get something in return — at the very least, good will and influence, and beyond that to get invited in turn, to hear the gossip, and perhaps even to get the job.

Jesus' advice is to invite the poor and the handicapped (v. 13) who can't repay you (v. 14). The only real way to give is the way God did it: He gave because He so loved the world. The recompense for one who gives from that supernatural motive lies in a growing likeness to God Himself. And one who performs, even for an instant, an unselfish kindness, inevitably knows a blessedness that can come in no other way. That blessedness is, as Jesus said, a foretaste of how God will repay in the resurrection of the just.

Although the details of humility are uniquely Christian, the idea of humility was foreshadowed for a long time before: in today's first reading, for example. It's from the Book of Sirach, which contains samples of the collected sayings of a famous teacher around 180 B.C. Sirach is as up-to-date and timeless about humility as he is about much of his other advice. Because his overall advice is hard to beat, in the early Church converts often received their moral training from his writings, and the book came to be known as "The Book of the Church" (Ecclesiasticus, from *ecclesia*, the Latin word for church).

Sirach realized that pride is the temptation of all pagan culture — such as the Hellenistic culture in Alexandria in Egypt to which the Jews were attracted. The same is true of the "self-image" concept of today's pop psychology. "I'm okay, you're okay," says this psychology. But then why is there so much wrong with the world? In the normal sense of the term, psychology aims to build up confidence in areas where we should be self-confident. Spirituality, on the other hand, is to move us in a faith direction by undermining confidence in the self so that we gain a confidence in God for Whom we have a bottomless need.

Sirach taught that humility gives a true estimate of self (vv. 17ff.). Humility is especially important for those in higher social strata (v. 18). Whereas through humility people perform their duty and avoid what's beyond their understanding and strength (vv. 20ff.), pride begets misjudgment, stubbornness, sorrow, affliction, and even perdition (vv. 23-27).

Sirach says that humility helps us be attentive to God's word (v. 28). And the water of kindness to the poor will quench the burning fire of puffed-up pride — which results mostly from a non-reflective approach to life and its challenges (v. 29). Pride requires only a false sense of superiority and aggression. Humility, on the other hand, demands true strength of character.

Pride is within us and all around us; that's why psychiatrists are jokingly referred to as "head shrinkers." Ours is a world of assertiveness training, the hard sell, status-winning, jockeying for position, the power luncheon, and general one-up-manship. Our world, despite its lip service to the contrary, exists on the principle of the powerful and wealthy exploiting the poor and the lowly, and business carried on ruthlessly and without concern for any resulting human wreckage.

Our world puts its faith in Uriah Heep in the Charles Dickens novel *David Copperfield* who, when he perceives it to be to his advantage, contemptibly insists that he's "an 'umble man," and with a "hook humility" fishes for compliments with a snare that shows through his false humility to a closet boaster. We're sometimes afraid of our own personal truth and keep secrets from ourselves. Through it all, our best lies are the ones we tell ourselves. So the call for humility requires special attention.

In brief, we need to remember that a mule doesn't stop being dull just because he's carrying the precious cargo of a king. We're that mule. Realizing that, may we exercise authority with true humility; may we never manipulate, abuse, or victimize others; may we discover ways of strong and at the same time gentle responsibility for each other. And may our humility bring God's love to all those we meet this week.

TWENTY-THIRD SUNDAY IN ORDINARY TIME
Ws 9:13-18   Phm 9f., 12-17   Lk 14:25-33

The Price of Being a Christian
The World's Street-Smart Wisdom vs. God's;
Commitment, Self-Control, and Detachment

The ancient Romans easily found a sufficient figurative connection between commerce, theft, and eloquence to place merchants, thieves, and orators under one and the same deity: the god Mercury. Whether this connection between merchants, thieves, and orators is correct or not, we leave it to you to judge. But in our day one thing's sure: Everyone — business-person, thief, or orator; doctor, lawyer, or Indian chief; rich man, poor man, beggar man, or thief — has to find out if he's willing to pay the price to come under the god he says he serves.

The great crowds (v. 25) surrounding Jesus in today's Gospel passage contained the exultant, sensation-seeking people streaming from the streets and alleys of the towns: the poor, the crippled, and the blind (v. 21). They thought Jesus was on the way to an empire; he knew he was on the way to the cross. They thought discipleship had no costs; he, now on his way to Jerusalem to suffer and die, was aware of its demands.

He had to say something to put them straight. People had to know what they were getting themselves into. So he gave three conditions for following him: putting commitment to him above everything else, including family ties; maintaining self-control; and developing detachment from possessions. Those are the opposites, then and now, of worldly people — who go for lack of commitment, self-indulgence, and attachment to all you can lay your hands on.

To sift through the complex demands, both before Christ's time and after, we need a wisdom from above. Today's reading from the Book of Wisdom tells us that. At the time this book was written, about a hundred years before Christ's birth, the Jewish community at Alexandria in Egypt, the place where it was written, lived in a world where different religions and philosophies were vying for converts. The devout Jew felt out of place in that world. To counter that feeling, this book taught that there was no need to envy other ways of life: Commitment to God, even when His plan lay beyond our understanding, is the true way to wisdom.

The name that had been connected with wisdom was King Solomon. The author of this book presents part of his version of Solomon's prayer for wisdom (vv. 1-18). Solomon wanted to build a magnificent Temple to God. The text suggests a question: How can anyone perform a task like that without that wisdom that was with God when He set about the work of creation? The answer given is that no one can arrive at God's counsels without wisdom (vv. 13-18).

Some would question Solomon's wisdom on two grounds. First, he had 700 wives and 300 concubines, and some men have problems with one wife! And second, his method of constructing the Temple was monumentally unwise. He funded the Temple's construction with massive new taxes and forced his subjects into labor — but exempted his native southern region of Judah from both taxes and labor. This led the nation to split along its ancient north-south fault line into Judah in the south and Israel in the north.

With regard to the first of Jesus' conditions for following him — putting commitment to him above everything — anyone who would become an intimate disciple must have the wisdom to prefer Jesus' kingdom to his family, and even to his own life (v. 26). In return, the kingdom promises life more fully; it transforms the commitment into a new, personal fulfillment. Many people like the promise but not the price. Just as it's possible to be a hearer of lectures without being a student, a listener to homilies without being a doer of the word, and a taker without being a giver, so it's possible to be a listener to Jesus without being a committed follower.

Temporary enthusiasm isn't enough. The true disciple can't act on impulse, but only on a carefully considered program of involvement. To teach that, Jesus told two stories. The first, about a man who wanted to build a tower-overlook to protect his vineyard (vv. 28-30), dealt with private life. The second, concerning a king about to march (vv. 31f.), pertained to political life.

Concerning private life today, everyone knows that if a youth wants to become a doctor, lawyer, or Indian chief, he or she must be committed to long hours of study. Concerning public and political life, examples of failure of wise commitment abound. In the closing days of World War II, for example, one of the reasons why the Soviet Union was able to occupy Eastern Europe and cause the long Cold War was that the Allied planners for the Normandy invasion hadn't wisely committed General George S. Patton's Third Army beyond the French beachhead, and the army ran out of gas and ammunition halfway across Europe.

Currently commitment leaves much to be desired. On a personal level, we don't seem to realize sufficiently that commitment is the foundation, the bedrock of any genuinely loving relationship. Anyone who is truly concerned for the spiritual growth of another knows, consciously or instinctively, that he or she can significantly foster that growth only through a relationship of constancy. While deep commitment doesn't guarantee the success of the relationship, it does help more than any other factor to assure it.

On the level of societal commitment, daily we see pictures of people throughout the world, especially children, so starved because of wars or natural disasters that they have arms like splinters and ribs pressing out of near-transparent flesh; infants with heads and bellies grotesquely large for their shrunken torsos; mothers numb with grief waiting for their babies to die in camps that look like garbage dumps; and seemingly weightless little bodies being carried to shacks that pass for morgues. In other situations of random and massive slaughter, people step over corpses that lie in the streets of ruined cities.

In what passes for the international community, shouldn't it be possible to be committed to plans such that when these horrors occur we can immediately come to the aid of the distressed and be present for them? In our national community, shouldn't we be more committed to alleviate the human victims of hurricanes, tornadoes, earthquakes, and other tragedies? Are we sincere about our commitment? That word "sincere" means to be "without wax" (*sine cera*): Ancient actors' masks were made of wax.

About Jesus' second and third conditions for following him — self-control and detachment — today's Second Reading makes good points. It's the only reading in all the liturgy from this shortest (25 vv.), very touching, and very personal letter of St. Paul. It illustrates a self-control and detachment that are not cold and aloof, but warm. Addressed to a rich Christian slave-owner named Philemon, it's a compassionate intercession by one Christian, Paul, in behalf of another, Philemon's slave Onesimus.

To understand this reading, it helps to know the story behind it. Because there were at the time 60 million slaves in the Roman Empire, fear caused the citizenry to make the laws concerning them strict. Runaway slaves could be punished by torture, death, or both. Philemon's slave Onesimus had stolen something from his master and run away. Onesimus was therefore in deep trouble: Now in jail in Ephesus, he was to be returned to Philemon as soon as possible. Anyone who harbored him would be liable for any loss that his master suffered.

It happened that Onesimus was put into the same jail as Paul. Paul converted, instructed, and baptized him, and the two had become close. That made it necessary for Paul to do some assessing. Should he, for example, condemn the very institution of slavery? He couldn't accomplish much by doing that. He was in jail, and condemning slavery would only make matters worse. Should he command Philemon as a fellow Christian to accept his servant Onesimus back? He clearly hadn't the authority to do that.

No, Paul's appeal to Philemon would follow the advice he gave elsewhere, as in his "hymn to love" (1 Cor 13). In the 25 verses of his letter to Philemon there are four references to love, plus two to Paul's heart. Paul appealed to Philemon to look at his slave in a new way (v. 10). By baptizing him, Paul had given Onesimus spiritual birth; the Jews looked upon spiritual birth as being more important than physical birth. For Christians, baptism establishes a new and radical relationship between Christians before which all others, including that of master and slave, give way in favor of a new kinship in Christ.

Paul wasn't a fuzzy-headed bleeding-heart denying the wrong Onesimus had done. And though Paul, a lonely missionary, would have liked to keep Onesimus for himself (v. 13), he deferentially acknowledged the master's right, and would do nothing without Philemon's consent (v. 14). Christianity doesn't have as a purpose to help people run away from their past: Christians are to face their past and overcome it. Christianity isn't escape from self: It's conquest of self.

In the entire affair, Paul saw the hand of providence (v. 15). This was because both slave and master were now through baptism adopted sons of God, and therefore brothers (v. 16). Considering Philemon's high social status, this tender and compassionate appeal may have been hard for him to recognize — but then he, and all good Christians, are expected to be open to new vistas. Although it wasn't until the nineteenth century that the human race showed that it realized that slavery is the evil thing that it is, slavery's death-knell had been sounded when a slave-owner was requested to treat his slave as a brother on the grounds of religious love.

All of us who face the invitation of God's grace have to balance the costs and make decisions about our commitment, our self-control, and our detachment. In the process, we have to ask hard questions. Are the demands of the code of morality that accompanies the Christian creed too hard for us? Would it be better to follow the pleasures of self-indulgence? In the tension between the wisdom of this world and the wisdom of God, should we compromise with a presiding deity who, like the Roman god Mercury, will cover all our options? In answering, let's remember that, in the end, our choices form us. And the reason why wise people still choose to follow Jesus, despite the price, is that, all things considered, that means choosing life over death.

TWENTY-FOURTH SUNDAY IN ORDINARY TIME
Ex 32:7-11, 13f.   1 Tm 1:12-17   Lk 15:1-32 (or 15:1-10)

Being Joyfully and Mercifully Forgiving
God's Unique Kind of Forgiveness; Relying Upon and Imitating God's
Forgiveness; Rise and Go to the Father; Forgiveness, the Final Form of Love

With good reason, someone has said that humankind's deepest need
and highest achievement is forgiveness. Today's excerpt from the second book of the Bible, Exodus, speaks of one incident of a provoked
God forgiving His people. Throughout the Exodus from Egypt, God's
people griped and whined: They complained that the pursuing Egyptians were going to overtake and kill them; they complained that they
didn't have enough to eat; when God gave them manna to eat, they
complained about its monotonous taste; they complained that they
didn't have enough water (so God gave them water from the rock); they
complained that the inhabitants of the Promised Land would be too
strong for them; and so on and on.

Now, while Moses was on Mt. Sinai, they complained that Moses
had abandoned them, so they molded the golden calf-idol. God announced that He would destroy the people for this, and so Moses appealed to Him to forgive. Because of God's loving-kindness (*hesed*)
for His people, He forgave. Of course, God doesn't "get angry" or
"change His mind" or "repent." But in our efforts to understand God,
we have to use human language, as did the writers of the First Testament. So what began as a story of a people's sinfulness really became
a story of God's forgiveness.

God's forgiveness on Mt. Sinai foreshadowed what Jesus would
do and teach. Today's portion of St. Luke's Gospel begins with the
Pharisees' complaint that Jesus was eating with sinners. In truth, Jesus'
dinner companions were what the cat dragged in: They would never
make the guest list at White House banquets or appear in newspapers'
society pages. And the Pharisees had a point. Whereas to us it may
appear simply that Jesus was being friendly, in their culture sharing
food together meant that the people at the table show that they accept
one another. To counter the Pharisees, Jesus told three stories about
God reaching out and about forgiveness.

Because the three stories are of the lost — the lost sheep, the lost coin, and the lost son — some flippantly call this section the "Lost and Found Department." It should more properly be called "God's Joy in Forgiving Sinners." Jesus' three stories have as their essential purpose the revelation that God's love is broader and deeper than people's love, and can forgive even when people would refuse to do so. But they don't all say exactly the same thing.

The beautiful "Story of the Lost Sheep" (vv. 3-7) contains the distilled essence of Jesus' Good News. To be a shepherd wasn't easy. Many of the flocks were owned by poor villages, which left two or three shepherds in charge. If at the end of the day a sheep was lost on the grassy plateaus, steep cliffs, or vast stretches, returning shepherds would get word out that one shepherd would be late because he was taking his turn at searching. When a villager reported seeing the shepherd with the lost sheep across his shoulders, there would be joy and thanks in the whole community. Jesus said in effect, "That's the way it is with God and a repentant sinner!"

Then (vv. 8-10) Jesus told the "Story of the Lost Coin." It wasn't hard to lose a coin in a house of that time. The house, often built into a hillside, was dark, lit by one window (which was small, the better to keep out the elements at a time before glass was used for windows), with a floor of hard earth covered with dried reeds. The woman who lost the coin perhaps needed it, small though its value, to feed her family. Or perhaps it had great sentimental value because it was one of the ten little coins she received on the day of her marriage and wore on her forehead. In either case, when she saw the glint of the coin her joy would be great. When dealing with lost people God, said Jesus, is like that woman, too.

These two stories went against the tradition, which never conceived of a God Who went out to search for sinners. The Pharisees, in fact, had a saying that "There is joy in heaven over one sinner who is obliterated before God." (And isn't that the way we think sometimes?)

After these stories' portrayal of God as one Who actively seeks what is lost, Jesus told a glorious story of the Father Who seems content to wait for a sinner to come to his senses and return home (vv. 11-32). Here the image of God is subtly different from the previous. Often called the "Parable of the Prodigal Son," it might better be called the "Story of the Prodigal Father" — for "prodigal" means spendthrift, and when we think about it we see that it's indeed the Father Who is spendthrift, lavishing His love, welcome, and forgiveness.

It's been said that the ingratitude of a child is more hurtful to a parent than the assassination attempt of a servant. What concerned this father most was that, whether he complied with his young son's heartless and callous request for his inheritance (v. 12) or not, he was going to lose his child.

Eventually, the son's misery brought him to his senses (v. 17). Here he was, this kosher boy, in a pig sty, envying the food of an animal that was itself not fit to be food. He had hit rock bottom. He had reached the first stage of seeking forgiveness. He determined — albeit selfishly — to do what we said in today's Responsorial Psalm: He would rise and go to his father.

The father's options with his returning son were many: He could scold him, or demand an apology, or be condescendingly accepting, or disown him. Or he could demand that the son make restitution by working as a hired hand, which was what both the son and Jesus' audience expected.

But the father chose forgiveness.

Now, there are many ways of forgiving. It's often done reluctantly, holding back, conveying continuing guilt to the recipient. Sometimes forgiveness is done as a favor. Worse, at times the forgiver, in a form of blackmail, implies that the other's sin will still in some way be held over him. With this father, though, the forgiveness was total, offering to treat the son's sins as though they had never happened. And it was joyous: To celebrate it the father broke forth into typical Semitic poetry (v. 24). He threw his arms around his son, kissed him (v. 20), and instructed his servants to dress him as befits his son (v. 22): to give him a ring, a token of honor and authority, and sandals, the mark of a freeman, since only slaves went barefoot. (The American slave's dream of heaven in the Afro-American spiritual is, "All God's Chillun Got Shoes.")

Whereas the father had interrupted the younger son's prepared confession out of love, the elder son in turn interrupted the father's expression of forgiveness because of small-spiritedness. Part of his thinking was possibly that the money for this party was partially coming out of his share of the estate! He complained about having done his duty (v. 29), and he undoubtedly had — but grimly. If over time his father hadn't heaped marks of affection upon him, it could well have been because his son's coldness made that impossible.

The elder brother showed meanness of speech in referring to his brother as "your son" (v. 30) rather than as "my brother." He alleged without evidence that the younger brother had swallowed up the father's property with prostitutes (v. 30). This is the kind of rash judgment in which the self-righteous often indulge. The father's answer was heart-rending: "My son, everything I have is yours" (v. 31).

The story of the Prodigal Son actually has no ending. We don't know whether the elder brother goes into the house to join in the cel-ebration, or whether he nurses his self-righteousness outside. There's no ending because it's not just a story: It's a challenge — to each one of us. Would you go in or stay outside?

Today's reading from the first letter of St. Paul to Timothy shows one result of what God's forgiveness can do. It shows Paul to be full of gratitude over the great mystery of mercy whereby he, the arrogant and fierce persecutor of Christian communities, had been forgiven. And God's forgiveness included trust. When people forgive, often they won't trust the forgiven again. After totally forgiving Paul, God ap-pointed him to responsible service in His Church.

Nothing speaks of the radical nature of Jesus' message more than his teachings on forgiveness. Forgiveness is the final form of love, and wholehearted forgiveness is so loving that it's God-like. Those real-izations should inspire us to see our need for Jesus' gift of the Sacra-ment of Reconciliation for God's forgiveness of our sins, saying, "I will rise and go to my Father."

And we're to imitate God's kind of love in joyful forgiving of other people. In individual cases that may be difficult. To those who brood over injuries, it may be easier to learn Chinese than to say "I'm sorry" or "I forgive you" in our own language. Remember, though, to pray for the grace to forgive, even when we don't feel like forgiving. The very fact that we sincerely want to forgive means we've actually forgiven the person in our heart. Good feelings will follow, though not necessarily right away.

Consider the honest testimony of a woman damaged by one of the most psychologically ruinous experiences possible to women: Her husband left her. She said, "After that I was angry, bitter, and filled with resentment and hatred for my ex-husband. I went through ques-tions like, 'What have I done?' and could come up with nothing: I had always tried to please him. So I asked, 'Lord, how could you let this happen to me?' I cried, I sobbed, I moaned, and I wailed. I beat my breast and asked for forgiveness for the spiteful feelings I had toward my ex-husband, and for the anger. Then, one sleepless night, I prayed aloud, 'Father, forgive me. I want to trust and have faith like a child, but right now I don't. Please help me really mean that I want to truly wish my husband all the best that life has to offer. You know I don't mean this now, but I want to.'"

She had unconsciously followed the advice of St. Augustine, who said: "Do what you can do, and pray for what you cannot yet do."

Remembering that forgiveness is humankind's deepest need and highest achievement, let's look into the concealed places where lost people tend to hide, and contribute to the healing forgiveness that we and our world so greatly crave.

TWENTY-FIFTH SUNDAY IN ORDINARY TIME
Am 8:4-7   1 Tm 2:1-8   Lk 16:1-13

Social Justice
Christian Cleverness; Money and Religion; Wealth Possessing the Possessor; Can We Have Both Money and God?

You might dislike sharp business practices, but you can't help but admire the cleverness of some of them. They range from the rather simple level of bait and switch techniques and loss-leader bargains in department stores to sophisticated stock market put-and-call options, bankruptcy proceedings for personal profit, corporate take-overs, and speculations in commodity market futures — sometimes making deals that are hard even to understand, much less perpetrate.

It was on a middle level of sophistication that we find the main character in today's Gospel, which consists of as interesting a group of knaves as you'll see outside a rogues' gallery. To begin with the manager, he wasn't only not a nice person: He was a villain. He had full authorization to make binding contracts for his master — a common custom of the time. He had to show a profit for his master, but he could make some profit for himself, too, by adroit loans and loan-shark rates of interest. He could find many ways around the Mosaic Law against taking interest on a loan, one way being to accept payment in commodities instead of cash.

Under the blow of his disgrace in having his sharp practices reported, he showed himself lazy, accustomed to deference from his master's workmen and customers, and soft: not strong enough to dig, and ashamed to beg (v. 3). A wily wheeler-dealer who was far from feeling repentance when he was caught, he turned to embezzlement, theft, and forgery to escape his predicament. But he managed it so cleverly that he made others commit the actual forgery. He directed a debtor who owed the yield of about 150 olive trees to write that he owed only half that. He reduced the obligation of the debtor who owed the yield of about 100 acres of wheat.

The debtors, too, were scoundrels: They were ready to take advantage of every opportunity they could, moral or not. But the manager knew that now they couldn't inform on him; on the contrary, if he were dismissed by his master, he could go and ask favors now of one, now of another, and if they didn't oblige him willingly they would have to do so unwillingly lest he report them.

The master also was something of a knave. When he entered the picture, he wasn't shocked by what the manager had done and, rather than giving attention to his devious employee's dishonesty, he gave him credit for being enterprising (v. 8). Jesus went on to point out that the children of this world are more astute in dealing with their own kind of people than are the children of light. That's the point — the only point — that Jesus praises.

An up-dated but innocent example of the children of this world being enterprising is the department-store clerk who had broken all sales records. Modestly disclaiming credit, he explained to his boss, "A customer came in, and I sold him some fishhooks. 'You'll need a line for those hooks,' I said, and sold him some line. Then I told him, 'You have to have a rod to go with the line,' and I sold him a rod. 'You ought to have a boat so you can use your new rod in deep water,' I suggested, and sold him a boat. Next I told him, 'You'll need a boat trailer,' and he fell for that, too. Finally, I said, 'How will you pull the trailer without a car?' And guess what? He bought my car." And the boss said, "But I assigned you to the greeting-card department." "That's right," the salesman nodded. "This customer came in for a get-well card for his girl, who had a broken hip. When I heard that, I said to him, 'You haven't got anything to do for six weeks, so you might as well go fishing.'"

Often the other-worldly — those who believe in God, attend

church, and try to live morally — don't give anywhere near as much attention to donating their services to God's work as the worldly give to making more money, living in the correct neighborhood, and hob-nobbing with the right people. Why is that? Is religion "the opium of the people" that provides an escape into a dream-like trance? Or do the "children of light" have phlegmatic personalities? Or are they lazy? Or without courage? Or smug? Or do they fail to see the wisdom of the axiom that "the only thing necessary for the triumph of evil is for good people to do nothing"?

Perhaps they don't see that evil people hate the light because it reveals themselves to themselves. They hate goodness because it re-veals their badness; they hate love because it reveals their laziness. They will destroy the light, the goodness, the love in order to avoid the pain of their own awareness of their state.

The Lord wants us to be even shrewder than the children of this world. He wants of us day-by-day fidelity — saying that the person who is trustworthy in very small matters is also trustworthy in great ones (v. 10). And he wants total dedication — telling us that we can't serve two masters, both God and mammon (v. 13). Like fire, money can be a good servant, but a bad boss.

Money's such a tyrant that the prophets frequently used it as one of the main barometers of religious concern. Today's reading from Amos (who's sometimes called "God's angry prophet") is an example. The earliest writing prophet, Amos wrote from near Bethlehem about 750 years before Christ. At a time of an ever-widening chasm between the wealthy few and the destitute masses, he had the courage to protest openly against the materialistic, rich, and sophisticated leaders who were so greedy as to exploit the poor. Amos is a prophet for our time.

Many of the Israelites were so greedy that their worship of God was only an empty ritual. Like Scrooge at Christmas, they couldn't wait for the end of the holy days so that they could get back to work for business profits (v. 5). Not only that: They would make greater profit by cheating their customers. They would short-weight the bushel by adding stones to tip the scales. They would sell debtors into slavery for failing to pay for even a pair of sandals (v. 6). They would mix the refuse of the wheat with the good grain they sold.

Amos spoke of social injustice as being blasphemy against God, and today's reading from a pastoral letter of St. Paul to young Timo-thy reminds us that when we worship, it must be with blameless hands

(v. 8). "Blameless hands" means positive involvement as well as distinct attempts at fairness. The silence of ordinary people has been the most decisive political act of our time. A short time ago, a church was broken into and desecrated: The tabernacle was forced open and the Sacred Hosts scattered and trampled underfoot. A shocked group of people went to inform the pastor. "Father," they said, "even the Body of Christ was trampled upon." "That's certainly awful," replied the pastor, "but what about the other Body of Christ, the poor? They're trampled underfoot every day, and nobody complains."

Christianity isn't a rushed three-quarter-hour attendance at worship once a week followed by a week of commitment to mammon. It's been estimated that an average American of 70 years of age has spent 6 years eating, 11 working, 8 amusing himself, 24 sleeping, 5 and 1/2 washing and dressing, 3 talking — and six months in church. Split personalities who try to serve two masters are always running — running after things. Such people isolate themselves from others in a world of non-concern. And they slowly wind up with a numbness — a numbness which shows up in their relationship to other people. And Christianity is about people — respecting people, loving people, helping people. It's by helping people that we can cure the running and the numbness — especially the numbness.

The liturgical prayer of the faithful community, Paul's letter insists, should show justice as well as charity to all people, up and down the social scale, from the rich and powerful to the poor. Although there are laws against the most egregious injustices, lack of charity is not an offense against law — even though charity is the greatest of the virtues. Let's remember that money is an article which may be used as a universal passport to everywhere except heaven, and as a universal provider of everything except happiness.

In front of the Brooklyn Museum is a huge statue of a lady who was intended to allegorize Manhattan. She strokes a peacock with her hand and rests her foot on a locked cash box. Many people think that the sculptor, Daniel Chester French, got the ethos of Manhattan just right, and extend the pride and greed to the rest of the contemporary scene. We still have short-change merchants, people for whose lives the bottom line is money, embezzlers, petty thieves, executives who cook the books, crooked managers of widows' investment portfolios, and business people who sell products they know to be harmful, even fatal. Our age has gone way beyond today's Gospel manager to such "big con" business methods as subliminal suggestion, pressure advertising, the creation of useless needs, market rigging, and the exploitation of weakness. Many people, if they had their way, would choose the front of the bus, the back of the church, and the center of attention.

We must see to it that that way of thinking is removed from our personal lives. Though we can't escape the economic and political world in which we live, we must apply Christian principles to the world. Living well lavishly may be the best revenge in some people's minds, but living well lovingly pays greater dividends in the long run. People remember Francis of Assisi, the *"poverello,"* better than they do his money-centered father.

TWENTY-SIXTH SUNDAY IN ORDINARY TIME
Am 6:1, 4-7   1 Tm 6:11-16   Lk 16:19-31

Responsibility to the Underprivileged
Awareness above Complacency; Tenderness over Hardness;
Justice; Hospitality and Its Abuse

As a symbol of justice, we take for granted the blindfolded lady in long-flowing robes holding scales in one hand and a sword in the other. The blindfold allegedly prevents Lady Justice from looking at such conditions as whether a petitioner is old or young, rich or poor, black or white. The sword indicates the swiftness and decisiveness with which she can mete out the punishment with which she can back up her decisions. Her equally-balanced scales are reminders that justice is dispensed equally to all. Modern cynical wags interpret the symbol differently. They say that justice looks so stolid in her long-flowing robes because she never moves. And they see it as good that both her hands are occupied, because then she can't take bribes.

Today's liturgy concerns itself with justice, and the prophet Amos had a different symbol for it. In a land where water was precious, his symbol of justice focused on a mighty mountain stream — which could renew, refresh, give life, and bring to fruition. Applied to justice, this torrent, surging with thundering power, meant the elimination of any kind of oppression that keeps people, especially the poor, from fully developing as human beings.

Amos, addressing the Jewish leaders, depicts the rich as Jesus did: self-satisfied, pampered, insensitive — and complacent (v. 1). The debauched rich were letting the good times roll. They luxuriated in elaborate furniture inlaid with ivory (v. 4), ate choice foods, and dedicated their lives to wine, women, and song at their most decadent. With matchless sarcasm, Amos mocks their banquet music by comparing it to David's — whose music praised God (v. 5). He prophesies that their inattention to the poor around them will bring about their doom.

In the Gospel, Jesus addresses the Pharisees, "who loved money" (v. 14). He tells the story of two men: Lazarus, the poor man, whose Hebrew name means "God is my help," and Dives, from the Latin adjective meaning "rich" — one of the "beautiful people" who went "first class" all the way: right out of the pages of *Esquire*. Dives's outrageously expensive outer garments were made of wool died in a purple that came from shells on the beaches of Tyre, so cherished that the veil of the Temple was made from this purple. From time to time attempts were made to reserve it exclusively for the togas of the emperor. At a time when the poor and hard-working populace were lucky if they got the cheapest cut of meat once a week, Dives dined sumptuously (v. 19) every day.

At the gate to his palace — right off the sidewalks of any modern city, where he lies in his cardboard shelter against the winds — lay Lazarus the beggar, almost a permanent fixture (v. 20). In abject poverty he longed to eat the scraps (v. 21) from Dives's table. Lazarus wasn't only poor, but helpless — so helpless that hungry dogs licked his sores, and he couldn't chase them away!

Then death came. Lazarus was taken to heaven as a reward — not for poverty, but for his trust in God as his help. Dives went to a place of terrible torment (v. 23), where he was wracked with hunger and thirst. This was not because of molesting Lazarus in any way: He didn't. In a sense, he did nothing wrong; but he did nothing about the rights of the poor. He was condemned not because luxury is evil, but because of apathy. Dives-types — his five brothers (v. 28) — continue to roam the earth, looking on the world's misery but not feeling it, and seeing fellow human beings in pain without involvement.

With Lazarus in heaven and Dives in hell, the arrogant Dives doesn't change! The tongue that had tasted the finest wines, now longing for a drop of water, demanded the saintly Lazarus — whose identity he knows exactly, even though he had never done anything for him in his days and nights of need — as his head waiter or errand-boy to do something to slake his thirst (v. 24)!

"As we live, so shall we die," is frightening but true. A famous bullfighter, hoist on a bull's horn, thought, "Now the lousy bull's ruined my whole afternoon." A motorcycle rider, his leg severed, sobbed in the ambulance, "What am I gonna tell my girl friend?" A sailor, bleeding to death on a California highway beside his wrecked car, mumbled before closing his eyes, "This would have to happen on my birthday."

In the Gospel, Abraham's answer to Dives's pleas for special help was the equivalent of those saddest of words, "Too late! Too late!" Wondrous events — a voice from the grave, even Christ's resurrection from the dead (v. 31) — won't automatically save people. Like Lazarus we must have a faith that affects the way we live.

The letter to Timothy advises the young bishop about his new role as leader of the community. It also reveals the kind of persons we ought to be. We're to have integrity, which means putting everything together for God and fellow human beings. To God, three virtues are especially due: piety, a quality of realizing that we're God's children whose life is lived in His presence; an unswerving fidelity in the darkness as well as the light; and love, which is the spontaneous response of our hearts to God's overwhelming love for us. Toward people, we owe the virtue of a gentle spirit — that overlooks wrongs done to oneself and challenges the injustice done to others, along with a temperament that's always ready to forgive.

Where do we actually stand? Will Christ find us among the complacent rich? Hand-in-hand with wealth and power must go responsibility. If we have no sense of responsibility or concern for others, there follows the blindness and coldness of heart exemplified in today's readings and in the modern bumper-sticker, "Life Is Cheap; Toilet Paper Is Expensive."

The truth is that all of us, even the poorest, are of great value, as the poet (Anonymous, *The Touch of the Master's Hand*) says of the auction of an old violin:

> 'Twas battered and scarred and the auctioneer
> Thought it scarcely worth his while

To waste much time on the old violin,
But he held it up with a smile.
"What am I bidden, good folks?" he cried
"Who'll start the bidding for me?
A dollar — a dollar — now two, only two,
Two dollars, and who'll make it three?
Three dollars, once; three dollars, twice,
Going for three" — but No!
From the room, far back, a gray-haired man
Came forward and picked up the bow;
Then, wiping the dust from the old violin,
And tightening up all of the strings,
He played a melody pure and sweet —
As sweet as an angel sings.
The music ceased, and the auctioneer
With a voice that was quiet and low,
Said, "What am I bid for the old violin?"
And he held it up with the bow.
"A thousand dollars — and who'll make it two?
Two thousand — and who'll make it three?
Three thousand once, three thousand twice —
And going, and going, and gone," said he.
The people cheered, but some of them said,
"We do not quite understand —
What changed its worth?" The man replied:
"THE TOUCH OF THE MASTER'S HAND!"
And many a person with life out of tune
And battered and torn with sin,
Is auctioned cheap to a thoughtless crowd,
Much like the old violin.
A mess of pottage, a glass of wine,
A game — and they travel on,
They're going once, and going twice,
They're going — and almost gone!
But the Master comes, and the foolish crowd
Never can quite understand,
The worth of a Soul, and the change that's wrought
By THE TOUCH OF THE MASTER'S HAND!

Unfortunately, our society hasn't changed essentially from the time of Amos 750 years before Christ. We reward our entertainers with lavish bounty while resenting persons on welfare; we give golden parachutes to failed CEO's and nothing to workers laid off as a result of their failure. Our society gives millions of dollars a year to corporate heads of clothing companies that pay fifty cents an hour to poor women who make the clothing.

Today's readings challenge all of us. We're not to adopt an attitude of resigned acceptance of the status quo that has us wait for "pie in the sky bye and bye." All of us are to be at one with Lazarus who placed his hope in the Lord, sensitive to the needs of others as Amos, and the person of God whom Timothy would recognize. The question to be asked of us is not, "Are you rich or are you poor?", as if one or the other would make us morally better, but, "Do you care, or are you complacent?" Are we persons of God, or have we created an abyss between ourselves and the Lazaruses of the world, putting ourselves among Dives's people still roaming the earth?

TWENTY-SEVENTH SUNDAY IN ORDINARY TIME
Hab 1:2f., 2:2-4   2 Tm 1:6-8, 13f.   Lk 17:5-10

Stir Into Flame Faith and Faithfulness
An Animating, Vigorous, and Courageous Faith; Faith and Courage;
Genuineness of Faith; Hang In There!

We've come to think that modern technology has vastly changed our world. At the same time, there's an old adage that the more things change, the more they remain the same.

Take insulation as one example. Long before human beings ever thought of such a thing as controlling temperatures by special types of insulating materials, the praying mantis was surrounding its eggs with a frothy mass of bubbles to protect them from the weather. The bubbles work on the same principle as our thermos bottles. No matter how cold or how warm the air gets, the tender eggs within are protected. Or take air conditioning as another example. Honey bees maintain a constant

temperature and a specific condition of airflow in order that their lar-
vae may be properly reared and honey successfully cured. Muscular
exertion of certain bees produces heat from their bodies, and then other
bees — the fanners — anchor themselves to the floor of the hive and
vibrate their wings to create and maintain the exact amount of air circulation needed.

All three readings of today's liturgy support the old adage that
the more things change, the more they remain the same. From at least
600 B.C., about when the prophecy of Habakkuk was written, through
100 A.D., roughly when the second letter to Timothy was written, right
up to the present, there have been problems with faith and faithfulness.

Habakkuk's times were as internally wicked and internationally
threatening as any before or since. It looked as though nothing would
stand in the Assyrians' way to conquer more of the world, including
the Jews' southern kingdom of Judah, where Habakkuk lived. Meanwhile, Nebuchadnezzar and his Babylonian armies became the new
mighty world power to contend with. Unfortunately, Jehoiakim, the
King of Judah, had backed the Assyrians, the losing side.

Habakkuk was a deep thinker and, according to the picturesque
phrase of St. Jerome, a "wrestler with God." A faithful man, Habakkuk
is all the more real to us because he knew what it is to experience temptations to faithlessness. Daringly but respectfully in today's dialogue
with God, he wanted to know some of the same things we'd like to
know.

Why, for example, is God so silent while the faithless conquer
and the wicked devour the good? Why doesn't God intervene in the
world — especially when suffering and evil seem to be triumphing?
Why does God tolerate the wicked? The Judeans had sinned, to be sure,
but why should God choose to punish them by means of monstrous
people who were more wicked than themselves?

God gave many interesting answers. He said that final justice will
surely come (2:3) — in God's own good time. Meanwhile, in ways we
don't understand, God is preparing the final victory of justice. Bringing the message down to individuals, God said that the evildoers shall
pass away, but good people shall live, because of their faithfulness (2:4).
Faithfulness in general is an unswerving adherence to someone or something by way of a union such as marriage, friendship, honor, oath, or
promise. It goes hand in hand with faith.

Faithfulness in the face of negative situations doesn't demand that we see these as being "the will of God" and remain passively accepting. In the face of outrage and violence, God affirms agonized search and active questioning like Habakkuk's. That search and questioning don't necessarily lessen faith or loyalty. Also basic is the truth that God has many fair-weather friends: those who are with Him as long as everything goes their way. Real faith is proved by steadfast loyalty to God in times of adversity. Today's Responsorial Psalm urges us not to harden our hearts to God, in bad times as well as good: "the human heart takes the shape of what it loves" (*Catechism of the Catholic Church*, 2404).

In today's Gospel we see the Apostles asking the Lord to increase their faith (v. 5). They had guessed correctly that theological faith is a gift: No one buys it, earns it, conquers it, or wins it. It comes from God, and one can only do what the Apostles in fact did: Pray for it, and for its increase when it's weak, especially when assailed by indifference or doubt.

Jesus used the picture of a tiny seed to move a mighty sycamore tree as a metaphor for faith being the greatest force in the world. Even on a purely natural plane, things that look impossible become possible when approached with faith. Examples abound: the invention of the simple electric light bulb, the airplane, space travel, medical marvels, television, and computers are but a few.

In the supernatural order, faith is the only power that can save the world, a seemingly impossible task. The rest of the Gospel passage (vv. 7-10) teaches the disciples the necessity of being humble in the service of God. In words that don't apply to other areas like labor-management relations, Jesus says that we can never have any claim on God. Our greatest response to the Giver of divine faith is works of service.

But faith is never definitively acquired; it must ceaselessly be reanimated. That's part of the message of today's excerpt from the second letter to Timothy. It's the beginning of a series from this letter for the next few Sundays. In about 100 A.D., its author made this letter out to be St. Paul's pastoral directions to a young, timid, sickly bishop. By attributing authorship to Paul, the author brings forward the authority of Paul, needed to guide the Church in a transitional age.

That reminds us of the humorous story of an updated piece of advice to a new pastor. On his very first day in office, this new pastor got a call from his predecessor. He congratulated him on his new charge and told him that in the center drawer of the desk in the office he had left three envelopes, all numbered, which he was to open in order when he got into trouble.

After a short-lived honeymoon with the congregation, the heat began to rise and the pastor decided to open the first envelope. The note inside read: "If it will help, blame me for the problem. After all, I'm gone and have new problems of my own."

That worked for a while, but then things went bad again. The pastor opened the second envelope, which read: "Blame the congregation. They have a lot of other interests. They can take it."

That too worked well for a while, but then the storm clouds gathered again, and in desperation the pastor went to the drawer and opened the third envelope. The message read: "Prepare three envelopes!"

Today's advice to Timothy begins by reminding him — and us — to stir into flame the gifts God has given (v. 6). Because Timothy is young and heresies and other dangers great, he must keep his courage high (v. 7). He's given a version of the message of Habakkuk: Bear hardships for the sake of the Good News, relying on the power of God. In your efforts, be strong, in order to have the power to cope; be loving, especially for the sake of those with whom you will deal; and be wise — with saintliness keeping control in the face of temptations to panic.

Anyone loyal and faithful to Paul toward the end of Paul's life would automatically be tempted to lose faith. For one thing, loyalty to Paul meant loyalty to one considered a criminal (v. 8): The aged Paul was in a Roman jail. For another thing, there was the hardship which the Gospel entails — difficult in the face of the world's self-indulgence. In the long term, however, we have to remind ourselves that faithfulness to the Gospel is rewarding. The biblical notion of faith, of course, means a commitment of the entire person to Jesus: This means action as well as intellectual assent. It's steadfast loyalty to God no matter what comes.

So Timothy must keep the sound teachings of the faith inviolate. The model is, at bottom, the teachings of Jesus himself. Though Jesus' doctrines can grow and develop, they remain fundamentally the same through all ages and fads. We adhere in faith, and with a loyalty ever true, and a hope that never loses confidence in God. And we must cooperate with the help of the Holy Spirit that's within us (v. 14) to guard the rich deposit of faith.

In ancient times, before banks as we know them, one of the places where people often deposited their valuables was the Temple. The deposit's safekeeping was considered a sacred trust. Faith, the greatest force in the world, is the richest deposit possible, and the most sacred of trusts. Paul had entrusted his work and his life to God. While a criminal in a Roman jail, treated at best indifferently by his barbarous keepers, he didn't change his faith, or his loyalty and steadfastness to God's plans for him. Why? Because it was inconceivable to him that God, Whom he had come to know intimately, would let him down. God's message to Habakkuk and Paul and Timothy and the Apostles is just as important to us now as ever in history.

TWENTY-EIGHTH SUNDAY IN ORDINARY TIME
2 K 5:14-17   2 Tm 2:8-13   Lk 17:11-19

Gratitude and Praise
Humility in Faith; The Silliness of God; The Saving Power of God;
God's Healing; On Being an Outcast

Occasionally, babies are born with a congenital illness of insensitivity to pain. Fortunately rare, the disease is called the Biemond Syndrome, or Analgia. In one family, where two children were born with it, the two-year-old boy, Paul, had already suffered third-degree burns, broken his arm, and sustained contusions and concussions — to all of which he responded with indifference. When his sister Victoria was born, he was jealous of her because people were making a fuss over her. When no one was looking, he would slug her in the face, or punch her in the stomach, or bite her on the arm, or throw her out of her crib and jump on her. Because she, too, had Analgia, she didn't even wince: She just looked up at him and smiled. Their father had to quit his job, because someone had to stay with them all the time, especially the boy. Children born without pain sensors rarely live to an old age; they often die of self-inflicted injuries.

But what is pain? Some see three views of it in the annals of Western culture: the classical idea that pain is ennobling, the romantic idea that it's the source of art and truth, and the modern, mechanistic, idea that it's nothing but an electrochemical disturbance in some neurological pathway. Because pain is often a crucially useful diagnostic tool for physicians, they're often not inclined to blunt it completely. If they do, they may lose a great source of day-to-day information on which to base their treatment. In today's readings we see that pain and suffering, while not necessarily good, can be.

Our First Reading is from a collection of short stories about the prophet Elisha (ninth century B.C.). In today's story Naaman, the army general of Syria, Israel's hostile northern neighbor, was handicapped at the height of his military career by a skin disease which at that time was called leprosy, but was apparently not bad enough to exempt him from his commission in the Syrian army.

Having tried every possible remedy without success, Naaman was sent by his king to seek a cure that was reported to be available from the Jewish prophet Elisha. Naaman came — with all his magnificent retinue — with a letter from his king to the king of Israel. He took along all kinds of expensive gifts: ten silver talents (each roughly a pound of silver), six thousand gold pieces, and ten festal garments. Naaman's approach scared the king of Israel out of his wits: He thought that the king of Syria was trying to say, "Cure my general Naaman or else!" Elisha heard about his king's plight and asked that Naaman be sent to him. The king was glad to oblige.

Humiliating though it was for the army commander of a great power to seek help in a vassal state from what appeared to be a religious eccentric, Naaman had high expectations. But he was disappointed. Accustomed as Naaman was to discipline and protocol, the prophet Elisha didn't even come out to meet him, and then made what appeared to be a silly recommendation: that he bathe in the Jordan River seven times. Naaman knew that the muddy waters of the Jordan were no hygienic match for the crystal-clear mountain spring waters of his native Damascus, and he refused. God's requests to all of us seem equally silly at times: to put up with disagreeable relatives, to mortify ourselves, to have patience with people with whom we don't see eye-to-eye.

Eventually Naaman, conforming to the pleas of his servants, performed the commanded ritual bath in the Jordan (v. 14). That's the point at which today's reading begins, telling us that thereupon Naaman's skin became as clear as that of a little child. And his cure was more than physical: It had reached his whole person. So he immediately did two things. First, he acknowledged that the God of Israel is the only God. Second, full of praise and gratitude, he felt compelled to offer the prophet a fitting reward. When Elisha firmly declined Naaman's generosity, Naaman asked for some Israelite earth to carry home, on which "holy ground" he could stand before an altar for continual praise of Israel's God.

St. Luke's Gospel story clearly echoes the Naaman story. Jesus was on his resolute journey to die in his city of destiny, Jerusalem (v. 11). He displayed extraordinary concern toward ten lepers, one of whom was doubly an outcast: not only a leper, but a Samaritan, considered by Jews a second-class heretical dog a step below the rest of Gentiles. He was brought to Jesus by his great need in the face of a disease that didn't yield some of its mysteries until only a little more than a century before our time, with the research of the Norwegian scientist G.A. Hansen. The leprosy of Jesus' time didn't necessarily mean Hansen's disease as we know it: What they called "leprosy" included skin blemishes like psoriasis and acne.

According to their Law (esp. Lv 13:45f.; Nb 5:2), which insisted upon cleanliness for the people whom God had set apart as His own, anything unclean was to be avoided, including lepers. Whereas Naaman's freely moving about indicated that he wasn't afflicted by the isolation-demanding type of leprosy, the ten lepers in Jesus' case were. Jesus told these ten marginalized people to show themselves to the priests (v. 14), because it was the priests who certified people as "clean": They were the representatives of both medicine and religion, both of which for a long time in human history were intertwined in attempts to cure the whole person.

We're only now beginning to return to that point of view. A growing number of physicians today question whether medicine should remain frozen in Cartesian and Newtonian worldviews — worldviews that envision the body as mere matter severed from spirit. These views negate the role of mind and emotions — some would say God — in healing. Growing numbers of health care professionals are acknowledging that good spiritual health and medical attention is an unbeatable combination.

Through prayer, which in this application is a new way of listening, the relationship between patient and physician can heal the physician as well: Physicians' egos have to be prepared to have the patient's eyes turned to God. And those engaged in alternative medicine should draw on their healing traditions, such as the laying on of hands.

At any rate, Jesus' command that the ten show themselves to the priests at this early stage appeared at least as silly as Naaman's being told to bathe seven times in the muddy Jordan. Nevertheless, they took Jesus at his word. Thereupon all ten were cured. And one of the signs of being cured of leprosy is the restored ability to feel physical pain.

But to only one was a complete cure of his whole person announced by Jesus' telling observation that the man's faith had saved him. That was the despised foreigner whom the Jews would have thought least likely to give thanks; the one who had no claim to the cure, especially from the hands of a Jew; the one whose cure involved an expansion of vision. This one, the Samaritan, returned to thank God the Father and to praise Jesus (vv. 15f.). Loud though his voice was, his gesture of throwing himself down before Jesus was louder. The man underwent the process of conversion necessary for all of us: realizing that we're nothing, acknowledging God and His gifts, being aware that we need God, and desiring to turn to Him and serve Him with all our heart.

The Samaritan's being healed, like Naaman's, was more than skin deep. There are other similarities between the Samaritan and Naaman: both were foreigners away from their home base; both were asked to do something that went against their grain; both knew enough to be full of praise and gratitude for their cure; and for both the cure involved an expansion of understanding.

The second letter to Timothy, which may come from the hand of a disciple writing in the spirit of St. Paul, provides another good example of whole-person cure: Paul. Paul, the old veteran now being treated as a common criminal (v. 9) and facing death in prison, bids an affectionate farewell to Timothy. In the first part of today's section he says that Jesus was divinely raised from the dead, an event that results in not just the inspiration of a memory, but the power of a presence: the presence of God. Paul's sufferings, like ours, aren't pointless: Paul's were helpful in spreading the Good News. For such sufferings, we're grateful.

Somehow we often find it difficult to praise either God or other people. Praise presupposes two elements: the recognition of good in whatever form it comes, and the due acknowledgment of that good through some gesture or action. And we should realize that gratitude isn't only the greatest of attributes, but the parent of them all, and that if we aren't grateful to God we can't taste the joy of finding Him in His creation. Like Naaman, the Samaritan, and Paul, we should also acknowledge and praise the goodness and tireless efforts on our behalf of other people who are instruments of God, especially our family. And like them, we should recognize that even pain and suffering can be cause for praise and gratitude, because they can bring blessing and redemption.

Too often we're like the doting grandmother who was walking with her young grandson along the shore in Miami Beach when a huge wave appeared out of nowhere, sweeping the child out to sea. The horrified woman fell to her knees, raised her eyes to heaven, and begged the Lord to return her beloved grandson. And, lo, another wave reared up and deposited the stunned child on the sand right in front of her. The grandmother looked the boy over carefully. He was fine. But then she stared up angrily toward the heavens. "When we came," she snapped indignantly, "he had a hat!" Personal obstacles can be advantageous. If we didn't feel pain, that might be dangerous.

TWENTY-NINTH SUNDAY IN ORDINARY TIME
Ex 17:8-13   2 Tm 3:14-4:2   Lk 18:1-8

Persistence, Especially in Prayer
The Place of Scripture in the Christian Life; Seeking Justice; Pray and Act

One of the most adaptable words in the English language is "persistent." When flies or bees or ants are persistent during a Summer picnic, we call them pesty. When children are persistent in wanting something, we consider them bold. But when politicians are persistent in pursuing the electorate, we call them astute. And when business people are persistent in following up sales prospects, we admire their tenacity. Today's liturgy connects persistence with religion, especially in our prayers of petition.

In today's Gospel, Our Lord tells one of the stories that shows his sense of humor: the story of the unjust judge and the forlorn widow.

The judge was the typification of the person of influence whom one would be reluctant to antagonize, and the widow the stock Older Covenant typification of the vulnerable and helpless. She's fragile in body but strong in faith.

In our idiom, we might picture her as a little old lady in tennis shoes, weighing less than ninety pounds, speaking perhaps with a high-pitched and cracking voice. The original Greek suggests that the violence that the unjust judge feared was a black eye. Jesus makes the point that the only thing that will move this judge is persistence. And if this can happen with a widow before an unjust judge, how much more with the poor in spirit before the all-just God!

St. Luke is famous for his widow stories. The reason is that the widow of that time and place was more to be pitied than most widows of any time. She was considered in many ways to be still married to her husband. If he died without leaving children, she was expected to marry his brother, if there was one, in order to bring forth children to carry on her husband's name. She was in no way provided for financially. She was left defenseless to fend for herself, without the possibility of finding work, and completely at the mercy of friends and relatives.

Today, widows at the death of their husbands have rights — such as her husband's will and social security programs. Nevertheless, immediately after her husband dies life for her is a black pit of loneliness. She wants to die too (and some countries accommodate that wish). She feels vulnerable, unattractive, and unloved. She misses the friend she could say everything to, misses the buddy who was really in her corner. The more she was in love with her husband, the greater her sadness now. The Church still gives widows an honored place, and with good reason.

Widows don't like to be called widows, because of the possible connotation of a lady in a long black dress who has retired from the world. If she goes out and laughs in a restaurant, people look at her as the Merry Widow, which makes things even worse. The statement of many widows is, "You don't ever get over the loss of your husband: You survive it."

Sad to say, projections from United States census data suggest that nearly 80 percent of all married women can expect to survive their husbands by about 16 years. Underlying those projections are two trends: Women live longer than men (7 years on average), and men tend to marry women younger than themselves.

In Jesus' story, the only weapon the widow had against the judge's injustice was persistence. That's a virtue all of us should have. Years ago in Illinois, a young man with six months' schooling to his credit ran for an office in the legislature. As might have been expected, he was beaten. Next, he entered business but failed at that, too, and spent the next 17 years paying the debts of his worthless partner. He fell in love with a charming lady and became engaged — and she died. He had a nervous breakdown. He ran for Congress and was defeated. He then tried to obtain an appointment to the U.S. Land Office, but didn't succeed. He became a candidate for the Vice-Presidency and lost. Two years later he was defeated for Senator. He ran for office once more and was elected. The man's name was Abraham Lincoln. And it took Winston Churchill three years to get through the eighth grade, because he couldn't pass English — of all things! Ironically, he was asked many years later to give the commencement address at Oxford University. His now famous speech consisted of only three words: "Never give up!"

Today's First Reading backs up the Gospel's urgings of persistence with the story of the first military activity of the newly-freed Hebrew people: the Israelites against the Amalekites. A nomadic tribe, the Amalekites dwelt in the Negeb in the desert between Sinai and Canaan. In the battle, the perhaps fanciful story had it that, as long as Moses prayed with his arms outstretched, the Israelites were victorious. When he became tired and let down his arms, the Israelites began to lose. So Moses' assistants Aaron and Hur held up his tired arms until victory was assured.

The Hebrew Scriptures always emphasize, though, that we don't win battles only by our own force of weapons. As the refrain of today's Responsorial Psalm says, our help is from the Lord. To this day, Rephidim, the place where today's event happened, is as sacred to Jewish memory as places like Valley Forge are to Americans. Indeed, the memory of Valley Forge isn't only of tired, bedraggled, poorly clad, hungry soldiers fighting for freedom, but also of the memorable painting of George Washington kneeling in prayer in the snow.

Today's portion of the second letter of Timothy reminds us of another dimension of our prayers: that they be other-directed. We should live and pray wholeheartedly for what we think we want. But we should at the same time pray and act not that our will predominate, but that "God's will be done" — leaving it to God to differentiate between what we want and what we need.

What does it mean to do God's will? St. Cyprian (*Treatise on the Lord's Prayer*) put it this way: "Humility in our daily lives, an unwavering faith, a moral sense of modesty in conversation, justice in acts, mercy in deed, discipline, refusal to harm others, a readiness to suffer harm, peaceableness with our brothers, a whole-hearted love of the Lord, loving in him what is of the Father, fearing him because he's God, preferring nothing to him who preferred nothing to us, clinging tenaciously to his love, standing by his cross with loyalty and courage whenever there's any conflict involving his honor and his name, manifesting in our speech the constancy of our profession and under torture confidence for the fight, and in dying the endurance for which we will be crowned — this is what it means to... do the will of the Father."

When and if we're in doubt about what's God's will and what's our own, today's portion of the letter advises Timothy to go, for one, to his teachers — in his case, principally his mother and grandmother. The home is the first school of faith. The letter emphasizes also the usefulness of the inspired word of God in the Scriptures. When the letter speaks of Scripture being good for revealing God's wisdom, for salvation, for teaching, for training in holiness, and for helping to correct ourselves, it's speaking of the Jewish Scriptures, for the New Testament hadn't yet been collected. How much more does this advice apply now that we have the New Testament as well! Ignorance of the Scriptures is ignorance of Jesus!

We wonder: How long must any current Moses hold up his weary arms until the people of God will prevail? When will God vindicate His elect? Not long yet, says Jesus in the Gospel. But he promised that a long, long time ago. Can we still believe it? The truth is that the promise was fulfilled when Jesus, sharing the lot of pleading humanity, was crucified and rose from the dead: Jesus' resurrection vindicated all sin and evil, and even death. The decisive battle in any war may have already occurred in a relatively early stage of the war, and yet the war still continues. Although the decisive effect of that battle is perhaps not recognized by all, it nevertheless already means victory. In the ministry of Jesus the decisive battle has been fought and won, Satan has fallen and the power of the evil spirits is broken. Yet the battle still goes on.

So we always gather in our assembly on Sunday to strengthen our faith, to remember God's judgment, to hear it again spoken in all its power, and to encourage one another to live in accord with that judgment. That requires perseverance.

A little-known man who exemplified that is John Harrison (1693-1776). Until the eighteenth century sailors navigated by following parallels of latitude and roughly estimating distance traveled east or west. Ships routinely missed their destinations. In 1714, England's Parliament offered a large reward to anyone who provided a "practicable and useful" means of determining longitude.

Most astronomers believed the answer lay in the sky, but Harrison, a clock maker, imagined a mechanical solution — a clock that would keep precise time at sea. By knowing the exact times at the Greenwich meridian and at a ship's position, one could find longitude by calculating the time difference. However, most scientists, including Isaac Newton, discounted Harrison's idea. Harrison persisted. He spent decades — decades! — of his brilliant life through skepticism and ridicule, working on a timepiece. Even after completing his timepiece, an instrument we now call a chronometer, in 1759, he underwent a long series of unfair trials and demonstrations. Ultimately he triumphed.

Starting right now, let's make a firm commitment to persevere in those areas of our lives where perseverance is most needed: relationships, family, faith, self-esteem, work, prayer. But let's temper our perseverance with the petition that, after all is said and done, "May God's will, and not mine, be done!"

THIRTIETH SUNDAY IN ORDINARY TIME
Si 35:12-14, 16-18   2 Tm 4:6-8, 16-18   Lk 18:9-14

How to Pray
The Lord and the Cry of the Poor; True Religion;
Humility in Approaching God; Preferential Option for the Poor

Sociological studies show many things about prayer, among them the following. This week more of us will pray than will go to work, or exercise, or have sexual relations. Many spouses readily discuss their sex lives, but have to struggle to talk about prayer. The studies show that serious prayer usually begins after the age of about thirty, when the illusion that we're masters of our own fate fades and adults develop a deeper need to call on the Master of the Universe. The studies show, further, that even on talk shows that deal with the controversial, prayer is never mentioned.

Today's liturgy discusses some aspects of prayer and life. In the First Reading, written about 180 B.C., the Book of Sirach takes up the theme. Jesus ben Sira, its author, wrote for Jews who were a minority dispersed among Gentiles, living — as many Christians do today — in an alien culture. Because the early Church adopted so many of his ideas, his book was also called *Liber Ecclesiasticus*, "The Book of the Church."

Sirach said that our prayer life will inevitably be connected with the rest of our lives. You can't act one way and pray another. So one requirement for prayer to be acceptable to the God of justice, says Sirach, is that our lives be just: that is, righteous, upright, wholesome, virtuous (v. 12). Sirach reminds us that God knows no favorites except toward the poor, the powerless, and the oppressed (v. 13). Why them? Because they don't have the illusion that the world turns around them. They're able to do what God wants of all of us: to concentrate on the interior disposition of the heart rather than externals. "The Lord hears the cry of the poor," as today's Responsorial Psalm puts it, and that and this lesson from Sirach is the background of today's Gospel.

In today's Gospel, Jesus tells of the Pharisee and the tax collector (v. 9), a story that shows the way to being right with God. These two went up to what was in Luke's Gospel a very privileged place, the Temple, to pray (v. 10). Or, as the humorist put it, "Two men went up to the Temple to pray; one did, and the other didn't!"

The Pharisee was a good man. He came from the *parisim*, meaning a group separate, apart. They tried to live up to their sacred Law completely. You would like the Pharisee as your next-door neighbor. You could count on him to be honest, to respect your property, and to do everything right. Yet the people gave some of them unflattering nicknames: "Blood-headed Pharisees," for example, because in their attempts to avoid looking at women in the street they bumped into walls; "Bookkeeper Pharisees" for those who kept an exact record of their good deeds to offset their bad ones; and "Wait-A-Minute Pharisees" for those who told people wanting to speak with them to "wait a minute" while they went to perform a good deed. But the true Pharisees were called "Pharisees of Love."

In today's story, the righteousness of the Pharisee considerably exceeded the standards prescribed by the Mosaic Law. For instance, the Law prescribed one day of fast a year (the Day of Atonement), but he, like many Pharisees, held a complete fast, with no food or drink until after sundown, twice a week: Mondays and Thursdays. The Law commanded tithes of farm produce profits; this Pharisee tithed himself on everything.

The Pharisee of Jesus' story attributed all his many virtues to his own merits, reminded God of all the good he was doing, and made God out to be in debt to him. He was full of himself; the key word in his prayer was "I." And he used his prayer to speak ill of his fellow human-beings. To look down on everyone else when we're doing good, as the Pharisee did, is easy. Our society gives ample opportunity to look down: on people guilty of abortion, for instance, and on homosexuals, indulgers in sex outside marriage, street beggars, drug users, AIDS victims, drunkards. Difficult though it may be to admit, there's something of the Pharisee in each of us.

Tax-collectors of that time, on the other hand, were as a group social outcasts. They were considered robbers for Rome. But the very body language of the tax collector of Jesus' story — keeping his distance, raising his eyes to heaven, beating his breast — showed his attitude in prayer. He used for his prayer the opening verse of the Psalm composed by King David to ask God's mercy after his adultery with Bathsheba — a prayer so simple and yet so perfect: "God, be merciful to me, a sinner." He knew himself.

It's as difficult to know ourselves, and often as painful, as it is to peel an onion, which makes us cry. Examination of the world without is never as personally painful as examination of the world within; because of the pain involved in a life of genuine self-examination, many people steer clear of it. Yet when you're dedicated to truth, this pain seems relatively unimportant — and less and less important (and therefore less and less painful) the farther you proceed on the path of self-examination.

But from childhood on, we acquire superficial identities which, like an onion, layer us as we become what our parents, teachers, and friends want us to be. Desperate for love and approval, we respond to other people, "Yes, I'll bury who I really am and become who you want me to be." But the real us doesn't go away: It lives in the center of our soul and pounds to get out. Then grace, often in the form of a crisis, moves us to start peeling the onion, and maybe start crying. When we strip away our false identities, we're left naked until we search for, discover, and treasure our real selves: God's idea of what He wanted us to be when He brought us into being in the first place.

The result of Jesus' story? He startled his audience by having the Pharisee the villain of the piece and the tax collector the hero (v. 14). The tax collector's self-knowledge and humility brought him home in a right relationship with God.

Which of the two are we?

As a model of what both Sirach and Jesus were talking about in humbly unifying prayer life and active life, we have today's reading from the second letter to Timothy. It presents a portrait of St. Paul in prison. Paul had been arrested before; he was aware that this time he wouldn't come out of jail alive: Martyrdom was imminent. Paul had already offered everything he had — his money, his scholarship, his work, his time — and now he was offering all that he was: his very life. Just as after their meal the pagans offered a sacrificial ritual of spilling wine upon the ground, so too Paul's life was being poured out (v. 6). The words of the murdered Archbishop Oscar Romero of El Salvador are apt here: "If I am killed, I will rise again in my people. My voice will disappear but my word, which is Christ's, will remain."

Paul called it the time of his departure. For Paul the tent maker, it meant taking down his earthly tent for a better place. For Paul the missioner who had often sailed the Mediterranean for Christ, it meant launching out to cross the waters of death for the haven of eternity. Death is all these things: an act of worship, a libation, an act of freedom, striking one's tent, and a launching into eternity.

Paul could face the end with equanimity. He expressed it in images of the athletic games. He had competed well (v. 7): Win, lose, or draw, he had done his best. That he had "finished the race" was a satisfaction: A race, like other efforts in life, is easy to begin, hard to finish. The world's most famous race is the Marathon. At the original Marathon in 490 B.C., the Greeks won a very hard victory. After the battle, a young Greek soldier ran all the way, day and night, to Athens with the news. As he finished the race and delivered his message of victory to the magistrates, he fell dead.

Like that Marathon runner, and like the competitors at the games, Paul had "kept the faith." Now, he merited the reward of a winner. The crown he looked forward to, however, wasn't the laurel crown (v. 8) given by men, which withered, but one given by God, which would never die. Paul knew that he was soon coming to the emperor Nero's judgment, and he knew what that judgment would be. He hoped for a favorable verdict from God.

For both Nero's and God's verdicts, he waited. And he waited alone. Not one of his friends stood by him (v. 16): It was too dangerous. During that time Paul's prayer contained reminiscences of the psalm-prayer that was on Jesus' lips on the cross (Ps 22): "My God, my God, why have you forsaken me" (v. 2), it began, and continued, "I have no one to help me" (v. 12), and "Save me from the lion's mouth" (v. 22). Paul derived courage from the knowledge that the Lord would bring him to his heavenly kingdom (v. 18).

Each of today's readings teaches us something about how we should pray and live: From Sirach, that our prayer must be connected with the rest of our lives, especially our conduct toward the powerless; from Jesus, that our prayer must be humble; from Paul, staying power. A good life, like a good prayer, comes from emptying ourselves of ourselves to let God in. That means a realization of the truth of the words scribbled long ago by an anonymous soldier of the Confederacy:

> I asked God for strength, that I might achieve — I was made weak, that I might learn humbly to obey.
> I asked for help that I might do greater things — I was given infirmity, that I might do better things.
> I asked for riches, that I might be happy — I was given poverty, that I might be wise.
> I asked for all things, that I might enjoy life — I was given life, that I might enjoy all things.
> I got nothing that I asked for — but everything I had hoped for.
> Despite myself, my prayers were answered. I am, among all men, most richly blessed!

FEAST OF ALL SAINTS
Rv 7:2-4, 9-14   1 Jn 3:1-3   Mt 5:1-12

Role Models, Heroes, or Celebrities?
What Are You Looking For?; Act Now, Before It's Too Late

Which would you prefer to have as a guide for your life: a hero, a role model, or a celebrity? Heroes are people who possess a noble task and who perform it for the sake of God, or country, or fellow human beings, and, in doing that, become larger figures. In today's mixed-up world, not many people agree upon who heroes are.

Virtually the last literary frontier for the American hero is mystery and crime fiction. Its male and female heroes aren't always as shiny as their mythic models. Even the "persons of honor" who would walk down these stories' mean streets often adhere to a code of behavior that plays fast and loose with the law. Their allegiance isn't necessarily to the law, but to something else — perhaps order, or a sense of the way things ought to be.

To modern fictional detectives, the law often appears impotent, its minions often corrupt, and the universe in chaos. Readers just want them to be people who see that something has gone badly wrong with the social structure and fix the mess we've made of our world — reminiscent of the Naval officer's daughter who, when asked what she'd learned at Sunday School, replied, "We studied about the ten commanders. We learned that they're always broke."

When people talk about heroes, they open small doors to reveal their own private visions of the world. A boy who says his hero is Batman "'cause he can't die" teaches something about his fears. A woman who says she never thought of having a hero because heroes are for boys teaches something about her thoughts on gender.

A role model doesn't have the same grandeur as the hero. Because many people consider hero-worship and role-model pursuit too bland, they've come to putting celebrities, instead of heroes, upon a pedestal. Celebrities are people who get a great deal of publicity, but aren't necessarily any better than anyone else — in wisdom (in which

---

Note: This homily is on Revelation. For 1 John, see Cycle B; for Matthew, Cycle A.

they may in fact be extremely poor), in intellect (in which they may be inferior), or in moral life (in which they may be only selfish pleasure-seekers). In our culture, celebrities — singers and actors and athletes — are shipped into our children's schools to deliver brief inspirational talks and then disappear into their limousines.

Nevertheless, we have so many negative images bombarding us that it's essential to have something positive to guide us. Hence the importance of reminding ourselves of the saints — how they got to be what they became, and how we can become the same. In this connection, we easily understand today's Second Reading, in which St. John reminds us of our privilege to be called God's children, and the Gospel, where Jesus informs us that practicing the Beatitudes is the way to heaven.

Today's reading from the Book of Revelation is more difficult, but dramatic. The type of literature to which this book belongs is called "apocalyptic." We don't have this kind of writing now, any more than ancient writers knew about comic strips or westerns. Apocalyptic was written during a time of crisis as a survival manual, to strengthen and console. For protection, it pretends to have been written by some venerable person as a "prediction" of the future, but that "future" is actually unfolding in the author's own time. Revelation's two visions in today's reading contain material that's simultaneously a warning, an assurance, and a promise.

The first vision pictures the People of God on earth placed under God's protection against coming adversity. The vision is based upon a Jewish concept of the world at the time the book was written. They thought of the earth as flat, resting on the sea, and square. Picturesquely, at the earth's four corners awaiting God's command as His agents were winds of potential destruction — especially the dreaded Sirocco, the blast of hot air from the southeast that destroyed vegetation. The ancient Israelites knew nothing of secondary causes like variations in atmospheric pressure or land configurations causing winds and rain. To them, God does it all. They're correct in the sense that God does act through the laws He put into His universe.

In the East was the protecting angel. The East is, first of all, the source of light. And it was from the East that the Messiah was expected to come. The protecting angel in the East held "the seal of the living God" with which to mark God's people. To the minds of early readers that seal would conjure up concepts of importance: like a king using his special seal on his signet ring, guaranteeing royal power; or a merchant putting his seal on a package of goods to certify his ownership; or a vineyard owner putting his seal on jars of wine to provide his personal guarantee that they came from his own vineyard.

"The living God" has put His seal on us because we're precious to Him. This is an encouragement: in times of difficulty we can realize that He's with us. Being God's, however, doesn't imply our escape from difficulty or death: The bad angels who have power to damage the land and the sea and all living things are still with us.

The number of God's sealed persons, the saints, is great. "How many people are going to be saved?" is a perennial one among us. Elsewhere, Revelation mentions 144,000, which is a symbolic number, not an actual one — standing for perfection, completion, and all-inclusiveness. Those called to be saints come from every nation, race, people, and tongue (v. 9) — all people through the ages, right down to ourselves.

Our view of the saints is not as a ladder, some sort of lesser deities upon whom we must climb to get up to God; we view them as in a circle, together with us in and through and with Christ, all of us giving praise to the Father. We're all kinds: smart and dumb, tall and short, fat and lean, young and aged, rich and poor, royal and peasant, lay and religious, quiet and loud, mystical and down-to-earth.

Many of the canonized saints can boast only of their suffering, martyrs to sickness and misunderstanding, or martyrs in times of persecution. The validity of St. Bernadette Soubirous' visionary experience at Lourdes was ratified in her heroic suffering with tuberculosis of the bone. At the end of his life, St. Alphonsus Liguori found himself at odds with the members of the very religious order he'd founded, the Redemptorists. All the saints show that those whom the world considers the movers and shakers, the top brass, holders of the Gold Card, and the "beautiful people" don't necessarily have the inside track in the race of life. We're all members of the Communion of Saints: We pray for one another, assist one another, care for one another, and affirm one another. And our union doesn't cease with death.

The short-range purpose of Revelation's second vision was to hearten Christians then undergoing persecution in the Roman Empire; its long-range purpose is to encourage all of us servants of God to persevere unto death. Even as it was being written, Christians were being martyred. One of the few pictures of heaven that Scripture offers, it's a vision that wonderfully sees the Church in heaven after the terrible trial on earth has passed and the saints have come through it. They're a people at peace, with joy and satisfaction in the presence of God.

The vision of them wearing white robes and holding palm branches (v. 9) signifies their triumph. In the Bible, white robes stand for purity — a life which is cleansed from sin — and for glorious victory, a life which has won over all the powers of evil. A Roman general always celebrated his triumphs clothed in white. Palm branches were a sign of the victory and thanksgiving.

A triumphal entry into a city of a Caesar or an Alexander would make a Hollywood producer jealous. For a Caesar or an Alexander, the parade would start with 1,000 lancers on the finest horses, followed by 2,000 trumpeters who could be heard for miles. Then would come the charioteers with their polished armor and helmets glistening in the sun; then 1,000 swordsmen followed by 40,000 foot soldiers marching in unison, followed by 2,000 more trumpeters. Then would come the great conqueror, riding a white stallion robed in crimson. Preceding him would be soldiers spreading the garments of the conquered enemies; and following them would come the defeated army in chains.

At the beginning of Holy Week, however, Jesus entered the city of Jerusalem in peace on a donkey. For Jesus, the crowds of the saints loudly give (v. 10) a triumphant shout of salvation — which means not a victory of escape, but of conquest; the sense of victory doesn't save people from trouble, but brings them through it; it doesn't make life easy, but makes life great. All the angels joined the shout of the saints (v. 11). These are all the members of the Church who have remained faithful and have survived the time of distress (v. 14).

The highly symbolic language of the Book of Revelation puts before us as heroes and role models those who, with the same difficulties and the same weak flesh as ours, have become saints. Unique as every one of them is in their different life-journeys, they've walked the world's path in simple garb and now wear the white robe of purity and victory. Like all the saints, we grow strong or weak not on one great occasion, but silently and imperceptibly; and at last some decisive event comes to show us what we've become. Let's each of us allow the saints to guide us and let's do what we can to join their ranks.

THIRTY-FIRST SUNDAY IN ORDINARY TIME
Ws 11:22-12:1   2 Th 1:11-2:2   Lk 19:1-10

To Whom Does Salvation Come?
The Table as Place of Salvation; Taking the Long View;
The Long and Short of It; Mercy as the Way to Salvation

About sixteen miles northeast of Jerusalem is Jericho, a town that in
Our Lord's time was beautiful and important. It was the last stop for
pilgrims going the steep climb up to Jerusalem from the east. Here the
weather was almost balmy. In winter, it was a relief from the damp,
bone-chilling winters of Jerusalem — a New Testament Miami, Riviera,
Estoril, or Rio. It contained a great palm forest, balsam groves that
perfumed the air, and famous gardens of roses. The Jewish historian
Josephus called it "a divine region," and others called it "The City of
Palms." Herod the Great had placed his winter capital on a hillside there;
there is even today on a hillside in Jericho a hotel called "The Winter
Palace." The Romans carried Jericho's dates and balsam world-wide.

All this resulted in wealth: customs had to be paid on the many
items that passed through, and agricultural taxes on produce from the
lush groves. That required the presence of a high tax official, with several ordinary ones under him. That chief tax collector — and a rich
man — was Zacchaeus (v. 2).

The terms "rich" and "poor" are particularly frequent in Luke.
Luke's Jesus is critical of the rich man who was tempted to eat, drink,
and be merry (12:6). He criticizes the host who invited only rich neighbors (14:12). But it's in those passages in which he contrasts the rich
with the poor that Luke has Jesus' teaching at its starkest: Jesus' blessings to the poor and woes to the rich (6:20, 24); the rich man and
Lazarus (16:19); the poor widow who gave her all (21:1-4). All the
incidents are challenges to abandon the blindness of riches while other
people are poor.

Zacchaeus' wealth had come at a price: Like Matthew and all
other tax collectors, he had had to love money enough to defy the hatred of his people in order to collect taxes for Rome. Because he was
an outcast he was lonely and, though he had become wealthy, he wasn't
happy. His conduct with Jesus was born of the courage of desperation.

It was his courage that led him into the crowd. He knew that many citizens would take the chance to get in a kick, a push, or a shove at him, and he would probably wind up black and blue with bruises. As the masses of our day might tend, with little evidence, to conclude easily that a rich man cooks his books to avoid paying taxes, the crowds of that time believed the worst of Zacchaeus the tax collector.

The crowd took special delight in taking care that this short man running in front of them wouldn't be able to see anything. But he who had climbed over difficulties on his road to riches found it relatively easy to climb a tree that had a short trunk and low-forking branches. Jericho tax-payers might have been amused to see their diminutive tax commissioner perched on a branch like a cat waiting to spring. Jesus, when he came to the spot, might have laughed as well, as might Zacchaeus himself when he was caught.

There is no recorded instance of Jesus' ever refusing an invitation to share food and drink, but here he surprisingly invited himself to stay at Zacchaeus' house (v. 5). Whereas the crowd saw in Zacchaeus a tax thief who earned his large commissions on the backs of the poor, and a shrewd manipulator who had climbed a tree to see the man they all wanted to talk to and had perhaps been following for months, Jesus saw Zacchaeus' heart and his hope. Zacchaeus looked at Jesus, and Jesus looked into Zacchaeus. Like all true seekers after God, Zacchaeus got more than he bargained for, and he was delighted (v. 6).

When Jesus arrived at Zacchaeus' house (v. 7), the gossips of Jericho clucked their tongues, murmuring against Jesus and showing the hardness of the society's class distinctions and its merciless coldness toward fallen members. After all, the jawbone of an ass was just as dangerous a weapon then — and is today — as it was in Samson's time.

Sharing food and drink is one of the easiest means of conversion and reconciliation. Many of Jesus' parables show that he used eating at table to picture fellowship with God. So delighted was Zacchaeus at the Lord's visit that he promised to give half his belongings to the poor (v. 8). "If I have extorted anything from anyone," he continued (and he could have added "and I have") he would pay him back fourfold — which weren't things he ordinarily did. Zacchaeus was showing himself to be a man of feeling, deeply touched by Jesus' kindness. He responded to a moment of truth — the moment he knew that God's love was bigger than the whole world — by letting go of his accumulations of a lifetime. And he went way beyond his religious laws. The rich man was becoming merciful; he was getting through the needle's eye!

Jesus, not to be outdone in generosity, promised that that very day salvation had come to Zacchaeus' house (v. 9). Just as Zacchaeus' entire household had suffered from his unjust practices, now it would benefit from his conversion. The Son of Man was saving what was lost (v. 10): that is, not necessarily what was damned, but what had been put in the wrong place. Persons are considered lost when away from God, and found when put back in their rightful place in God's household. That's frequently us.

And that's God's mercy. In modern religious usage we tend to associate mercy only with the judgment of God, as if we were criminals facing the judicial system and throwing ourselves on the mercy of a court. But the classical meaning of mercy (*chanan* in Hebrew, *eleeo* in Greek) is much wider in scope; it means kindness, graciousness, loving helpfulness. And that's the implication of the final sentence of this passage, which encapsulates Jesus' ministry to save.

The immensity of God's loving mercy that Jesus demonstrated, the Book of Wisdom spoke of. Today's First Reading is at the heart of that book. Written about a century before Christ at Alexandria in Egypt (where the Jews were a minority in a Hellenistic culture), it indicated that salvation doesn't necessarily come only to those fixated against sin, which is negative, but to those who are open to God's love, which is positive. This passage begins by putting everything in perspective: Before the Lord the whole universe is as a grain on a scale (v. 22) — a very small weight on an extremely sensitive measure — or as a drop of morning dew. It's a reflection on one of our greatest paradoxes: on the one side God's utter transcendence — His being over all of His mighty creation — and, on the other side, the individual attention His mercy accords to persons.

God's mercy is a prolongation of His creative power (11:24-12:2) and of His mastery over His own might. God is like a strong tall man who's so secure in his person that he can afford to be gentle. He loves all the things that His creative power has made, for only love can explain His having created and preserved them. Because of this love God pardons and is patient with all kinds of people so that they might repent (vv. 23ff.). We, in turn, should feel so secure in our person as to be able to imitate God's mercy. This should stimulate in us an attitude of reverence for everything within creation: how we're to behave toward the universe, toward animals, and toward all other aspects of ecology. As the bumper sticker says, "God doesn't make junk."

As regards animals, we're the recipients of two old traditions. The mainstream Western tradition has been that animal nature is not like ours, so animals simply don't matter, and people can do what they like with them. The other tradition treats animals as our fellow-creatures, having feelings.

In our religious tradition, hostility to animals grew out of the preoccupation with establishing monotheism and avoiding nature-worship. Pagan religions had made much use of animal symbolism, and had often revered particular animals and plants as sacred. The gods had them as companions: Jove had his eagle, Athene her owl, Odin his ravens and his eight-legged horse. Moreover, pagan writers such as Plutarch who had championed animals had sometimes used arguments from the reincarnation of souls — that the souls of deceased people who proved themselves unworthy went into lower forms like animals — which was contrary to Christian doctrine.

So the defense of animals smelled of heresy. St. Francis got away with going against that tradition, but his influence in this respect — despite today's blessing of animals on his feastday — wasn't wide. At the beginning of the seventeenth century Descartes, in laying the foundation of modern science, exalted human reason as the only genuine form of consciousness. Animals, having no reason, he said, are just automata. This convenient doctrine was invoked to justify crude vivisections which even the conscience of the age found shocking.

What prevailed was Spinoza's notion that animals, though conscious, can't concern us, because they're simply too different from us for any sort of duty of consideration to be possible. This went far beyond Christianity. Exalting reason as humankind's link with God, humankind's self-worship by reason of intelligence became to some extent an overt religion, as when the French revolutionaries enthroned the naked Goddess of Reason on the altar of Notre Dame cathedral in Paris. Auguste Comte set up a formal Religion of Humanity.

Upsetting the general body of scientists as much as upsetting Christianity was Charles Darwin. What worried many scientists about Darwin was not God's dignity but humankind's: For them, Darwin's idea that human dignity is compatible with an earthly origin was unbearable.

The truth is that we live here surrounded by our animal relatives.

In order to understand ourselves, we need to take animal parallels seriously, though of course not simplistically. Doing so doesn't degrade us: Dignity depends on truth. In a beautiful Polish, Lithuanian, and Slovak Christmas custom, as each of the many dinner courses is served, a small portion is set aside for the animals. This reminds all that at the first Christmas, when Christ was born, the animals were the only honored "eye witnesses" and deserve to be remembered.

Today's reading from the second letter to the Thessalonians carries the same theme in yet a different way. This and the first letter to the Thessalonians were written about 51 A.D., and constitute the earliest writings in the New Testament. The first letter had taught that the day of the Lord would come "like a thief" and might catch some people off guard (1 Th 5:5). Some were therefore teaching that the final days were already there. This gave rise to two sets of errors. Some said, "Let's live it up — eat, drink, and be merry, and the devil take the hindmost." Others sank into despair, feeling that in the time available they would never be able to reform their lives and so would be damned.

This second letter intended to overcome these ideas. The author, not necessarily St. Paul though certainly with the authority of his name, encouraged these frightened Christians to square their shoulders, throw back their heads, leave the end of the world to God, and carry on with life. The letter wants them not only to endure their circumstances patiently, but to master them and use them to strengthen their nerve.

Today's section begins with a prayer that is a concise expression of the delicate coordination of both divine initiative and human effort in the work of our salvation. Our glory is Christ, all right, but his glory is us. Just as the glory of teachers is in the students they form and parents' glory is in the children they beget, Christ's glory is in those who have learned to be little lights of the world, lit by his great light. It's a prayer that could very well be used by everyone.

That we be gathered to Jesus is, of course, the deepest hope of all of us. If we're to be numbered among Jesus' assembly, we must rely upon the mercy of God. Most of all, we look upon Jesus' mercy to Zacchaeus, and the mercy of the new and converted Zacchaeus to others, perceive how different that mercy is from society's attitude, and imitate it. Salvation comes to the merciful!

Thirty-Second Sunday in Ordinary Time
2 M 7:1f., 9-14   2 Th 2:16-3:5   Lk 20:27-38

Is This Life All There Is?
The Resurrection of the Body; Life after Death;
Resurrection to Life; This World and the World of Resurrection

Ghosts and goblins — and life after death — are an attractive source of stories, novels, and movies. Many famous people have wrestled with the idea of life after death. "If there is no immortality, I shall hurl myself into the sea," wrote Tennyson. Bismarck was calmer: "Without the hope of an afterlife," he said, "this life is not even worth the effort of getting dressed in the morning." Even Freud called the belief that death is the door to a better life "the oldest, strongest and most insistent wish of mankind." Some modern literature is different. In Ionesco's *Amédée*, the plot concerns a corpse that blows up larger and larger until it floats away in the shape of a balloon — a balloon that's on the way to nowhere.

It's no wonder that we have concern about something so important as life after death. We haven't experienced it, and it seems to exceed the bounds of reason. But many important things exceed the bounds of reason: our parents' love, for example, and the trust of children, and genuine friendship — to all of which we give great attention.

Now, as the end of the Church year arrives in two weeks, it's natural for our thoughts to turn to life after death. The Judeo-Christian tradition has a lot to say about it. Belief in a bodily resurrection after death started even before the events of today's liturgy.

With the Maccabees in today's First Reading, the belief reaches a definitive statement. These events took place when the Seleucid Antiochus IV, King of Syria from 175 to 164 B.C., ruled the Holy Land. Antiochus decided to eliminate the Jewish mindset by introducing pagan Greek thought and ways into Palestine. Like Alexander the Great before him and other ethnic purist dictators since, he wanted one culture for his kingdom (Hellenism), one language (Greek), and one religion (the Greek pantheon). That culture included the Greek dramas, which were really liturgies offered to pagan gods and goddesses. It included the athletic games and the gymnasium; these were in the nude, which was offensive to Jewish morals. Worst of all, Antiochus blasphemously erected a statue of Olympian Zeus in the Temple itself — the ultimate desecration (the "abomination of desolation" referred to in Dn 8:13 and again in the Gospels).

As with any such attempt, there was a group willing to cooperate to save their prestige, their wealth, and their lives. But most Jews resisted. So Antiochus's armies attacked them; 80,000 Jews died and another 80,000 were sold into slavery. It became a capital offense to possess a copy of the Mosaic Law; mothers who had their children circumcised were crucified with their children hanging around their necks. Antiochus turned the Temple courts into brothels, pilfered the Temple treasury, and turned the Temple's great altar into an altar to the Greek god Zeus, on which he added the further insult of offering pigs' flesh to the pagan gods.

The Jewish resistance fighters were led by a single family, the Mattathias — or, as they were called, "The Hammers": the Maccabees. Today's reading is part of the inspiring story of their bravery. (For the sake of the squeamish, the reading omits verses 3 through 8, telling the details of their inhuman martyrdom: cutting out the tongue of one who had spoken up, scalping him, cutting off his hands and feet, and frying him while still alive; and with a second, tearing off the skin and hair of his head.) Each of the seven brothers, as he approached death, was inspired by their mother. She urged them all to be strong, put their faith in God, and die like men. Their hope was in the glory of the resurrection to come.

The Maccabees and their band won their epic struggle. Joyous lights were put up in the Temple and in every Jewish home, giving the feast its second name, the Feast of Lights — appropriate because of its meaning to the light of freedom. Judas Maccabaeus decreed that the days of the rededication of the altar should be observed with joy and gladness on the anniversary every year for eight days (1 M 4:59). The feast is still commemorated as Hanukkah, and to this day Jews celebrate it with lights in their windows.

One of the many New Testament affirmations of the resurrection of the body is the dialogue between Jesus and the Sadducees in today's Gospel passage. The only immortality they would accept was for the community of Israel; they didn't believe in individual resurrection. They posed to Jesus a trick question, disguised in the form of a rabbinical

debate. It was so phrased that Jesus would either be caught in the quag-
mire of rabbinical casuistry or be forced to deny the reality of the resurrection of the dead.

It was natural that the Sadducees should bring forth the Law of
Moses: For them, that was the sole religious authority. What they
brought up was the "Levirate Law," whereby a widow was to marry a
brother of her dead husband in order that through their children her
husband's name and family line mightn't be obliterated (Dt 25:5) —
another way of bringing about immortality. Their point wasn't the
Levirate Law itself, which was no longer in effect, but the matter of
being raised from the dead. For them, the impossibility of a woman
being reunited after death with seven husbands was proof enough that
no resurrection was possible. Modern living poses similar cases: How
is resurrection of the body possible, for example, for people bombed
into apparent nothingness by a nuclear explosion?

In the first part of Jesus' answer, he took the opportunity to give
a deeper understanding of the nature of the resurrected life. He said
that we shouldn't speculate about the other side of the grave in terms
of this earth. Life there is quite different. The resurrected life, for example, is the life of a completed human person, no longer defined in
marital or generative terms. In the resurrected life, we're not just resuscitated, but resurrected — not the kind of life we have here, but rather
a life fulfilled on a wholly other plane. When Jesus spoke of the resurrected becoming in a sense like angels, he didn't mean that we will no
longer have bodies in the life to come, or that we won't recognize or
be interested in seeing each other as well as God. But at that point, any
further discussion with the Sadducees — who were materialists incapable of conceiving of anything spiritual — had to come to an end.

Then, since the Sadducees held only to the Law of Moses, Jesus
returned to that, citing the remarkable incident of Moses encountering
God in the burning bush. God called out to Moses from the bush, identifying Himself as the God of Abraham, Isaac, and Jacob (Ex 3:1-8).
When Moses heard from God, Abraham, Isaac, and Jacob were dead.
Yet God had said, "I am the God" of these three patriarchs: not "I was,"
but "I am" their God. So Abraham, Isaac, and Jacob still lived! So the
creative power of God brings about life after death! The Sadducees
became silent. Jesus had met them on their own ground and won.

While we should be concerned about our life after death, we
needn't be overanxious. That's what St. Paul wrote to the young Church

at Thessalonica, which was upset because many expected the end of
the world and Jesus' Second Coming in a short time. Today's reading,
which comes from the center of St. Paul's letter, preaches peace of soul.
The prayer (2:16f.) is that God may comfort and strengthen the people
at Thessalonica as they strive to live out the Gospel in their lives. After his own prayer for them, Paul in turn movingly requests the weak
Thessalonians' prayers for himself and his work.

The stories in today's liturgy present human situations which cry
out to teach us the resurrection of the dead. Innocent suffering on behalf of truth, as depicted in the Maccabees, demands that the just God
give a final rationale for human suffering. The human situation behind
the Gospel story — that is, the attempt to have one's name remembered and passed on to the future — recognizes a basic human yearn-
ing to give life a sense of purpose.

All of us have a desire for immortality, which some seek in various surrogate ways. There's the immortality of fame, like that of movie
stars whose names live on after death. There's an immortality of influence, like that of rich people who might donate art, politicians who
might have a lengthy obituary, and statesmen who have monuments
erected in their honor. And there's an immortality of power, usually
accomplished through the establishment of foundations or charitable
institutions.

Christian belief in immortality, on the other hand, is unique and
special. The Gospel of Jesus Christ is the Good News of fullness of
life in this age, and of resurrection in the age to come. For us death is a
door, not a wall — not a wall that ends growth and action like the Berlin wall, but a door into a Christmas-tree room full of surprises. Someone has compared death to standing on the seashore. A ship spreads
her white sails to the morning breeze and starts for the open sea. She
fades on the horizon, and someone says, "She's gone." Just at the moment when someone says, "She's gone," other voices who are watching her coming on another shore happily shout, "Here she comes." Or
to use another metaphor, what the caterpillar calls "the end," the butterfly calls "the beginning."

When in a moment we say the last line of the Creed, "We believe in the resurrection of the body and life everlasting," we're asserting our belief that, in a way that no one fully understands, at our resurrection our body joins with our spirit to continue our existence in eternal life. So our body as well as our spirit is holy, and for both of them
this life isn't all there is.

THIRTY-THIRD SUNDAY IN ORDINARY TIME
Ml 3:19   2 Th 3:7-12   Lk 21: 5-19

Patient Endurance
The Lord Comes to Rule the Earth with Justice;
Live Life Fully; The Day of the Lord

People will demonstrate for or against just about anything. Some time ago, a woman was walking up and down in front of the White House in Washington, D.C., with a sandwich sign that said absolutely nothing. A curious passerby asked her what she was demonstrating about, and she answered, "None of your business!" One of the most popular causes for demonstrations is the end of the world, demonstrators' signs usually reading something like, "Repent! The end of the world is near!"

Whenever one tries to base definite predictions about the end of the world on Scripture, the texts become rather vague. Whenever, for example, the Apostles asked Jesus for some information about the end of the world, Jesus deliberately talked simultaneously about the destruction of the Temple and the city of Jerusalem along with the world's end.

In today's Gospel, Jesus and the Apostles were looking at Jerusalem — the object of Jesus' mission — from the Mount of Olives. They were looking especially at the building which was one of the wonders of the ancient world, the Temple. A beautiful refurbishing of the Temple had begun about forty-six years before Jesus by Herod the Great, who was expert at trying to curry the favor of the people by doing just this kind of restoration. Some of the granite stones in the Temple walls, as big as modern freight cars, were so expertly linked together without mortar that it was hard to see the joints.

The sun reflecting from the Temple's brilliant white marble and gold ornament, set on a hill, made it visible for miles. It was as difficult to conceive of this building not lasting as to conceive today the same fate for the Lincoln Memorial in Washington, D.C., St. Peter's in Rome, the Eiffel Tower in Paris, the Prado Museum in Madrid, or Buckingham Palace in London. Yet because of the wickedness of Jerusalem, Jesus prophesied that not one stone of the Temple would be left on another. Completed in 63 A.D., the building's destruction was accomplished seven years later, about forty years after Jesus' prophecy.

At that time a thirty-year-old Roman general named Titus stood on about the same spot as Jesus did in today's Gospel. Titus and his vicious army of between sixty and eighty thousand men surrounded the city. It was early May when they began, intending to starve the unyielding Jews out. Soon, pitiable bands of Jewish deserters left the city daily, their bellies distended from starvation. Rumors had started among the bandits on the fringes of the Roman soldiery that the Israelites' bellies were distended from swallowing their jewelry, so the bandits slit them open in hopes of becoming rich. The Roman soldiers crucified so many others that the local forests were denuded of trees.

All day and into the night the sound of battering-rams against the gates shook the earth. When their summons to surrender went unheeded, the Romans stacked large stores of food within the sight of the starving Jews on the walls.

In the beginning of July, the Romans were able to enter part of the city. They saw that the inhabitants were steeped in the horror of factional fights among themselves. Fanatics, extreme nationalists, and bandits held various quarters of the city. When the Romans opened cellars and closets in the hope of finding gold which rumor said was hidden, they found instead grisly corpses stacked high — corpses which the Jews had become too weak to fling over the walls as they had done in the beginning of the siege back in May. Josephus, the Jewish historian, tells of one rich matron who was reduced to looking for grains of corn in the animal dung in the streets. He tells of another pitiful woman who killed and ate her baby nursing at her breast.

At first, Titus, realizing the importance of the Temple in the life of the worshiping Jews, tried to save it from his soldiers. But when his attempts to have the Jews surrender met only with counter-offers to negotiate, he was so enraged that he unleashed the fury of his soldiers' hatred of the Jews. They destroyed everything in sight, finally managing to enter even the Temple's Holy of Holies and set it afire. Even today, you can see on the Arch of Titus at the old forum in Rome friezes proudly depicting the Roman soldiers returning with booty from the Temple: the gold candelabra, the gold table for offerings, and other sacred vessels.

Inasmuch as Luke wrote in about 80 A.D., shortly after Jerusalem was destroyed, we needn't look for the "signs" he gives of the end of the world — false messiahs, wars, earthquakes, plagues, persecutions, betrayals — because they all happened before he wrote. Several false messiahs had already promoted themselves, the Jewish War was over, the Persians were threatening invasion of the Roman Empire, Judaism had excommunicated Christians from the synagogue, families were betraying each other, the terrible eruption of Mt. Vesuvius had cast darkness over much of the Mediterranean world, and Roman persecutions had begun.

What are we to think or do about the last things, then? There have been many different approaches. Some people, like those addressed in today's First Reading from the Book of Malachi (his name in Hebrew means "God's spokesman"), were proud, vain, and smug. Consideration of the last things never penetrated their hard shells. Their enthusiasm had cooled and selfishness abounded.

Malachi addresses perennial problems. Why do evildoers prosper? How long must the just endure? Of what value is the hard-won virtue of pious men and women, if all their faithful observance of God's law is cynically scorned by their irreligious contemporaries? Malachi uses the metaphor of the sun, which scorches and sets afire but also warms with its healing rays. So will be the "Day of the Lord": The end of the world and the judgment will be terrible for the evildoer, but joy for the faithful.

Things were essentially no different for the Thessalonians to whom the letter of today's Second Reading was written. They were, like other ordinary persons of those times, mostly victims. For most of the people, life was mere existence. People had to work from dawn till dark. Children began working as soon as they were able. And there was always the threat of disease, insurrection, and death.

The Christians among them were expecting the end of it all with the Second Coming of Jesus; in fact, because most of the early converts were from the lower classes, they looked forward with more than ordinary eagerness to the "Day of the Lord." But — mistakenly — they stopped working. Those who had nothing were sponging from those who were better off, and spent their time as gossiping busybodies. The letter informs the non-workers that, no matter when the Second Coming arrives, people are expected to meet their daily responsibilities.

There have been other reactions to the prospect of death through history. Take the Black Death, for example, which spread through Europe beginning in 1348. People were dropping dead everywhere, in some cities far more than half the population. No one was without a relative or friend who had died, and all could well expect that their turn might be next. It was worse than the AIDS epidemic or any other epidemic in any part of today's world. Knowing nothing of bacteria, many people at that time thought the Black Death was a scourge from God. Their reactions? While it's true that some turned to God and prayer, others invented defiant "Dances of Death," and lived according to the philosophy, "Eat, drink, and be merry, for tomorrow we die."

So what do we do now about our thoughts on the "last things"? For one thing, within ourselves we ought to develop a deeper spirit of responsibility so that we seek to become dependable rather than dependent, givers rather than takers, generous rather than addicted to self-interest. Should we become painfully anxious about our future — whether because of ill health, unemployment, economic hardship, career choices, broken relationships, bereavements, or other reasons — we should be consoled by the Lord's promise that "not a hair of your head will be harmed." Outside ourselves, we're to be busy with the calamities around us; not just to deplore the world's trouble spots, but to help their victims.

Above all, we're to remember the Lord's promise in the last sentence of today's Gospel that our endurance will win us our lives. Perseverance is an essential quality of character in high-level leadership. Much good that might have been achieved in the world is lost through hesitation, faltering, wavering, or just not sticking with it.

To illustrate perseverance, there's a good story. One morning, a couple of cowpunchers went out to bring in a wild steer from his range in the mountains. They took along one of those shaggy little gray donkeys — a burro. Now a big three-year-old steer that's been running loose in the timber is a tough customer to handle. But these cowboys had a technique. They got a rope on the steer and then they tied him neck and neck, right up close, to the burro. When they let go, that burro had a bad time. The steer threw him all over the place: against trees, over rocks, into bushes. Time after time they both went down.

But there was one great difference between the burro and the steer. The burro had an idea: He wanted to go home. And no matter how often the steer threw him, every time the burro got to his feet he wound up a step nearer the corral. As the cowpunchers left, this was going on and on. After about a week the burro showed up at ranch headquarters. He had with him the tamest and sorriest-looking steer you ever saw.

Arthur James Center
    O. St. Univ. Hospital

JP   When God gives life
    He gives it forever

Xims:
    In the midst of winter
    always Think of spring

Benjamin Franklin once observed (in *Poor Richard's Almanac*): "The noblest question in the world is, 'What good may I do in it?'" To do anything good, it's necessary to patiently endure reverses, and to persevere in loyalty to Christian values.

FEAST OF CHRIST THE KING
2 S 5:1-3   Col 1:12-20   Lk 23:35-43

True Leadership
Life's Two Ways; The Full Meaning of Jesus as our King

The sentence "Mary had a little lamb" has many memories for us. But if it didn't, and you were hearing it for the first time, what would it mean to you? That Mary owned the lamb, or that she ate it, or gave birth to it? Without knowing more background, it can mean all those things. The meaning of the sentence, if fed into a computer, would be problematic.

Some of the sentences of the Bible, even for knowledgeable people, can be similarly difficult. One of the most difficult jobs in the world is translating the Bible into modern languages. The biblical scholar takes the ancient Hebrew and Greek texts and forms them into today's words whose meanings change from day to day. The greater the concepts, the more difficult the translating. One good example is today's Feast of Christ the King.

When the New Testament gives us the word "king," it's typically in the mouth of a pagan — like Pontius Pilate. Other words have been used to describe Christ the king. He's the Good Shepherd, who gives his life for his sheep. He's the "man for others," the one who came "not to be served, but to serve."

What word can we use in modern languages? Chief? Leader? Ruler? Sovereign? Perhaps the words "shepherd" and "commander," as in today's First Reading, are the closest. But, applied to Jesus, all are inadequate. Jesus is all those words in their best sense — not like the subaltern about whom a British officer facetiously wrote, "I don't doubt that there are men who will follow this officer anywhere, but it will only be out of curiosity."

Pope Pius XI established this celebration in 1925, when all of Europe had nightmare memories of what they called then "The Great War," a time of an explosion of hatred, and blindness, and a torrent of blood that wiped out much of the European population. At that time, the swastika — a disfigurement of a cross — was ready to lurch across Germany, and in Russia a high ideal was being destroyed by tyranny, corruption, and mismanagement. Piercing the sound of these ideologies' bands, marches, and hate-filled speeches, the pope's new message of justice, peace, community, and love was lighting a new spark. In initiating this feast, the Church wanted to take our worship of Jesus from the privacy of our hearts and to proudly proclaim his public sway as well.

The connotations of the word "king" were then unquestioned by a society that knew many kings and accepted them. Later, kings went out of fashion. A media-saturated world lost respect for kings whose foibles were exposed. Applied to Christ, feminists objected to the masculine word "King" and wanted instead words like "Ruler of the Jews" or "Sovereign One." In our democracies, we see it as social progress to vote monarchy to little more than a nominal status under a parliamentary system. And many aren't satisfied with the word "King" to express the nature of the intimacy of their relationship with Jesus. No matter what words we use, the title of today's feast is intended to convey the relationship between Christ's rule and all creation.

Calling Jesus "King" is actually less than calling him Christ. When we say "Christ," we're tapping into all the rich historical connotations of Jewish tradition. A thousand years before Jesus, David was the first great "Christ" or anointed ruler of Israel, their great ideal of kingship. King David, to whom the Scriptures constantly refer in speaking of Christ the King, and who is the subject of today's First Reading, showed that, though a reign might be looked upon as a Camelot, its love doesn't preclude intelligence.

It was through the thirty-year-old David's intelligence, as well as his ability to judge people, that he became king of all the tribes of the Jews. Although his united kingdom lasted only to the death of his son Solomon, for that brief time the Jewish people had their Camelot: a glorious and golden age.

David's reign had become a model, and the pastoral image of "shepherd" described him. Some day, the people hoped, there would be another great shepherd-king like the most-beloved David. The reason why the Church chose this reading for this feast is to suggest that Jesus, of the line of David, is that other great king.

As our Church year comes to its close today and begins our preparation for Christmas next week, we can't help but look at both the kingly crown and the Christmas creche: The theme of Christ the King is already apparent in the motifs of Jesus' conception and birth. At his conception, the angel said to Mary, in words we repeat in the Creed at Mass, that of his kingdom there will be no end (Lk 1:32f.). And when Mary gave birth to Jesus the angels announced to the shepherds that a savior had been born who is Messiah and Lord (Lk 2:11). And the thesis of life's two ways — the way of accepting and coming to God and the way of taking care of self — was also already apparent: It was present, for example, with the people who turned their back on Mary and Joseph, and with the shepherds who rejoiced and believed.

That theme of life's two ways is continued in today's Gospel. In it, St. Luke paradoxically, yet dramatically, highlights the kingly rule of Jesus in the scene of the crucifixion. The very first line (v. 35) tells us that whereas the leaders were rejecting Jesus, the people were accepting him. The theme was present also in the soldiers, some of whom made fun of Jesus (v. 36), but others of whom, like the centurion spoken of later, said that this was truly the Son of God (Mt 27:54). The full inscription over Jesus' head (v. 38), which he had to carry to the place of execution, was the assertion of his crime: "This is Jesus of Nazareth, the King of the Jews." What had been intended as the last best insult became for the Gospel writers a triumphant proclamation.

The two criminals, too, contradicted each other on Jesus. Both were guilty and deserved punishment. One, however, out of an ingrained ignorant habit of cursing and blaspheming took up the taunts of the leaders and of some of the soldiers against Jesus (v. 39). The other criminal not only refused to rebuke the Lord, but berated his companion (v. 40f.) and touchingly kept asking that Jesus remember him when Jesus came into his kingdom (v. 42).

Jesus' gracious response to the contrite criminal was to assure him that that very day he would be with him in paradise (v. 43). Jesus put an emphasis on "this day": that is, before the sun sets. The penitent will be "with him" — not simply following Jesus in his retinue, but sharing his reign. "Paradise" is a lovely word of Persian origin meaning "a walled garden." When a Persian king wanted to do someone a special honor, he invited him to walk with him in his garden.

That a person like Jesus is a great King has always been for some people hard to understand: He doesn't appear strong enough, or materialistic enough. From the beginning, some haughty people like the Gnostic heretics haven't been satisfied with ordinary Christianity; they've wanted something more sophisticated, more intellectual, more exclusive.

The letter to the Colossians argues against that. It states that God alone rules the universe, Christ is its cosmic Lord and King, and those who belong to him share his mastery over the world. Referring to the ancient custom of victor nations transporting entire defeated populations to their own country, the letter explains that God has transported us from the power of darkness to light, and transferred us from the kingdom of Satan to the kingdom of Jesus (v. 13).

Then the letter shows an exalted awareness of Jesus as King and Judge of the world, endowed with divine redemptive power, and containing the fullness of God's effective presence among people. Whereas every human being is patterned after the image of God (Gn 1:26f.), Jesus is the actual likeness of God (v. 15). Jesus not only shows who God is, but also who we're meant to be. Far beyond angels whom the Gnostics called thrones or dominations or principalities or powers (v. 16), Christ is God who shared in the creation of all things and is therefore supreme. It's to him that creation owes all that it has been, is, and will be. Christ isn't only the agent of creation in the beginning, but also its goal in the end, and in between these two it's he who holds the world together (v. 17).

And Christ is supreme over the Church, which without him is unthinkable and unrealizable (v. 18). He's the beginning of the Church not only in the sense of sequence, like "a" is the beginning of the alphabet and "1" is the beginning of numbers, but in the sense of being the source of everything. By virtue of his victory over death, he's Lord of all. The absolute fullness (*pleroma*, v. 19) that resides in him means that everything that makes God to be God resides in Jesus. Only in his kingdom do we find majesty without tyranny, power without domination, glory without terror. Though he's nothing like the earthly kings we've heard about, what else can we call him but our King?

Altogether, Jesus' kingship holds out a vision that takes us beyond imagination. It's a vision of a place beyond nations' mountains of arms and our own private worries; it provides a recipe for human contentment out of peace and hope for the future. Quite unlike dictators or politicians who intuit which way the human parade is heading and getting in front of it, Jesus came to turn the parade in a different direction. The kingship of Jesus is always different from that of earthly kings, and its meaning doesn't crumble away with the passing modes of earthly politics. His kingship depends on our willing acceptance of his rule in our hearts and in our lives. We make him welcome and ask him to lead us, as the Shepherd-King of our souls.